REINSURANCE

FOR THE BEGINNER

by

R. Philippe Bellerose
F.C.I.I., C.Dip.A.F.

revised by

Christopher C. Paine, M.S.T.I.

5th Edition 2003

WITHERBY

PUBLISHERS

ISBN 1 85609 239 9

All rights reserved

Published and Printed by:
Witherby & Co. Ltd.
32-36 Aylesbury Street, London EC1R 0ET
Tel No: 020 7251 5341   Fax: 020 7251 1296

British Library Cataloguing in Publication Data
  R. Philippe Bellerose F.C.I.I., C.Dip.A.F.
  Christopher C. Paine, M.S.T.I.
  Reinsurance for the Beginner
  1 Title
  ISBN 1 85609 239 9

All rights reserved. No part of this publication may be reproduced, stored in a retrieval system, or transmitted, in any form or by any means, electronic, mechanical, photocopying, recording or otherwise, without the prior permission of the publisher and copyright owner.

While the principles discussed and the details given in this book are the product of careful consideration, the author and the publishers cannot in any way guarantee the suitability of recommendations made in this book for individual problems or situations, and they shall not be under any legal liability of any kind in respect of or arising out of the form or contents of this book or any error therein.

REINSURANCE

FOR THE BEGINNER

Fifth Edition

by

R. Philippe Bellerose
F.C.I.I., C.Dip.A.F.

revised by

Christopher C. Paine, M.S.T.I

All rights reserved
Witherby & Co. Ltd.
32-36 Aylesbury Street,
London EC1R 0ET

1st Edition 1978
2nd Edition 1980
Reprinted 1984
3rd Edition 1987
4th Edition 1998
5th Edition 2003

WITHERBY

PUBLISHERS

© R. Philippe Bellerose

1978

ISBN 1 85609 239 9

Printed and Published by
WITHERBY & CO. LTD
32-36 Aylesbury Street,
London EC1R 0ET
Tel No: 020 7251 5341   Fax No: 020 7251 1296
International Tel No: +44 20 7251 5341
International Fax No: +44 20 7251 1296
www: witherbys.com

Introduction to the Fifth Edition

I worked for a short time at Reinsurance Evaluations Limited where Ken Louw was the long-standing managing director. He retired in the later part of 2001 and subsequently offered me the opportunity, with Alan Witherby's approval, of revising the Fifth Edition of this excellent publication.

Sadly, Ken died on 1st August 2002 whilst on holiday in St Petersburg, Russia, and we never had the opportunity to collaborate on revisions to the text. Many of us had received the benefit of Ken's wisdom, knowledge and encouragement throughout the years (and my own association with him goes back to the mid-1970's), so I would like to dedicate this Fifth Edition to his memory and hope that my own revisions match Ken's exceptionally high standards in conveying the concepts and philosophy of non-marine reinsurance.

I have left Ken's 'Notes on Usage' unchanged as they are still relevant and have continued his method of identifying the construction and application of reinsurance, rather than the usage and bureaucratic requirements of any particular market. I am sure that both Philippe and Ken would approve.

As time progresses, so do dates, values and the use of the English language itself. I have therefore taken the opportunity to update many of these aspects, but not change the original ideas, concepts or methods being described. Wherever possible, I have also attempted to lay out certain word examples in a more visual format.

I have also added a new chapter in which I have tried to identify certain problems that have arisen since Ken revised the Fourth Edition. Many of these contentious issues will become the subject of much consideration and discussion in years to come.

Reinsurance is formed by a series of concepts. I tend to describe them as being "intangible". As society, technology and business all develop, new insurance and reinsurance products are created or adapted to reflect those developments. It was never the intention that "Bellerose" should address all the "issues of the moment", but this explanatory book deserves to take its place alongside other well-known publications on reinsurance – *The Law and Practice of Reinsurance* (Dr. Golding, revised by Ken Louw) and *Reinsurance in Practice* (Kiln & Kiln).

Christopher Paine, M.S.T.I.
January 2003

Introduction to the Fourth Edition

Philippe Bellerose F.C.I.I., was a Director and General Manager of the Sydney Reinsurance Company Pty. Limited, a member of the QBE Insurance Group Limited, Australia. He had been in reinsurance for some 25 years, the last 15 being as Reinsurance manager of the QBE Group which operates in 26 countries. Sadly he died in early 1995. As a result Alan Witherby asked me to prepare a new edition of this excellent little book

Many and major changes have taken place in the world in the 9 years since the previous edition was published. Increasing industrialisation, changing patterns of commerce, wider legal obligations and the use of sophisticated technology have made their presence felt in all parts of the world. This is reflected in the reinsurance business by the development of strong regional centres. It is also reflected in the increasing use of highly developed reinsurance mechanisms and the awareness of practices which had been previously confined to few first world activities.

We have extensively re-cast the book (while trying to maintain its original simple and direct approach) to adapt it to the needs of a new generation of readers, whether new to the business or undergoing education as a specialist or one of those whose lives are increasingly impacted by reinsurance as financial adviser, accountant, lawyer or regulator. We have directed the major changes to a more extensive discussion of the various types of excess of loss reinsurance. This has become an increasingly popular form of reinsurance for all classes of business in all parts of the world, despite its inherent complexities and difficulties.

The proper practice of reinsurance is something you will only learn by experience. This book is intended to provide you with an explanation of the basic elements of the business of reinsurance

Ken Louw
1998

Foreword (to the Original Edition)

I met Mr. Bellerose's little book long before I met its author and immediately adopted it as a teaching aid in the annual Reinsurance Study Course, which I directed on behalf of the NSW. Insurance Institute.

I find its great appeal lies in its simplicity of utterance and illustration which makes it eminently suitable for beginners in reinsurance or persons who need a working knowledge of the elements of reinsurance.

In recent years, the author became a resident of Sydney and as well as practising its craft with a leading Australian Insurance Company with an international portfolio of business, I am happy to say he lectures on Reinsurance for the Insurance Institute at both State and Federal level.

I am privileged to be able to recommend this book as a very useful contribution to the teaching of Reinsurance.

John Allison

Publisher's Note

This compact little book on reinsurance has proved enormously useful, not only to those closely allied to reinsurance but also to those new to the industry who want to know more about this interesting subject.

Many companies, brokers and training schools have adopted the book both here in Britain and overseas for training purposes. The success of what has now become known as "Bellerose" is born out by the increasing succession of new editions and reprints since the initial publication.

Alan Witherby
2003

Notes on Usage (Ken Louw)

The reinsurance business is often accused of being imprecise in its terminology. This can arise because a single term needs to perform a number of tasks. Thus, a word may have a specific meaning in one class of insurance and a quite different meaning in another class. Lots of problems can arise from the use of the word "risk". It can mean the uncertainty whether or not a loss will arise ("the risk of loss") or refer to the property being insured ("any one risk any one location") or describe the peril being covered ("fire risks"). In this book we try to use the term "risk" for the property or liability being insured (or reinsured) and "peril" for that which is insured (or reinsured) against.

In most classes of reinsurance business the contracting parties are referred to as the "reinsured" (the insurer who buys the reinsurance) and the "reinsurer" (who provides the protection). However Life and Marine business tend to use the terms "reassured" and "reassurer". Many Lloyd's reinsurance contracts also use these terms. For consistency we have used "reinsured" (and ceding company) and "reinsurer".

This study directs itself mainly towards the study of the reinsurance of non-life business. Even here there can be differences in terminology; what is known as "surplus reinsurance" is sometimes referred to as "excess of line reinsurance" in Marine business. The structure of Life assurance is different to that of non-Life insurance and the practice of Life reassurance will reflect that difference.

This book uses "slips" to illustrate the terms and conditions which would apply to various types of reinsurance contract. A "slip" consists of a summary of the terms and conditions of the proposed coverage which is used in many parts of the world for the placing of reinsurance contracts. It is not, however, a universal method. For some classes of coverage, there is an increasing use of formal questionnaires.

We have tended to use a single generic currency term (Dollars = $) in the various examples which appear in this book. These are intended purely for illustration and have no connection with any currency, living, virtual or dead. Other figures and material which appear in these examples should also be treated as illustrations and not as guides to underwriting or to rating.

We have not included any reference to the more esoteric forms of reinsurance such as "signed line excess", "tops and drops", "cascades", etc. This is, after all, a Beginner's Guide. In the same way, and for the same reason, a number of topics have not been developed in detail.

Contents

		Page
Introductions to various Editions		v
Foreword		ix
Publisher's Note		x
Notes on Usage		xi
Chapter 1	Introduction	1
Chapter 2	Facultative	7
Chapter 3	Treaties	21
Chapter 4	Proportional Treaties	25
Chapter 5	Quota Share Treaty	49
Chapter 6	Surplus Treaty	67
Chapter 7	Pools and Facultative Obligatory Treaty	71
Chapter 8	Non-Proportional Reinsurance	75
Chapter 9	Event Excess of Loss	91
Chapter 10	Risk Excess of Loss	121
Chapter 11	Catastrophe Excess of Loss	133
Chapter 12	Stop Loss and Aggregate Excess of Loss	151
Chapter 13	Reinsurance Planning – Basic Principles	159
Chapter 14	Reinsurance Planning – Practical Application	177
Chapter 15	Basic Contract Wordings	205
Chapter 16	Treaty Wordings – Proportional	237
Chapter 17	Contract Wordings – Excess of Loss	259
Chapter 18	Developments Since the 4th Edition	281

1

Introduction

The function of an insurance company is to protect the original insured against potential heavy losses. The reinsurer provides a similar protection to the insurance company.

Reinsurance therefore plays a very important, if not a vital, role in the insurance industry. That role can be summarised under three headings:

1. Providing Capacity
2. Creating Stability
3. Strengthening Finances

Providing Capacity

The provision of capacity is the primary reason for reinsurance.

In every branch of insurance there are risks where, because of their size or their nature, an insurance company cannot afford to keep the whole of the insured value for its own account. Such risks are numerous: oil rigs and jumbo jet aircraft are some of the best examples.

In certain insurance markets, large risks are insured on a sharing basis by several different insurance companies, all operating in that particular market. Each insurance company takes a share of the risk that it can absorb, and the remainder is insured with other insurance companies. This practice is known as co-insurance. Care must be taken in the use of the term co-insurance. In certain markets, the concept of co-insurance does not exist, as different insurance companies prefer to accept 100% of an original risk. In these circumstances, the term "co-insurance" means that the original insured co-insures the risk with its insurance company. We could also describe this philosophy as self-insurance.

In many instances, the insurance company insures the whole risk itself; lays off some of the amount it has accepted to other insurance or reinsurance companies; and keeps, or retains, only what it can absorb for its own net account. This practice is called reinsurance.

Thus, it is necessary for an insurance company to effect some form of reinsurance protection where the amount of any exposure, whether it be one individual risk or a group of similar risks, is such that it is beyond the limit prudent for that insurance company to carry.

In its simplest form, the following diagram explains the transaction.

The original risk exposure is passed

From	to	who then passes part to
Original Insured	Insurance Companies	Reinsurance

An example of such a transfer would be:

Original Insured has factory worth $10,000,000	Insurance Company issues a policy for $10,000,000	Retains $2,000,000 for Own Account

and

Cedes $8,000,000 to Reinsurer

Creates Stability

The next most important reason for reinsurance is to even out the underwriting results of the insurance company over a period.

Wide swings in the results of an insurance company can be very damaging to its image with the public and can also cause concern to its shareholders. Results fluctuate as a result of a very large and sudden catastrophic loss event or an unexpected accumulation of a number of losses occurring during an accounting period. Reinsurance minimises these fluctuations by limiting the exposure of individual risks to a loss and by restricting the losses to which a portfolio would be subject either for an event or over a year of account.

The following diagram illustrates that function:

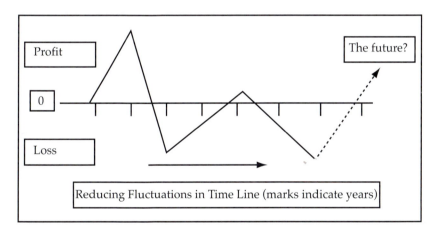

The peaks above and below the "0" line indicate the function of reinsurance in underwriting results during the period. The reinsurer shares in the fortunes of the insurance company by participating in the profits (portion above the line) and by contributing to the losses (portion below the line). The net result is a stabilised loss ratio (represented by the line) over the period of the cover.

Strengthening Finances

In a sense, all reinsurance is a form of financing. If a reinsured does not have access to reinsurance capacity, it might have to decline business and lose premium income. If it does not buy sufficient or the correct reinsurance, a major loss or an accumulation of smaller losses could send it out of business.

However, the financial function of reinsurance has another aspect. The measure of solvency is one of the yardsticks used by regulatory bodies in controlling insurance companies. This is often calculated as the percentage that the capital and free reserves of the insurance company bears to its net premium income (i.e. retained premium after deduction of premiums paid for reinsurance). Most regulatory authorities have minimum ratios below which they would not allow insurance companies to operate. This ratio is termed the "minimum solvency ratio". In some countries solvency is calculated on gross premiums (before allowances for reinsurances) and a separate reckoning is made for reinsurances, with a limit on the amount of reinsurance that is allowed.

The following example illustrates how reinsurance can help to improve an insurance company's solvency margin and therefore its financial strength.

An insurance company has paid-up shareholders' capital and free reserves of $100,000,000. These are known as its total free assets. It writes a total annual gross premium income of $250,000,000.

Without reinsurance, its solvency ratio would be 40%, being the division of its total free assets by its gross premium income.

$$\frac{\text{Total Free Assets}}{\text{Total Gross Premium}} \quad \frac{\$100,000,000}{\$250,000,000} \times \frac{100}{1} = 40\%$$

If it has reinsurance arrangements that allow annual

premium cessions of $125,000,000 to its reinsurers, its solvency ratio would be increased to 80% (total free assets divided by net retained premium income of $125,000,000, being $250,000,000 gross premiums less ceded premiums of $125,000,000).

$$\frac{\text{Total Free Assets}}{\text{Total Net Retained Premium}} \quad \frac{\$100,000,000}{\$125,000,000} \times \frac{100}{1} = 80\%$$

By ceding 50% of its premium income to its reinsurers the insurance company increases its solvency ratio by 200%. This example should not be considered as being a recommendation that an insurance company can use reinsurance to disguise its lack of solvency (although some insurance companies have attempted to do so to postpone the day when they are forced out of business). However, this function of financial support by way of reinsurance is very important. Over the years, many newly-established insurance companies or those entering upon a new class of business have relied upon their reinsurers for this type of financial support.

Forms and Types of Reinsurance

Reinsurance is conducted in many forms and types. The following diagram gives a summary of these forms and types which will be reviewed in detail in later chapters.

REINSURANCE	
FACULTATIVE	**TREATY**
Proportional	Proportional
	Quota Share
	Surplus
	Facultative Obligatory
Non-Proportional	**Non-Proportional**
(known as **"Excess of Loss"**)	Event Excess of Loss
	Risk Excess of Loss
	Catastrophe Excess of Loss
Stop Loss	Stop Loss

2

Facultative

There are only two forms of reinsurance – facultative and treaty. This chapter describes facultative reinsurance. Treaty reinsurance will be reviewed in later chapters.

Facultative reinsurance is the oldest method of reinsurance. It is perhaps less frequently used than treaty reinsurance although it is still necessary and useful.

Basic Features

The basic features of facultative reinsurance are the individual offer and acceptance of risks. Each risk that requires a facultative placement would be considered separately by the reinsurer.

The insurance company must give the reinsurer all material information about the risk to enable the latter to decide whether or not it would accept a share and to enable it to set an adequate reinsurance premium rate. The reinsurer has the option of either accepting 100% of the risk, just a proportion of it, or decline to participate at all.

Drawbacks

The main drawbacks of this method are:

(1) Large amount of administration involved. Full details must be provided by the insurance company and studied by the reinsurer for each and every risk

reinsured both at inception and at renewal. Therefore high administrative costs arise for both insurance company and reinsurer(s).

(2) Time taken to place a risk. The insurance company must contact several reinsurers for each risk offered and supply full details to all of them. It must then seek their agreement to accept or renew a share, or participation. Very often the insurance company has to negotiate with several reinsurers in order to complete placement on an individual risk.

(3) The insurance company may not be able to give immediate cover to an original proposer on risks that exceed its capacity of absorption if it must first complete the facultative placement of the amount which it wishes to reinsure.

(4) Due to the reasons above, the rates of commission (see note below) given by the reinsurer under facultative cessions tend to be lower than under treaties.

Note. Commission is a reimbursement paid by the reinsurer to the insurance company. An insurance company incurs costs in acquiring and administering the original business it accepts. It must pay brokerage to intermediaries producing the original business. The insurance company must also make an allowance in its original premium rates for preparation of policy documentation, marketing that business and all the general expenses involved in running the day-to-day affairs of that insurance company. Reinsurers recognise this aspect and contribute to those expenses by allowing a commission deduction. This is normally a function of the original gross premium, e.g. original gross premium less 30% commission. Commission is an important part of all forms of proportional reinsurance.

Purposes

In spite of those drawbacks facultative reinsurance is still used for the following main reasons to:

(1) Reinsure special risks which are outside the scope of normal treaty facilities.

(2) Reinsure amounts which are in excess of existing treaty limits.

(3) Restrict the insurance company's liability and that of its treaty reinsurers, especially where the physical hazard of a particular risk is abnormally high.

(4) Reduce exposure in areas where because of accumulation of risks the insurance company is already very heavily committed. This is very important if the original business is exposed to natural perils (earthquake, flood, storm etc.).

(5) Enable the insurance company to trade its business reciprocally against business of similar quality from other insurance companies. (Reciprocity is the exchange of similar reinsurance treaties between insurance companies located in different countries).

(6) Obtain capacity when the volume of business does not justify treaty arrangements, e.g. when writing new lines of business.

(7) Enable the reinsurer to evaluate the underwriting practices of the insurance company.

(8) Seek the expertise and experience of reinsurers on risks that are complex or of a special nature.

The following is a specimen placement slip showing details of a risk to be reinsured on a proportional facultative basis:

PLACEMENT SLIP

Reinsured:	ABC Insurance Co. Ltd
Type of Business:	Facultative Quota Share Reinsurance
Period:	12 months at 1st July 2003
Class of Business:	Fire, Cyclone & Riots
Original Insured:	Sweet Sugar Factory Ltd
Location:	Port Louis, Mauritius
Sum Insured:	Buildings, Machinery & Stock $20,000,000
	Loss of Profits $40,000,000
	TOTAL $60,000,000
Original Gross Rate	0.25% for Buildings, Machinery & Stock
	0.15% for Loss of Profits
Commission:	25% on O.G.R.
Reinsured's Retention:	10%
Percentage ceded to automatic treaties:	40%
Percentage reinsured hereunder:	50%
Conditions	Being a reinsurance of and warranted same gross rates, terms and conditions as and to follow the settlements of the Reinsured.
(Plans and full description of risks are usually attached)	

The original gross rate is the factor applied to the total sum insured to calculate the premium due by the original proposer to the insurance company. The insurance company in turn pays the reinsurer a proportion of that original gross premium in accordance with the proportionate share of the risk accepted by the reinsurer.

In the above example, the total original gross premium due to the insurance company is $110,000.

Item	Sum Insured		Original Gross Rate	Original Premium
Buildings, Machinery & Stock	$20,000,000	x	0.25%	$50,000
Loss of Profits	$40,000,000	x	0.15%	$60,000
Total Original Gross Premium (O.G.P.)				$110,000

Reinsurers have agreed to accept 50% of this risk. In return for accepting liability for 50% of the total sum insured, they would be entitled to accept 50% of the original gross premium. They would also reimburse the insurance company by paying their share of the original acquisition costs. This is known as commission (historically known as exchange commission).

Facultative placement	50% of $20,000,000	=	$10,000,000
	50% of $40,000,000	=	$20,000,000
Total Sum Insured	50% of $60,000,000	=	$30,000,000
Buildings, Machinery & Stock	50% of $50,000	=	$25,000.00
Loss of Profits	50% of $60,000	=	$30,000.00
Reinsurer's share of O.G.P.	50% of $110,000	=	$55,000.00
Less Commission at 25% of 50% of O.G.P.			$13,750.00
Reinsurer's share of Original Net Premium			$41,250.00

As we explained, the reinsurer pays a commission to the insurance (ceding) company to reimburse it for the expenses incurred in obtaining the original business as well as making a contribution to the insurance company's general management and administration expenses. The rate of commission varies between country of origin and the type of business involved. The insurance company deducts the agreed amount of commission from the original gross premium due to the reinsurer. In the above example, the rate of commission is 25% and we have shown the appropriate calculations.

In certain countries, because of high acquisition costs, commission is not calculated on "O.G.R." (original gross rate, i.e. the actual original gross rate applied by the insurance company to the total sum insured to obtain the original gross premium) but on "O.N.R." (original net rate, i.e. after deduction of brokerage or original commission paid to brokers or other agents). This "overriding" commission would be at a lower rate than that calculated on O.G.R. It is often sensible to define the term "O.N.R." as this would avoid disputes between the insurance company and its reinsurer(s). An example definition might be as follows "O.N.R. = O.G.R. less a maximum of 25% in all". This means that any overriding commission (or "overrider") would effectively be applied to 75% of the original gross premium. If we assumed a 5% overrider, then the commission terms might be expressed as O.N.R plus 5% overriding commission. The overrider could be calculated on either O.G.R. or O.N.R., and would be agreed on an individual case-by-case basis.

The placement slip is shown to each reinsurer. If a reinsurer accepts a share, it writes the percentage share or monetary amount it is prepared to accept on the placement slip and initials that acceptance in confirmation of the terms and conditions contained within the placement slip. With increased duties of compliance, the reinsurer would include the date the acceptance was made and indicate some form of reference. This important detail assists the creation of an audit trail for that individual placement.

The normal practice is for the insurance company to send closings to the reinsurer(s) giving brief details of all the risks accepted by that reinsurer either on a monthly or quarterly basis together with technical accounts which cover all the transactions between the insurance company and the reinsurer during that period. The transactions include premiums due less commissions and small paid losses that have occurred on earlier or current reinsurances. Large losses are often paid by way of a special cash call immediately the insurance company has settled the claim to the original insured without waiting for a monthly or quarterly account. The cash call amount is then credited back in a subsequent periodic account and appears as a paid loss item in that subsequent account.

If losses have occurred on a reinsured risk but have not been paid, the insurance company should advise the reinsurer of all potential outstanding loss amounts. This information would enable the reinsurer to establish a correct loss reserve for that outstanding loss.

Non-Proportional Facultative (Facultative Excess of Loss)

This type of reinsurance has developed quite extensively over the last few years. Original premium rates for many classes of business have reduced dramatically, often due to intense competition. Insurance companies have found it beneficial to use facultative excess of loss reinsurance as it allows them to retain more premium while still limiting their exposure to a quantifiable level. This method of assessing the allocation of liability and premium is known as deductible credit or exposure rating. Many reinsurers also favour this type of reinsurance as they can quote their own premium rates for a limit of liability in excess of a stated amount irrespective of the original premium rate being charged by the insurance company. Reinsurers use a series of rating tables known as "first loss scales".

Developing that phrase, let us look at the facultative quota share cession on the previous risk. Rather than place a proportional facultative reinsurance, the insurance company might decide that it could maximise its premium by purchasing a facultative excess of loss placement on the uncovered 50% element of the risk.

If the insurance company decided that it was comfortable retaining its $6,000,000 retention and would be willing to pay all losses up to that amount, then we could say that its retention was "first loss". It still has proportional treaty reinsurance for 40% of the risk, and would recover 40% of any loss before it needed to consider its own involvement.

Let us assume that the insurance company does purchase facultative excess of loss. The limits required are:

$30,000,000 in excess of $6,000,0000 or more simply $30,000,000 xs $6,000,000.

The amounts relate to the unplaced 50% of the original risk in excess of the insurance company's chosen retention of $6,000,000. In true percentage terms, this cover represents 50% xs 10%, but if we grossed those limits up to 100%, then 50% of 60% = 83.333% and 10% of 60% = 16.667%. The excess of loss cover could be expressed as 83.333% xs 16.667%. These figures would be used for assessing the deductible credit, or the disproportionate amount of premium the insurance company could keep for retaining its $6,000,000 on a "first loss" basis.

There are many scales in use today and readers should be aware of the scale or scales applicable to their own market, as there is no "standard" scale. In this example, the "first loss" or deductible credit scales might show that our insurance company could retain 65% of the original *net* premium rates for 16.667% of the liability. This puts a different perspective on the insurance company's option of purchasing quota share or excess of loss facultative reinsurance. Let us work through the calculations.

Buildings, Machinery & Stock	$20,000,000 × 0.25%	$50,000
Loss of Profits	$40,000,000 × 0.15%	$60,000
Total Original Gross Premium (O.G.P.)		$110,000
Less 20% *Original* Commission		$22,000
Total Original Net Premium (O.N.P.)		$88,000
60% of Original Net Premium (retention plus 50% facultative XL)		$52,800
Facultative Excess of Loss Reinsurance Charge 35% of O.N.P.		$18,480
Original Net Premium after Facultative Excess of Loss Reinsurance		$34,320

The full apportionment of the original risk and premium would be as follows (all in $):

Party	Liability	O.G.P.	Commission Out (20%)	Commission In (25%)	O.N.P.
Original	60,000,000	110,000	22,000		88,000
Retention	6,000,000	11,000	2,200		8,800
Surplus	24,000,000	44,000		11,000	33,000
Total (50%)	30,000,000	55,000	11,000	11,000	41,800*
Balancing 5% Commission (to benefit of insurance company)					2,200

There are obviously inconsistencies in the above. At the outset, the insurance company must pay 20% original commission on the full original premium to the producing source, normally a local broker. It is able to recover those original costs from its surplus reinsurers, plus an additional 5% contribution (in this instance). The $2,200 balancing commission goes therefore to the insurance company's credit. In effect, its original gross premium "increases" to $13,200 ($11,000 plus $2,200). The facultative excess of loss premium would be calculated in the following way (all in $).

60% of original net premium (110,000 less 20% commission x 60%)	=	52,800
35% charge for facultative excess of loss reinsurance	=	18,480
Original net premium retained by insurance company	=	34,320

Let us reconcile what gross and net premium the insurance company has available.

60% original gross premium	=	66,000
20% commission on that 60% O.G.P.	=	13,200
60% original net premium	=	52,800
Less facultative charge at 35% of O.N.P. (as above)	=	18,480*
Plus 5% commission refund from surplus reinsurers (as above)	=	2,200
Total net premium available to insurance company	=	36,520*

*(Please add the three figures marked * – the first is in the original apportionment – to reconcile the total of $88,000 original net premium income).*

Any loss affecting this risk would first be recovered on a proportional basis between the insurance company and its surplus reinsurers. The insurance company's involvement would then be set against its facultative excess of loss cover. If the net retained loss (which we discuss in later chapters) exceeds its $6,000,000 retention, then the insurance company would be entitled to recover any amount in excess of that figure. Let us look at an example.

Original loss for 100% of the original risk	=	$15,000,000 (25% of original)
60% retention (before facultative XL)	=	$9,000,000 (60% of original loss)
40% surplus cession	=	$6,000,000 (40% of original loss)

The insurance company would be able to set its net retained loss (gross loss after prior proportional recovery) against its facultative excess of loss placement.

Net retained loss	=	$9,000,000
Less excess of loss retention	=	$6,000,000
Recovery from facultative excess of loss reinsurers	=	$3,000,000

This example also highlights the different effects of proportional and excess of loss reinsurance. There is a true sharing of the original loss in the surplus treaty example, whereas the insurance company retains the entire loss up to its stated monetary retention in the facultative excess of loss example. There would be numerous changes to the detail contained in a facultative excess of loss placement slip and we have shown those details below:

Reinsured:	ABC Insurance Co. Ltd
Type of Business:	Facultative Excess of Loss Reinsurance
Period:	12 months at 1st July 2003
Class of Business:	Fire, Cyclone & Riots
Original Insured:	Sweet Sugar Factory Ltd
Location:	Port Louis, Mauritius
Limits:	To pay up to $30,000,000 ultimate net loss each and every loss in excess of $6,000,000 ultimate net loss each and every loss (in respect of 60% of original)
Rate:	35% Original Net Premium (in respect of 60% of original)
Premium:	$18,480 payable in full at 1st July 2003 (in respect of 60% of original)

Brokerage:	10%
100% Original Sum Insured:	Buildings, Machinery & Stock $20,000,000 Loss of Profits $40,000,000 TOTAL $60,000,000
100% Original Gross Rate	0.25% for Buildings, Machinery & Stock 0.15% for Loss of Profits
Reinsured's Retention after surplus cession:	60%
Percentage reinsured hereunder:	100% of limits shown, being in respect of 60% of original
Conditions:	O.N.P. = O.G.P. less 25% deductions in all

As we have seen, the main problem when using excess of loss facultative reinsurance is that the insurance company's loss potential increases far more than if it used proportional facultative reinsurance. This emphasises the insurance company's "first-loss" situation.

When only facultative reinsurance is used on a risk (whether proportional or excess of loss) and the remainder is for the insurance company' net account, then both parties are aware of their respective potential exposures. But where proportional treaty reinsurers are also involved, there could be further problems.

Often facultative excess of loss reinsurance is used for what is known as the "common account" of the insurance company and its surplus reinsurers. Whilst the insurance company might favour facultative excess of loss for the reasons explained above, treaty reinsurers might not have been told that facultative excess of loss had been used by the insurance company. Surplus reinsurers would not be aware of their potentially higher exposure – and on a "first loss" basis – until after a loss had occurred. This sometimes leads to complications, misunderstandings and possible legal problems.

The excess of loss method of facultative reinsurance should therefore be used only after treaty reinsurers had given their specific approval. An alternative for the insurance company is to treat the amount to be reinsured facultatively as a second retention and to reinsure that additional retention by the facultative excess of loss method. The concept is quite complicated and we shall leave an explanation for that until another time.

3

Treaties

We pointed out in the previous chapter that the individual facultative method of reinsurance suffers from several drawbacks. Treaty reinsurance developed as a way of effecting reinsurance that was not affected by these disadvantages.

Treaties are usually classified into the two categories – Proportional and Non-Proportional. Proportional treaties will be examined in Chapters 4 to 7, whilst reinsurances on a non-proportional, or excess of loss basis, will be examined in Chapters 8 to 12. Brief explanations of both types of those reinsurance arrangements are given below.

Proportional

A proportional treaty is an agreement entered into between an insurance company and one or more reinsurers whereby the insurance company agrees to cede and the reinsurer agrees to accept a proportional share of all original insurances within the agreed limits of the treaty. Those treaty limits could be expressed in monetary terms and could apply to a specific geographical area, branch of business, section of the account or specific type of risk. The insurance company is obliged to cede all risks that fall within the agreed terms of the treaty and the reinsurer is obliged to accept all such cessions. This means that automatic protection is secured for the insurance company. The insurance company is able to provide cover immediately for any original proposal that it wishes to accept and that falls within the identified limitations of the treaty.

The reinsurer does not examine each risk individually and has no power to decline or rate a risk that falls within the scope of the treaty. The reinsurer has to accept a mixture of risks, above average, average and below average. It used to be the practice for insurance companies to provide their treaty reinsurers with bordereaux (lists) that gave details of every risk ceded to a particular treaty and the relevant premiums involved. This enabled reinsurers to monitor all risks ceded to them. Often there would have been separate bordereaux lists of incurred losses as well.

Since percentage shares of risks are *ceded* under proportional treaties, and the whole concept of proportional reinsurance is sharing in all its associated aspects, the insurance company is often referred to as the "cedant" or "ceding company".

Non-proportional

Strictly speaking a reinsurance agreement made on a non-proportional basis is not a treaty. It is known as a contract of reinsurance.

A treaty provides for risks to be ceded by way of proportional reinsurance and the reinsurance arrangement normally follows the terms and conditions of the original policy of insurance it protects. Conversely, there is no cession or sharing of business in non-proportional or excess of loss reinsurance. An excess of loss reinsurance is an agreement made between an insurance company and one or more reinsurers whereby the reinsurer agrees to pay the balance of any loss which exceeds a certain specified monetary limit and that loss arises out of the portfolio of risks being protected. The reinsurance arrangement is therefore not based upon any individual proportional cession of the original sum insured but on the amount of any claim that occurs. The loss itself therefore identifies whether there is a claim to any excess of loss arrangement, not the policy of insurance it protects. The insurance company is therefore referred to as the "reinsured" in excess of loss contracts, as the premium terms are based upon the premium derived from the whole portfolio of protected risks, not the individual constituent parts.

Through proportional treaty reinsurance the reinsurer becomes totally dependent on the insurance company's underwriting judgement and skills. A new concept must now be considered, that of underwriting the insurance company instead of the risks themselves. This means that the insurance company's management methods, its underwriting and claims procedures, past business experience, often become more important than the individual risks forming part of the portfolio of business to be protected.

The main drawbacks of facultative reinsurance (high administration costs, time and uncertainty of capacity) are reduced by the automatic treaty method which is more efficient, simple to operate and more cost-effective. This cost aspect also benefits the reinsurer, as it no longer has to administer a large number of risks on an individual facultative basis. Moreover, the reinsurer knows in advance that it will have a certain identified volume of business of a particular category, type and quality. The following listing should serve as a reminder of the different ways of reinsuring a portfolio of insurance business.

PROPORTIONAL TREATY
Quota Share
Surplus
Facultative Obligatory (often referred to as "Fac. Oblig")

NON-PROPORTIONAL REINSURANCE CONTRACTS
Risk Excess of Loss
Event Excess of Loss
Catastrophe Excess of Loss
Stop Loss, Excess of Loss Ratio, Aggregate Excess of Loss.

4

Proportional Treaties

A proportional treaty is an agreement which binds the insurance (ceding) company to cede and the reinsurer to accept a share of all risks which are ceded to the treaty. The reinsurer shares proportionally in the premiums and claims as well as all other expenses incurred by the ceding company in respect of any risks ceded to the treaty. Once the terms and conditions for the treaty have been agreed, those terms become obligatory for both parties and are automatic and allow no freedom of action or choice. This applies to both Surplus and Quota Share treaties and they are often referred to as *obligatory treaties* (especially if this phrase is mentioned under the "Exclusions" section of any reinsurance agreement).

The information required to place a proportional treaty would appear on a placement slip under the following headings. Some items do not appear on Quota Share placements and others would only appear on Surplus treaties (as will be seen in the following chapters).

- Name of the Ceding Company
- Type of Treaty
- Class or Classes of Business being reinsured (and any risks which are excluded)
- Territorial Limits
- Period
- Notice of Cancellation Provisions

Maximum Limit per Line
Number of Lines
Maximum Liability (for 100%)
Basis of Premium (Original Gross or Net Rate)
Commission
Profit Commission
Accounts
Account Settlement Details
Cash Loss and/or Loss Advice Limit
Bordereaux
Reserve Deposits
Interest on Deposits
Portfolio Assumption/Withdrawal
Brokerage
Information
Statistics
Estimated Premium Income

Some of these terms have already been explained when we discussed facultative cessions. Other terms are specific to a particular type of proportional treaty and will be explained in later chapters or sections. The following paragraphs explain those terms that are common to all proportional treaties.

Period and Notice of Cancellation

Proportional treaties are usually arranged for an unlimited period, i.e. they continue for as long as both parties agree to maintain the treaties in force. Many proportional treaties identify the period as being a "continuous agreement from 1st January 2003". Either party may decide that it wants to review the results of the treaty or even to cancel its involvement. The treaty allows for this to happen, but it must be done before a specified date, known as the anniversary date. For example, if a treaty renews at 1st January, then the anniversary date is 31st December. Either party must give *written* notice to the other party of its intention to review the treaty arrangements or cancel a participation in that treaty. The required notice period is usually 3 months before the agreed anniversary date.

Maximum Liability

This is the monetary extent for which a reinsurer is liable for any one single risk. A limit could be expressed in terms of Sum Insured (S.I.), Probable Maximum Loss (P.M.L.) or Estimated Maximum Loss (E.M.L.). There are other assessment methods such as Maximum Probable Loss (M.P.L.) and Maximum Amount Subject (M.A.S.). These are all variations on a theme. If the limit is expressed on a sum insured basis, then in the event of a loss the reinsurer knows the maximum amount it would have to pay is the amount of the stated sum insured. This follows an important principle of insurance, namely that an item must be insured for its full value to allow an insurance company to charge a fair and equitable premium for that risk.

As risks become larger and more complicated, the full value sum insured might not be fully exposed if a fire or explosion were to affect that risk. The full value sum insured could perhaps be reduced to a lower amount much nearer to a more realistic loss potential. Specialist risk surveyors or engineers assess individual risks and they make their recommendations as to a likely loss scenario. The limits of many proportional treaties will therefore be expressed as P.M.L. or E.M.L. amounts, but please remember that these are only estimates, not a treaty term, condition or warranty.

A ceding company uses P.M.L. or E.M.L. assessments as an underwriting mechanism to retain more on a particular risk and utilise its reinsurance treaties for lesser amounts. In turn, the reinsurer relies on the judgment of the ceding company in determining the maximum amount that could be paid by the reinsurer. Unfortunately, large losses do occur which sometimes exceed the estimated P.M.L. amount. This means that reinsurers might end up paying far more than they had anticipated. If treaty limits were to be expressed in P.M.L.terms, then they should be qualified by a statement showing the estimated P.M.L. value as a percentage of the full sum insured, such as "Minimum P.M.L. (say) 50%". The treaty reinsurer would then know that its limit of liability would not exceed twice the P.M.L. limit in the event of a total loss.

Treaty limits should also be expressed in terms of 100% of treaty capacity. All sorts of confusion can arise from neglect of this simple precaution. For example, a ceding company might place 60% of its treaty directly with reinsurers in one market and 40% through a broker intermediary in another market. A reinsurer writing a 5% participation could become very confused if any participation was "part of *whole*", or "part of *order*" (i.e. 5% of 60% order = 3% of *whole* or 5% of 40% order = 2% of *whole*). This kind of misunderstanding has probably caused more recourse to lawyers and tears and tantrums in accounting and claims departments than any other reinsurance problem.

Profit Commission

This is a contingent commission which is allowed in addition to the ceding commission. (Please refer to Chapter 2 for comments on ceding commission). It is calculated as a percentage of the profit made by the reinsurer out of the treaty and is refunded to the ceding company at the close of each treaty year. The profit derived from the treaty is due to the skill and care exercised by the ceding company in the conduct of the original business, and it is natural for the ceding company to expect to share in the profit of the business ceded to the reinsurer. Profit commission could therefore be considered as a reward for good results. In its simplest form, the excess of Income over Outgo represents the net annual profit and the profit commission is expressed as a percentage of this balance. The items included in a typical Profit Commission calculation are as follows:

INCOME

1. Gross Written Premiums for current year
2. Losses outstanding brought forward from previous year*
3. Unearned premium reserve brought forward from previous year*

OUTGO

1. Commissions paid for current year (applied to gross written premiums)
2. Losses paid during current year
3. Unearned premium reserve for the current year
4. Losses outstanding at end of current year
5. Reinsurers' management expenses (expressed as a percentage of gross written premiums for current year**)
6. Any deficit brought forward from previous year or years*
7. Miscellaneous charges.

*These items would not normally appear in the calculation for the first year of operation of any treaty. However, if the treaty operates on a "clean-cut" basis with automatic assumption and withdrawal of portfolio premiums and outstanding losses then these items would also appear in the profit commission calculations. Please note that confusion often arises if the unearned premium reserve (for unexpired risks) is set at 40% and the premium portfolio at 35% (or another basis). The profit commission would reflect the actual unearned premium reserve, whereas the technical treaty accounts would be rendered on the basis of the agreed basis of the premium portfolio transfer. Similarly, losses outstanding would be included at 100% within any profit commission calculation, but might be set at a lower amount (90% or 95%) for any (outstanding) loss portfolio transfer in the technical treaty accounts.

**Reinsurers' Management Expenses are a percentage of gross written premiums. Reinsurers are allowed to charge these expenses against the profit commission calculation as it represents their own costs in administering the treaty. Amounts vary between 2.5% and 10%.

If Outgo exceeds Income in a given treaty year there is a deficit and no profit commission is due to the ceding company. The deficit of the previous year is often brought forward as Item 6 in the following year's profit commission calculation, whether or not the treaty shows a profit or a loss in that following year. Any deficit is usually carried to the following year or years until it is fully extinguished and replaced by a profit. In some treaties the deficit is automatically cancelled after a certain number of years (usually 3 or 5) so that it is not carried forward beyond the agreed time limit, even if any loss has not been extinguished by a subsequent profit on that treaty.

An example of a typical profit commission calculated at 31st December 2003 might be calculated as follows:

INCOME		OUTGO	
1. Gross Premium for 2003	150,000	1. Commission for 2003 (30%)	45,000
2. Outstanding Loss Reserve at 31st December 2002	25,000	2. Losses paid in 2003	60,000
		3. Unearned Premium Reserve at 31st December 2003 (40%)	60,000
3. Unearned Premium Reserve at 31st December 2002	40,000	4. Outstanding Loss Reserve at 31st December 2003	30,000
		5. R/I expenses (5%)	7,500
		6. Deficit from previous year	NIL
		Profit for 2003	12,500
	$215,000		$215,000

Profit commission payable to ceding company (at, say, 15%) = 15% of $12,500 = $1,875.

In certain profit commission terms, the profit commission is calculated on the average profit over a period of years (for example, the preceding 3 years) rather than having losses carried forward for a number of individual years or to extinction.

Sliding Scale of Commission

In some treaties a sliding scale of commission is used instead of a combination of ceding commission plus profit commission. In such instances the rate of commission payable is related to the actual loss ratio incurred under treaty at the end of the period of cover. This is an inverse relationship where a larger commission is payable when the loss ratio is low and the rate of commission actually decreases as the loss ratio increases. For example, the basis for calculation of the commission could be expressed in the form of a table, such as the following:

Loss Ratio	Rate of Commission Payable
Less than 46%	40.0%
47% or less but more than 46%	39.5%
48% " " 47%	39.0%
49% " " 48%	38.5%
50% " " 49%	38.0%
51% " " 50%	37.5%
52% " " 51%	37.0%
53% " " 52%	36.5%
54% " " 53%	36.0%
55% " " 54%	35.5%
56% " " 55%	35.0%
57% " " 56%	34.5%
58% " " 57%	34.0%
59% " " 58%	33.5%
60% " " 59%	33.0%
61% " " 60%	32.5%
62% " " 61%	32.0%
63% " " 62%	31.5%
64% " " 63%	31.0%
65% " " 64%	30.5%
Over 65%	30.0%

Under such an arrangement, a provisional rate of commission would be allowed in the quarterly (or half-yearly) accounts and an adjustment is made at the end of the treaty year depending on the actual results. In the above example, the provisional rate of commission might be 30%.

The loss ratio is calculated at the end of the year according to the following formula:

> Claims paid
> **plus** outstanding loss reserve at end of current year
> **less** outstanding loss reserve at end of previous year
>
> divided by
>
> Premium ceded to treaty less returns and cancellations
> **plus** unearned premium reserve at end of previous year
> **less** unearned premium reserve at end of current year.

In the above example the commission would not be more than 40%, even if the loss ratio were less than 46%. The commission would not be less than 30% if the loss ratio were above 65%. This ensures a reasonable sharing in the experience of the treaty, and leaves a fair rate of return to both parties in case of extremes. Thus, there is no need for profit commission as any adjustment is made immediately when the treaty result is known.

An example of how this works is as follows:

> P_1 Premium for the year — $150,000
> P_2 Unearned premium reserve at end of previous year — $40,000
> P_3 Unearned premium reserve at end of current year — $60,000
> L_1 Losses paid during year — $60,000
> L_2 Losses outstanding at end of current year — $30,000
> L_3 Losses outstanding at end of previous year — $25,000
>
> Commission already paid at provisional rate of 30% — $45,000
>
> The formula to be used would be:
>
> $$\text{Loss Ratio} = \frac{L_1 + L_2 - L_3}{P_1 + P_2 - P_3} = \frac{60{,}000 + 30{,}000 - 25{,}000}{150{,}000 + 40{,}000 - 60{,}000} = \frac{65{,}000}{130{,}000} = 50\%$$

According to the table used in the original sliding scale of commission, the final rate of commission should be 38%. There would be an additional commission payable of $12,000 (8%) over and above the agreed provisional rate of commission (30%). This results in a total ceding commission of $ 57,000 for the year, being 38% of $ 150,000.

Establishing the levels of ceding commission, profit commission and/or sliding scales of commission (and the mix between ceding and profit commission) is a matter of negotiation between the ceding company and the reinsurer. It is clearly in the interests of the reinsurer that some form of incentive should be built into the commission structure so that both parties benefit from profitable business being ceded to the treaty.

Periodic Technical Accounts

These are statements of the business transactions between the parties. They are prepared at regular intervals, usually on a quarterly or half-yearly basis (though some treaties provide for annual accounts). Accounts are normally of two types:

(a)   Year of Account basis
(b)   Underwriting Year basis.

(A)   Year of Account basis

These technical accounts deal with all premiums and losses in the year under review irrespective of date of origin or inception of any individual cession or loss on that cession. Accounts are usually closed at the end of the year in question by providing for portfolio assumptions and withdrawals of both premiums and outstanding losses.

We have shown below a simple example of quarterly periodic accounts for two treaty years of account. Commissions are set at 40% of premiums written and premium portfolio transfers are also at set 40%. Interest on the premium reserve (equivalent to the incoming premium portfolio transfer) is set at 2.5%. The premium reserve would be retained at inception and released at the end of the annual period. There is a slight rounding for interest in Year 2. There is no reconciliation for incoming or outgoing loss portfolio transfers.

Proportional Treaties

Year 1

	1st Quarter Dr	1st Quarter Cr	2nd Quarter Dr	2nd Quarter Cr	3rd Quarter Dr	3rd Quarter Cr	4th Quarter Dr	4th Quarter Cr
Premiums Written		266,000		126,000		238,600		128,500
Commissions	106,400		50,400		95,440		51,400	
Losses	31,200		20,700		32,070		22,140	
Premium Reserve	260,000							260,000
Interest on Reserve								6,500
Premium Portfolio		260,000					303,640	
Loss Portfolio		118,600					152,800	
Balance	247,000		54,900		111,090			134,980
	644,600	**644,600**	**126,000**	**126,000**	**238,600**	**238,600**	**529,980**	**529,980**

Year 2

	1st Quarter Dr	1st Quarter Cr	2nd Quarter Dr	2nd Quarter Cr	3rd Quarter Dr	3rd Quarter Cr	4th Quarter Dr	4th Quarter Cr
Premium Written		242,200		190,800		427,000		286,000
Commissions	96,880		76,320		170,800		114,400	
Losses	22,900		42,600		91,550		23,740	
Premium Reserve	303,640							303,640
Interest on Reserve								7,600
Premium Portfolio		303,640					458,400	
Loss Portfolio		152,800					248,800	
Balance	275,220		71,880		164,650			248,100
	698,640	**698,640**	**190,800**	**190,800**	**427,000**	**427,000**	**845,340**	**845,340**

This set of accounts shows the movement of premium reserves and premium and outstanding loss portfolio transfers in the first and last quarters of each year of account. Most technical accounts would show premium reserves accounted in each quarter. An agreed amount (here we have used 40% of premiums written) would be retained in one quarter of a particular year and the same amount would be released in the corresponding quarter of the following year.

In the above example, the positive balance in each of the first three quarters would be paid to the reinsurer. In the fourth quarter the balance is negative (due to the withdrawal of premium and outstanding loss portfolio transfers) and would be due to the ceding company.

There are no set patterns for rendering accounts, although many reinsurers have tried to impose identified time parameters for the ceding company to render a periodic account, allow it to be checked and then the resultant treaty balance paid to or from either party. Accounts would depend on the type of business covered, the country of origin and type of treaty involved.

(B)   Underwriting Year basis

Under this method of accounting (which is probably the most accurate) the period in which a risk incepts is of paramount importance. All premiums, claims (whenever they might arise), commissions and expenses are closed or accounted to the underwriting year in which the original risk incepted. Historically, many marine and aviation treaties were accounted on this basis as were the accounts of Lloyd's Syndicates. Advanced discussions are taking place to change the accounting of business at Lloyd's, and readers should follow developments in that famous market. Underwriting Year accounts are often closed after three years but some are left open for longer periods until all claims are fully settled. For obvious reasons, this might take many years and an underwriting year might involve numerous accounts. For example, if claims take 7 years to settle, then technically 28 separate quarterly accounts should be issued (4 x quarterly accounts in the underwriting year itself, plus 6 years x 4 quarterly accounts = 24, making 28 accounts in all – just for that one treaty period).

Accounts are often rendered quarterly but every quarterly account therefore contains a separate statement for *each* underwriting year that is still open. A typical example (on a calendar year basis for the period) would be:

3rd Quarter 2003			
Underwriting Year **2001**	Return	Premiums	(1,000)
		Commission (25%)	(250)
			(750)
		Losses	3,000
Due to ceding company			(3,750)
Outstanding losses			5,000
Underwriting Year **2002**	Written	Premiums	10,000
		Commission (25%)	2,500
			7,500
		Losses	37,500
Due to ceding company			(30,000)
Outstanding losses			60,000
Underwriting Year **2003**	Written	Premiums	100,000
		Commission (25%)	25,000
			75,000
		Losses	1,000
Due to reinsurer			74,000
Outstanding losses			75,000

This account is in respect of premiums, commissions and paid losses arising in the 3rd Quarter 2003, namely between 1st July 2003 and 30th September 2003. There are, in fact, three separate accounts for the individual 2001, 2002 and 2003 Underwriting Years, all of which might be open or current at this point in time. Readers should note the inclusion of outstanding losses for each open underwriting year.

This example shows that accounting on an underwriting year basis is complicated and requires good internal disciplines to track all movements on a particular underwriting year.

Cash Loss Limit and Loss Advice Limit

In most cases all losses and premiums under a treaty are accounted in the quarterly or half-yearly statement. However, when there are certain large individual losses, the ceding company might not wish (or be able) to wait until the issue and settlement of the normal account to obtain any money due because this might place an undue strain on its liquidity. It therefore asks the reinsurer for an immediate cash settlement of the amount of the claim it has paid. The total paid claim must exceed a stated limit to qualify for a cash settlement and this limit is called the *cash loss limit*. If a large claim occurs, the ceding company is obliged to report that claim to its reinsurers under the provisions of the *loss advice or reporting limit*. This puts the reinsurer on warning of its potential involvement in that claim and possible cash loss settlement. Amounts paid by way of cash losses appear as an adjustment (credit and debit) in a subsequent quarterly account to prevent the same recovery being made twice. There are no standard rules of identifying the level of loss advice and cash loss limits, but a reasonable figure would lie between 2.5% and 5% of the lower of the maximum treaty limit or total premium ceded to the treaty.

Bordereaux (a) Premium

This is a schedule or list of risks ceded to the treaty during a defined period. The ceding company provides details of all original insureds and their occupation, locations, original sums insured and amounts reinsured, rates of premium, etc. It is sent to the reinsurer at regular intervals and informs the reinsurer of all risks reinsured and whether the cessions conform to the terms and conditions of the treaty. These bordereaux often enable the reinsurer to monitor accumulations of (say) natural perils exposures in any one area or identified zone.

Bordereaux (b) Loss

This is a schedule or list of claims incurred on risks ceded to the treaty during a defined period. It gives details of each loss, circumstances, date of occurrence, nature of claim, extent of loss, amounts paid, amounts outstanding, etc.

Nowadays, the provision of treaty bordereaux is quite rare. This is largely due to the high cost of administration. However, bordereaux of outstanding losses at the end of the treaty year should still be supplied, as this would give important information on large individual losses affecting a treaty and possibly large event losses (e.g. a storm or an earthquake). A reinsurer might have treaty participations from a number of ceding companies in one country and might want to see the cumulative effects of a particular risk or event loss arising from several treaty involvements. This might assist the reinsurer in recovering from its own reinsurance protections, known as retrocession contracts (retrocession means a "reinsurance of a reinsurance").

The following are examples of Premium and Loss Bordereaux.

PREMIUM BORDEREAU FOR MONTH OF JULY 2003

Policy Number	Period of Insurance From	Period of Insurance to	Name of Insured	Type of Risk	Description and Location of Risks	Original Sum Insured	Rate Per Mile	Original Premium	Sum Reinsured	Premium Reinsured
FB 7685	01-Jul-03	30-Jun-04	Ronsonal plc	Fire/Bus Int	All concrete textile factory at 112 Herbert Street, Manchester	£20,000,000	2.00	£40,000	£15,000,000	£30,000
FB 7686	16-Jul-03	15-Jul-04	Mecalec plc	Fire/Bus Int	Electronic goods in pre-fabricated partition store covered with tiles at 16 Ranton Street, Leeds	£15,000,000	1.80	£27,000	£10,000,000	£18,000
FO 1016	16-Jul-03	15-Jul-04	Mercantile Ltd	Fire only	Electronic goods in concrete store covered with tiles at 16 Hussar Street, Bradford	£5,000,000	1.50	£7,500	£3,000,000	£4,500

LOSS BORDEREAU FOR MONTH OF OCTOBER 2003

Claim Number	Policy Number	Date of Loss	Name of Insured	Details of Loss	Gross Loss Paid	Outstanding	Loss to treaty Paid	Outstanding	Remarks
85/2003	FO 6312	08-Oct-03	Amotal plc	Fire in factory at 12 Lansdowne St, Burford. Cause unknown. Building severely damaged.	Nil	£1,500,000	Nil	£250,000	Police are investigating. Suspicious circumstances. Fire alarm disconnected before fire.
86/2003	FB 5162	21-Oct-03	Barber & Sons	Fire due to short-circuit in warehouse at 8 Victoria Road, Castle Hill. Stock of electronic goods completely destroyed.	£500,000	£100,000	£100,000	£20,000	Surveyors report attached. Amount outstanding is in respect of surveyor's fees.
87/2003	FB 4425	26-Oct-03	Chooks Ltd	Fire in cold room at 56 Smith Road, Liverpool. Cause unknown. Stock of frozen chickens damaged.	Nil	£100,000	Nil	£20,000	Police report will be released soon.

Premium Reserve Deposit

This is a proportion of the premium due to the reinsurer but is retained by the ceding company as a guarantee for the reinsurer completing its obligations under the agreed terms of any treaty. This reserve must not be confused with the reserve for unexpired risk (although the amounts are often the same). The reserve for unexpired risk is that portion of the premium required for risks that have started during the currency of the treaty period and would still be in force after the expiry date of the treaty. Thus a risk incepting on 1st October 2003 and issued for 12 months would continue until 30th September 2004. At 31st December 2003, the expiry date of treaty, there would unearned premium for the period 1st January 2004 to 30th September 2004. The ceding company would not be able to take credit for the unearned premium until the liability under the risk had actually expired, namely 30th September 2004 in this example.

There were a number of reasons for keeping a premium reserve deposit equal to the unexpired risk reserve as security. Initially, many countries did not want to allow their valuable currency to be sent overseas to distant reinsurers. This might have weakened their national economy. Regulations were created restricting the settlement of premiums to overseas companies and the concept of a legal premium reserve deposit was established. (As time, globalisation and improved communications have developed, there has been a marked decrease in the number of countries where premium reserve deposits are a legal requirement).

Over the last few years, many reinsurers have also become insolvent. This has led to complicated actions at law to recover various balances due to the ceding company. These events have highlighted the sensible decision to retain premium reserve deposits. Additionally, if a reinsurer cancels its participation on a treaty, then many treaties allow for the retention of a premium reserve deposit until the reinsurer has discharged its obligations. Whatever the reason, by retaining a premium reserve deposit the ceding company would be able to use that amount of retained premium to offset recovery of any claims due from its reinsurer, whether as a result of cancellation of the treaty or otherwise.

The ceding company retains the premium reserve deposit for one year and releases it in the corresponding periodic account for the next year. At that same time it retains a similar proportion of that next year's treaty premium as security for a further year.

Many reinsurers create *internal* premium reserve items in their own accounts. This allows for the principle of not taking credit for premium until the risk has expired.

(Outstanding) Loss Reserve Deposit

The purpose of a loss reserve deposit is to provide the ceding company with additional security. As with premium reserve deposits, by retaining a loss reserve deposit equivalent to the amount of outstanding claims at the end of the treaty year, the ceding company would be able to guarantee the reinsurer's obligations. Most of those outstanding claims would probably be settled in the following year or years. The loss reserve deposit is usually set at 100% of outstanding losses at the end of the treaty period, as this offers the ceding company an absolute guarantee of the reinsurer's performance. Historically, the loss reserve deposit might have been set at 90%-95%. This assumed a so-called claims redundancy, or saving, on reserved amounts to their ultimate settlement. Nowadays, most ceding companies are looking for certainty.

The mechanics of retaining and releasing loss reserve deposits are similar to premium reserve deposits. They would be retained for one year and released in the corresponding account one year later, or at different period by mutual agreement.

Two points are worth noting about both premium and loss reserve deposits:

1. They may be required by law, in which case the parties have no option but to include them in the arrangements.

2. Where they are not required by law, it is no longer common practice to include them. Results of proportional treaties in recent years have been very poor. In order to ease cash flow to reinsurers, reserve deposits are seldom retained by ceding companies.

Interest on Reserve Deposits

Reserve deposits are retained by the ceding company, but ultimately those deposits belong to the reinsurer. As the funds are being kept out of the reinsurer's pocket, the reinsurer loses a potential investment return on those funds. The ceding company allows a notional rate of interest on the retained amounts and credits the reinsurer in a later account, normally one year after the reserve deposit was retained. This interest compensates the reinsurer for income lost by not being able to invest the reserve deposit funds itself.

Historically, interest levels were notional and were often well below rates available in the banking world. Where reserves have to be withheld by law, reinsurers often insist on higher interest rates nearer to (or above) actual interest rates being paid by banks on their own deposits. At the time of writing, worldwide interest rates are at their lowest for 40 years and are likely to remain so for the foreseeable future. Interest rates on reserve deposits are therefore more a theoretical than actual problem.

An alternative procedure is for the reinsurer to supply a Letter of Credit equivalent to the amount of the premium or loss reserve deposit required. The ceding company can then draw down on the Letter of Credit if necessary. This procedure is favoured by many US ceding companies if their reinsurers are non-admitted (not resident in US).

Portfolio (a) Premium

The main reason for using premium portfolio transfers is to transfer the unearned premium for unexpired liability at the end of one treaty period into the next treaty period. It is a recognised accounting mechanism and simplifies the accounting procedure. The method of accounting is known as Year of Account. It is often used if a reinsurer cancels or changes its participation from one treaty period to the next. If a reinsurer cancels its participation at the end of the current treaty year, it is relieved of its liability, and would be *debited* with a percentage of the premium it had received during that treaty year. This would happen in the last quarterly (or other) account for that treaty period. The new reinsurer (who has accepted the business for the next treaty period) is *credited* with the premium that had been withdrawn from the previous reinsurer. The effect of this transaction is to release the previous reinsurer from any liability in respect of the *unexpired* portion of the risks accepted in the preceding year and the new reinsurer accepts this liability (for those risks which will expire in the next treaty period). The new reinsurer has effectively assumed liability for any claims that might arise on those unexpired policies that will *run off* in the next treaty period.

As we have said, premium portfolio transfers are also used when a reinsurer changes its participation at renewal. If this happens, the reinsurer is debited with its old share of the premium portfolio at the end of the treaty year and is credited with its new share of that portfolio at the beginning of the following year.

The premium portfolio transfer represents the amount of unearned premium for unexpired risk at an agreed point in time. It is generally accepted that premium portfolio transfers are made after deduction of commission.

The premium portfolio transfer was traditionally calculated at a rate of 35% or 40% of the year's written premium. These rates assume that risks in the portfolio incept evenly throughout the year. The calculation is arbitrary and inaccurate as the dates of inception of business in a portfolio are seldom evenly distributed.

The "twenty-fourth" method is a more accurate way of calculating the portfolio. Under this method, it is assumed that the average commencement date of all policies issued during a month is the 15th day of that month (half the policies would have been issued on days before the 15th and half would have been issued after that date). The average expiry date for these policies would therefore be the 15th day of the same month in the following year. For example, it is assumed that policies issued in January 2003 would expire on or about 15th January 2004. Hence, on 31st December 2003, the risks would still have ½ a month or $\frac{1}{24}$ of a year to run. Similarly, policies written in February would have 1½ months or $\frac{3}{24}$ of a year to run.

The same calculation can be made for all the subsequent months and the portfolio at 31st December would be on the following lines:

Risks commencing in month of	Premium for the month	Fraction unexpired	Unexpired premium
January 2003	$480,000	1/24	$20,000
February	120,000	3/24	15,000
March	84,000	5/24	17,500
April	240,000	7/24	70,000
May	96,000	9/24	36,000
June	72,000	11/24	33,000
July	600,000	13/24	325,000
August	120,000	15/24	75,000
September	108,000	17/24	76,500
October	360,000	19/24	285,000
November	72,000	21/24	63,000
December 2003	48,000	23/24	46,000
	$2,400,000		$1,062,000
Less reinsurance commission at, say, 25%			265,500
Portfolio			$796,500

In this example the premium portfolio to be transferred at the end of December 2003 would be $796,500. This amount is net of 25% commission.

With improved computer technology it has become possible to calculate the exact unexpired period of each policy written or accepted by the ceding company. Companies can therefore calculate the exact unexpired premium on an "actual days" basis. This is also known as pro rata or *per diem*.

Portfolio (b) Losses

In addition to the provision for the transfer of unexpired liability, a reinsurer may be relieved of known losses outstanding at the end of the treaty year. This transfer is often simpler than a premium transfer in that the reinsurer would be debited with either 90% or 100% of known losses outstanding at the end of the treaty period. The replacement reinsurer would be credited with the same amount. The effect of this is to release the old reinsurer from any liability in respect of claims that had occurred in the earlier treaty period, but would be settled in the next treaty period. The new or replacement reinsurer would accept this obligation to settle those outstanding losses by receiving a monetary credit equivalent to the known outstanding losses at the end of the previous treaty period.

Brokerage

Very often reinsurance brokers, who are the intermediaries between the ceding companies and their reinsurers, place proportional treaties. The broker's remuneration for this work is called brokerage and is paid by reinsurers on the basis of a fixed percentage of premiums ceded to the treaty. The usual level of brokerage allowed on proportional treaties tends to be between 1.5% and 2.5% of ceded treaty premiums.

Statistics and Information

These give details of the gross premiums, commissions, losses paid, losses outstanding, and portfolio transfers, if any, for the years preceding the year of negotiation of the particular treaty. The information often relates to five or more years experience or history of the treaty. This period is known as the *observation period*. The information should contain details of previous treaty and class retentions, large individual risk losses, together with any event losses, such as an earthquake or storm that might have affected the treaty in earlier years. Any important *changes* in the historic information when compared to the constitution of the present-day account should also be included. This information is intended to provide the potential reinsurer with data it can use to assess whether or not to accept a participation in the treaty and on what terms, conditions and exclusions that participation should be made.

The ceding company should also supply an estimate of the anticipated treaty premium for the coming year. Although only an estimate, it provides a potential reinsurer with a useful guide for budgetary, regulatory and internal monitoring purposes.

5

Quota Share Treaty

Quota share reinsurance is often known as the purest form of proportional reinsurance as it involves a simple percentage sharing of risks, premiums, commissions, expenses and claims between the ceding company and the reinsurer. A quota share treaty is an agreement whereby the ceding company is obliged to cede and the reinsurer is obliged to accept a fixed percentage proportion of every risk accepted by the ceding company within its stated retention. As with surplus treaties, once the terms and conditions of the quota share treaty have been agreed, they are automatic in their effect. Certain risks might be excluded, and these would be negotiated and agreed between the parties at the formation of the treaty. Excluded risks might relate to a specific type, class or those risks located in an identified geographic area. The reinsurer therefore shares proportionally in the risk, receives premiums, and pays commission, expenses and losses all in the same percentage proportion that the risk was ceded to the quota share treaty.

For example, a ceding company might arrange a 50% quota share treaty covering all its simple (personal, private, domestic or householder's) fire business. The retention of the ceding company would be 50% of each and every risk and the balance of 50% would be ceded to the reinsurer. Thus, the reinsurer would cover 50% of all simple risks, receive 50% of all premiums (less commission and expenses) and pay 50% of all claims falling within the terms and conditions of the quota share treaty.

It is customary for a quota share to specify a definite monetary limit beyond which the reinsurer would not be committed on any one risk.

In the above example this limit could be expressed as:

> To accept a 50% quota share of a maximum $1,000,000 (for 100%) any one risk
>
> Quota share cession hereon not to exceed a maximum of $ 500,000 any one risk.

Advantages and Disadvantages

The quota share treaty has advantages and disadvantages. Advantages for the ceding company might sometimes be disadvantages for the reinsurer and vice versa.

For a Ceding Company

Main advantages of a quota share treaty are:

(1) Simplicity of operation. Once the treaty has been arranged it requires very little administration.

(2) Higher commission and better terms are obtainable. This type of treaty gives the reinsurer a better spread of business without being selected against. Quota share treaties are generally more profitable than other proportional treaties and should attract better terms and commissions.

Main disadvantages are:

(1) Ceding company cannot vary its retention for any specific risk and thus pays away premiums on small risks it could retain for its own account.

(2) Retained risks are not necessarily homogeneous or similar in size. Ceding company retains a fixed percentage of all risks written and these will be of

varying sizes and different loss frequency and severity.

For a Reinsurer

Main advantages are:

(1) Reinsurer receives a share of each and every risk. There is no selection against the reinsurer and it participates to a far greater extent in the business written than under other types of proportional reinsurances.

(2) Reinsurer obtains a larger share of profits from the ceding company than it would have obtained under any other type of proportional treaty.

Disadvantages:

(1) Reinsurer has to pay a higher commission to the ceding company than under other types of proportional treaty. As this may be matched by a higher profitability and better spread of ceded business, it might not really be a disadvantage.

(2) Reinsurer has no protection against an accumulation of losses if a natural disaster were to affect a large number of individual risks covered under the quota share treaty. In an attempt to counter this problem, there is an increasing tendency for quota share (and other proportional) treaties to contain an *"any one event"* limit.

This **"Event Limit"** seeks to restrict the loss potential of one natural perils event affecting the treaty. Another mechanism used by reinsurers to restrict poor quality (or under-rated) business being ceded to a proportional treaty is known as a **"Cession Limit"**. These limitations could be used together or independently of one another, but both seek to minimise or restrict the reinsurer's exposure to an aggregation of risks covering natural perils. As quota share treaties are more likely to be affected by a natural perils event (because of the large number of small simple risks ceded to a typical quota share treaty), the restrictive event and cession limit clauses are perhaps more relevant to them than other forms of proportional treaties.

What must not be forgotten is that proportional treaties are as unlimited as the number of individual risks ceded to them. If reinsurers impose cession or event limits, then reinsurers have effectively imposed an artificial restriction on the operation of that proportional treaty, either in the form of the amount of business the ceding company is allowed to accept (cession limit), or the amount of any natural perils loss the ceding company is allowed to recover (event limit). It would be normal for the ceding company to expect enhanced commission terms if either limitation is imposed. More importantly, both parties should identify, in advance, what would happen if a series of different situations were to occur, especially if the situation involved the triggering of either or both limitations, and one or both had been exceeded or contravened at the date of any natural perils loss.

Main uses of Quota Share

A quota share treaty is best suited for:

(1) New insurance companies or companies entering a new class of business or in a new area or location. Reinsurers might have superior knowledge of that new line of business or area and their participation might assist the ceding company to develop its new account in a more profitable way.

(2) A ceding company might wish to accept reinsurance business itself. It could offer its business in exchange for similar business of another insurance company,

often located overseas. This is known as reciprocity, or the mutual exchange of business. Reciprocal exchanges between direct insurance companies enable each party to participate in a wider portfolio at minimal costs and balance the outgo of ceded premiums and liabilities for a similar amount of inwards reinsurance premium and associated liabilities. Reciprocity is often used by insurance companies within the same group, but located in different countries. It would be fair to say that reciprocity is not that common nowadays, but is still used in selected markets throughout the world.

(3) Increasing the solvency ratio of a ceding company by reducing the amount of retained premium for own account. This is sometimes termed "surplus relief". Please see the simple example in Chapter 1.

The placement of a quota share treaty also starts with the preparation of a placement slip. A slip would usually contain the following information (fictitious details have been used in the example):

Ceding Company:	XYZ Insurance Company Limited
Type of Treaty:	Quota Share
Class of Business	Fire and Allied Perils
Territorial Limits:	Republic of South Africa
Period:	Continuous Agreement from 1st January 2003
Notice of Cancellation:	3 months prior to 31 December in any year
Limits:	Maximum Liability hereon $1,000,000 (for 100%) Sum Insured any one risk (as defined)
Maximum Cession	50% Quota Share cession, subject to maximum cession hereon of $500,000 Sum Insured any one risk (as defined)
Rate	Original Gross Rate

Commission:	25%
Profit Commission	10%
	Reinsurers' Expenses: 5%
	Losses carried forward to extinction
Premium Reserve Deposit:	Nil, but 40% in event of cancellation
Loss Reserve Deposit:	Nil, but 100% in event of cancellation
Portfolio:	35% Premium
	90% Losses
Cash Loss/Loss Advice Limit:	$250,000 for 100% hereon
Bordereaux:	None
Accounts:	Quarterly (including Outstanding Losses)
Accounts Settlement	45 days for preparation, 15 days for reconciliation and further 30 days for settlement (90 days in all)
Brokerage:	2.0% on O.G.R.
Statistics:	(Usually attached for past 5 years or more)
Estimated Premium Income:	$5,000,000 (for 100% hereon)

It is customary to specify that the ceding company's stated percentage retention (50% in this example) should be retained by the ceding company for its own net account and not reinsured under additional *proportional facilities*. This prevents the ceding company from accepting poor business, reinsuring a large part under its quota share treaty and then further reinsuring its retention (perhaps by other quota share placements) and thereby keeping little or no liability for itself under that risk. The ceding company would be allowed to effect excess of loss reinsurance to protect itself against individual risks or an accumulation of losses on its net retained account, as would occur in a storm, flood or earthquake. Please see Chapter 11 on catastrophe reinsurance where we explore this topic in greater detail.

There are many variations of quota share usage and some

are often quite confusing. In certain countries, local regulations might exist that require a ceding company to make a compulsory cession to a national or regional reinsurance company. After making these compulsory cessions, the ceding company would be allowed to reinsure itself in the normal way. For example:

Original Sum Insured	$10,000,000
Less 10% compulsory cession	$1,000,000
Sum Insured net of compulsory cession	$9,000,000
50% quota share cession	$4,500,000
Original Gross Premium (O.G.P.)	$20,000
Less 10% compulsory cession	$2,000
O.G.P. net of compulsory cession	$18,000
50% quota share cession	$ 9,000

In the example above, the ceding company would cede liability and premium to any quota share treaty based upon the sum insured net of any compulsory cession. Here we have used a 50% quota share cession.

More confusion arises if the ceding company builds further proportional facilities on its gross retention (its retention without any quota share reinsurance) or its gross net retention (its retention after quota share reinsurance), or its gross retention together with its quota share reinsurers. For example:

Gross Retention	$1,000,000 (equivalent to one line)
Surplus treaty, maximum 4 lines	$4,000,000 (4 x $1,000,000)
Total automatic capacity	$5,000,000 (own line plus surplus capacity)
Gross Net Retention	$ 500,000 (Gross retention after 50% quota share)
Surplus treaty, maximum 4 lines	$2,000,000
Total automatic capacity	$2,500,000

Gross Retention (Net & QS)	$1,000,000 (Own gross net retention plus 50% QS)
Surplus treaty, maximum 4 lines	$4,000,000 (4 x $1,000,000)
Total automatic capacity	$5,000,000 (own line plus surplus capacity)

In effect, the first and third examples are the same, but the ceding company and reinsurers must identify which of the options is being used.

There is also a treaty known as a variable quota share. In certain countries, the insurance regulator does not allow the ceding company to expose its assets to more than a certain specified amount. In this case, reinsurers often allow the ceding company to cede higher quota share percentages as the risks themselves increase in size. For example:

Maximum gross net retention allowed	$400,000	
Risks up to $500,000 Sum Insured	20% QS cession	max. $ 100,000
Risks between $500,001 and $1,000,000	60% QS cession	max. $ 600,000
Risks between $1,000,001 and $4,000,000	90% QS cession	max. $3,600,000
In each category, the quota share reduces the ceding company's exposure to a *maximum* of $400,000 any one risk.		

6

Surplus Treaty

A surplus treaty is an agreement whereby the ceding company is obliged to cede and the reinsurer is obliged to accept the surplus liability over the ceding company's own chosen retention. The essential difference between quota share and surplus treaties is that:

> Under a quota share treaty the reinsurer accepts a fixed percentage share of each risk accepted by the ceding company within its retention.

> Under a surplus treaty the ceding company decides what to retain on each risk and cedes the balance over its chosen retention to the reinsurer.

A surplus treaty allows the ceding company to reinsure any part of the risk (the surplus) which it does not wish to retain for its own account. If a risk is wholly retained then no surplus cession need be made to the treaty. The maximum amount that could be ceded to a surplus treaty is usually expressed in terms of a number of "lines". A "line" is the amount of the ceding company's own chosen retention. Thus a "5 line surplus treaty" means that the treaty will accept a maximum of 5 times the ceding company's own chosen retention. Please refer to our comments in the previous Chapter concerning the automatic and obligatory aspects of proportional treaties and our later comments on gross or net line cessions. Surplus treaties are also obligatory treaties and automatic in their usage once terms, conditions and exclusions have been agreed between the contracting parties.

The way in which a surplus treaty operates can be seen in the following example.

Maximum own retention any one risk	$500,000
Maximum Surplus Treaty capacity	9 lines, each of maximum $500,000
Maximum Surplus Treaty capacity	$4,500,000 (9 lines x $500,000)
Maximum automatic underwriting capacity	$5,000,000 (own retention plus surplus capacity)

If the sum insured on a particular risk is $4,800,000, then the apportionment between the ceding company and the reinsurer would be:

Original sum insured	$4,800,000	
Ceding company's own retention	$ 500,000	(10.417% of original risk)
Surplus cession	$4,300,000	(89.583% of original risk)
Original gross premium at 0.30%	$14,400	
Ceding company's own retention	$ 1,500	(10.417% of original risk)
Surplus cession	$12,900	(89.583% of original risk)
Original gross loss	$1,000,000	
Ceding company's own retention	$ 104,170	(10.417% of original risk)
Surplus cession	$ 895,830	(89.583% of original risk)

In this example, the balance of $4,300,000 could be ceded to the surplus treaty. The actual multiple is 8.6 times the ceding company's own retention. This example shows that fractions or inexact multiples of a line can be ceded, providing they accord with the agreed treaty terms and do not exceed any stated maximum cession. Please note the percentage amounts shown. The premium, commission and expenses for the risk would be retained and ceded in those same proportions. If a claim were to occur on that risk, the same percentage amounts would also be used, irrespective of the amount of loss involved. Please see the examples above.

Most computer systems record cessions by percentage, rather than by monetary amount. This makes the apportionment of premiums, commissions, expenses and claims much easier to administer.

If the retention were to be set at $250,000 then the maximum amount that could be ceded to the surplus treaty would be only $2,250,000 (9 x $250,000). The remaining $2,300,000 would have to be reinsured under other (higher) proportional reinsurance arrangements.

Original sum insured	$4,800,000	
Ceding company's own retention	$ 250,000	(5.208% of original risk)
Surplus cession (9 lines of $250,000)	$2,250,000	(46.875% of original risk)
Total own retention and surplus	$2,500,000	(52.083% of original risk)
Balance to be reinsured in other facilities	$2,300,000	(47.917% of original risk)

In this example, premiums, commissions, expenses and claims would also be settled according to the new percentage amounts shown.

When an amount is shown as being the retention (the line) under a surplus treaty, this does not mean that the ceding company has to retain the stated amount stated in every instance. That limit is the maximum that the ceding company could retain and it is possible for the company to retain a smaller amount than the suggested limit. This possibility of varying the size of a selected retention enables the ceding company to calculate its retained liability in relation to the quality of the risk it wishes to reinsure. Thus, if it has accepted a risk which is of a very high quality, then the ceding company could retain a higher amount than if the risk were of lower quality. The ceding company utilises a *table of underwriting limits* to identify the quality of individual risks. Quality will vary according to the occupation, construction and location of an individual risk.

Where the ceding company maintains a high retention, a larger amount could be ceded to the surplus treaty. In the same way, if a retention on a risk is small, then the surplus treaty would have a limited capacity to absorb the surplus. Please refer to the examples below.

A ceding company accepts two risks, A and B. Each have a similar sum insured of $2,000,000. A is a desirable risk whereas B is a less desirable one. The ceding company's maximum retention is $500,000 and it has a surplus treaty of 5 lines. This gives the ceding company a maximum automatic underwriting capacity of $2,500,000 (own maximum retention plus maximum surplus capacity geared to that retention). The ceding company might decide to retain its maximum retention for risk A but only $200,000 for risk B.

The ceding company's retentions and cessions to the surplus treaty would be:

Surplus Treaty

Risk	A	B
Original Sum Insured	$2,000,000	$2,000,000
Own Retention	$ 500,000 (25%)	$200,000 (10%)
Surplus Treaty cession	$1,500,000 (75%)	max. $1,000,000 (50%)
Number of lines ceded	3 x 500,000	5 x 200,000
Balance over surplus treaty	Nil	$800,000 (40%)

In the case of risk B, the ceding company is unable to place the whole of the risk under the surplus treaty because it has decided to retain a lower retention. There is a substantial portion of the risk (40% in our example) without reinsurance. This could involve an individual facultative reinsurance. This might be difficult to obtain if the risk is of poor quality. In order to resolve the problem the ceding company could increase its retention to perhaps $300,000 so that only $200,000 would have to be reinsured facultatively. ($300,000 own retention plus 5 x $300,000 = $1,800,000 leaving $200,000, rather than $800,000 to be covered elsewhere).

The retention and limits can be based upon Sum Insured, Estimated Maximum Loss (E.M.L.) or Probable Maximum Loss (P.M.L.). We discussed the important differences between these methods in Chapter 4.

Advantages and Disadvantages

Advantages of surplus reinsurance for the ceding company are:

(1) Only the portion of the risk that exceeds the ceding company's retention is reinsured. Should the size of a risk be less than the ceding company's retention, then it is not bound to cede any share of that risk to the surplus treaty. The ceding company therefore retains all liability and premium for such risks (and pays all the claims).

(2) As the ceding company retains a fixed monetary amount (as opposed to a fixed *percentage* under a quota share), the retained portfolio becomes more homogeneous or balanced.

(3) By retaining a larger amount on good quality or above average risks and a smaller amount on risks of lesser quality, the ceding company is able to retain more profitable business for itself than ceding that business to its reinsurers.

The high cost of administration is the principal disadvantage to the ceding company as it needs to employ experienced individuals to determine the retention for each and every risk. The risks would be graded according to type (occupation, construction and location), quality (above average, average, below average) and exposure (other risks in same location or to identified perils). Premiums would then be calculated according to retained amount for own account and the amount to be ceded to reinsurers. The use of advanced computer technology has vastly reduced this administrative burden.

The disadvantages to the reinsurer are:

(1) As the ceding company retains a larger part of above average risks for its own account, it follows that the reinsurer might receive a larger share of less desirable risks.

(2) The reinsurer receives not only a larger share of poorer quality risks, but also a disproportionately large share of peak risks, as the ceding company has probably retained a large portion of the smaller risks for its own account.

Please note that peak risks are also known as "target" or "market" risks. The sums insured for these risks are so large that the combined capacity of an entire national insurance (and possibly national reinsurance) market might be required to insure the original risk. Obviously, if all insurance companies accept a co-insurance share on that "target", "market" or "peak" risk, then there could be a substantial accumulation problem if a reinsurer reinsured several insurance companies in that national market. In order to counter this problem, reinsurers have imposed a special "target risks" exclusion or restriction on many reinsurance treaties. The size of "target" risks differs between various national markets, but individual risks larger than $1,000,000,000 would be a reasonable indication.

There is little advantage for a reinsurer to accept a surplus treaty in preference to a quota share except that the rate of commission payable to the ceding company would normally be less for surplus than for quota share treaties. We explained this in the various disadvantages above. Surplus treaty reinsurers might have a similar exposure to quota share reinsurers if an accumulation of losses arising from a natural perils disaster were to occur under the surplus treaty. We described this aspect in Chapter 5 and our comments on Cession and Event Limits also apply to surplus treaties. Many surplus treaties now contain these limitations or restrictions that are in addition to an identified maximum exposure to any one risk (as defined and agreed between the parties).

Multiple Surplus Treaties

Ceding companies might have First, Second or even Third Surplus treaties. For certain categories of risk, a ceding company might have a first surplus treaty of 10 lines, a second surplus of 10 lines and a third surplus of 10 lines. The ceding company therefore has 30 lines of reinsurance capacity available (31 lines automatic underwriting capacity with its own retention and total of the three surplus treaties).

Why, then, not create one single surplus treaty with a capacity of 30 lines? It could be that the second and subsequent surplus treaties had been added over time as the ceding company's account grew and it required more capacity. Reinsurers (and/or any reinsurance brokers involved) might be able to accommodate that additional capacity in the form of additional surplus treaty arrangements, without disturbing the initial (first) surplus treaty.

There is another important reason that the ceding company might have deliberately arranged its proportional reinsurance programme in a number of different surplus treaties. In order to maintain the high commission obtained on its (first) surplus treaty, the ceding company might have to offer reinsurers a reasonable ratio of treaty liability to premium ceded to that treaty. This is known as the balance or exposure of the treaty. Effectively, the net outgo of premium could be less under 3 separate treaties rather than the total under a single treaty. The following example should explain this concept:

We shall assume that the retention of the ceding company is $100,000 any one risk, and that there is only one surplus treaty of 30 lines, and that the portfolio is made up of the following risks:

Surplus Treaty

No of Risks	SUMS INSURED PER RISK					PREMIUM INCOME			
	Original $	Retention $	%	Surplus $	Original %	Retention $	$	To Surplus $
1,050	10,000	10,000	100.00%	0	0	105,000	105,000	0
2,300	25,000	25,000	100.00%	0	0	575,000	575,000	0
1,222	50,000	50,000	100.00%	0	0	611,000	611,000	0
580	90,000	90,000	100.00%	0	0	522,000	522,000	0
150	150,000	100,000	66.67%	50,000	33.33%	225,000	150,000	75,000
100	200,000	100,000	50.00%	100,000	50.00%	150,000	75,000	75,000
60	1,000,000	100,000	10.00%	900,000	90.00%	450,000	45,000	405,000
40	1,500,000	100,000	6.67%	1,400,000	93.33%	450,000	30,015	419,985
20	2,000,000	100,000	5.00%	1,900,000	95.00%	200,000	10,000	190,000
10	2,500,000	100,000	4.00%	2,400,000	96.00%	125,000	5,000	120,000
5	2,750,000	100,000	3.64%	2,650,000	96.36%	27,500	1,000	26,500
1	2,900,000	100,000	3.45%	2,800,000	96.55%	2,900	100	2,800
0	3,000,000	100,000	3.33%	0	96.67%	0	0	0
TOTALS						3,443,400	2,115,615	1,314,285

Let us assess the relationship between the maximum surplus treaty capacity of 30 lines to the premium income ceded to that treaty. In this example, the maximum treaty limit is $3,000,000 compared to a total ceded premium income of $1,314,285. This produces an approximate ratio of liability to premium of 2.30 to 1. Reinsurers look at this relationship and assess the balance of the treaty (treaty premium divided by highest treaty exposure) or its exposure (highest treaty exposure divided by treaty premium income). The former shows that the balance of this treaty is 43.80% and the exposure is 228.26%. The ideal situation is where the balance or exposure is nearer to 100% or better. Subject to the claims experience of the treaty, this relationship might enable the ceding company to obtain a commission level of, say, 25%. After that 25% commission level, reinsurers would receive net premium of $985,714, being gross premium of $1,314,285 less $328,571 in commission.

If, instead of one surplus treaty of 30 lines, there were three surplus treaties as originally described above, then the apportionment of risks and premiums would be as follows:

Surplus Treaty

			SUMS INSURED PER RISK			PREMIUM INCOME		
Number of Risks	Original £	Retention (1 line) $	1st Surp (10 lines) $	2nd Surp (10 lines) $	3rd Surp (10 lines) $	1st Surp $	2nd Surp $	3rd Surp $
1,050	10,000	100,000	0	0	0	0	0	0
2,300	25,000	100,000	0	0	0	0	0	0
1,222	55,000	100,000	0	0	0	0	0	0
580	90,000	100,000	0	0	0	0	0	0
150	150,000	100,000	50,000	0	0	75,000	0	0
100	200,000	100,000	100,000	0	0	75,000	0	0
60	1,000,000	100,000	900,000	0	0	405,000	0	0
40	1,500,000	100,000	1,000,000	400,000	0	299,989	119,996	0
20	2,000,000	100,000	1,000,000	900,000	0	100,000	90,000	0
10	2,500,000	100,000	1,000,000	1,000,000	400,000	50,000	50,000	20,000
5	2,750,000	100,000	1,000,000	1,000,000	650,000	10,000	10,000	6,500
1	2,900,000	100,000	1,000,000	1,000,000	800,000	1,000	1,000	800
0	3,000,000	100,000	0	0	0	0	0	0
						1,015,989	270,996	27,300

Ratio for the first surplus treaty is approximately 1 to 1. $1,000,000 liability to $1,016,000 ceded premium income. Exposure is 98.43%, balance is 101.60%.	
Gross ceded premium	$1,016,000
Commission at 35%	$355,600
Net ceded premium	$660,400
Ratio for the second surplus treaty is approximately 3.69 to 1. $1,000,000 liability to $270,996 ceded premium income. Exposure is 369.00%, balance is 27.10%.	
Gross ceded premium	$270,996
Commission at 22.5%	$60,974
Net ceded premium	$210,022
Ratio for the third surplus treaty is approximately 37 to 1. $1,000,000 liability to $27,300 ceded premium income. Exposure is 3,663.00%, balance is 2.73%.	
Gross ceded premium	$27,300
Commission at 17.5%	$4,778
Net ceded premium	$22,522
Total gross ceded premium	$1,314,285
Total commissions	$421,352
Total net ceded premium	$892,933

The first surplus treaty shows a very good balance and, subject once again to claims experience, the ceding company might obtain a higher level of commission, perhaps between 30% and 35%. The second surplus might produce a commission of between 20% and 22.5% and the third surplus between 15% and 17.5%. We have shown above the gross ceded premium less commission for each of the three treaties and then the total if they are made on this basis. The ceding company would generate more commission when compared to the single 30 line surplus treaty, where commission was set at 25% and amounted to $328,571. We concede that it might be difficult to place the third surplus treaty, but our example shows the importance of relating exposure to ceded premium and carefully negotiating commission terms.

There is an accepted order in ceding a risk to a programme of surplus treaties. Having decided upon its own retention, the ceding company must utilise the available treaty capacity of the first surplus in priority to that of the second surplus, and then utilise the available treaty capacity of the second surplus in priority to that of the third surplus, and so on.

Assuming that the majority of risks fall below the maximum treaty limit, then we would see that more favourable treaty conditions could be obtained by the ceding company if it decides to use more than one surplus treaty.

There is however an administrative drawback. It obviously costs more to administer three surplus treaties rather than one. Any increase in commission for the ceding company might be offset by substantially higher administration costs. Clearly, the ceding company must consider all the advantages and disadvantages of having several small surplus treaties instead of one treaty. In their turn, reinsurers would view the construction of the proportional facilities from the opposite perspective.

The details of the treaty are submitted on a placement slip in the same way as a quota share treaty. A typical placement slip would usually contain the following information (fictitious details have been used in the example):

Ceding company:	DEF Insurance Company Limited, Singapore
Type of Treaty:	First Surplus Treaty
Class of Business	Fire and Allied Perils
Territorial Limits:	Singapore

Period:	Continuous agreement at 1st January 2003
Notice of Cancellation:	3 months prior to 31st December in any year
Maximum Limit per Line:	Maximum $200,000 P.M.L. any one risk (as defined). Minimum P.M.L. 40%.
Number of Lines:	20
Maximum Limit heron:	Maximum $4,000,000 P.M.L. any one risk
Rate:	Original Net Rate (O.N.R. = O.G.R. less maximum deductions of 30% in all)
Fire Brigade Charges:	3.00% on O.G.R.
Overriding Commission:	5.00% on O.N.R.
Profit Commission	15%. Reinsurer's Expenses: 5% Losses carried forward 3 years
Premium Reserve Deposit:	40%
Interest on Deposit:	3% per annum
Loss Reserve Deposit:	100%
Interest on Deposits:	3% per annum
Portfolio Assumption/ Withdrawal	Premium 35% Outstanding Losses 90%
Cash Loss/Loss Advice Limit:	$250,000 for 100% of treaty
Bordereaux:	Nil
Accounts:	Half Yearly
Accounts settlement period:	30 days for preparation, 15 days for reconciliation, plus further 15 days for settlement (60 days in all)
Brokerage:	3.0% on Original Net Rate (=2.10% on O.G.R.)
Statistics:	(Usually attached for past five years or more)
Estimated Premium Income:	$5,000,000 (for 100% treaty hereon)

7

Pools and Facultative Obligatory Treaty

Pools

The principle of a reinsurance pool is that all members of the pool contribute the whole or part of their premiums for a specific category of business into a common fund. They then share the claims that arise, either in the same proportion as they contributed premiums (to the fund) or in some other agreed manner. Profits, losses and administration expenses are shared in the same way. In simple terms, a pool acts as an insurance or reinsurance company created by its members but without those members having to find the necessary capital to form such a company.

Advantages and Disadvantages

Pools are established for a variety of reasons.

The main advantage of a pool is the creation of capacity to handle risks of a catastrophic nature or special category. Atomic or nuclear energy risks are a good example. Most insurance policies exclude nuclear energy risks, but many governments use nuclear power to generate electricity for the benefit of their country, so nuclear pools are created within regions or individual countries to protect those generating plants. Recently, many governments have encouraged their national insurance and reinsurance industries to create special pools to cover the increasing threat of terrorism. If pools did not exist, it probably would not be possible to insure or reinsure those risks and the government might have to act as an insurer of last resort.

Pools have also been created in certain countries or regions to reduce the flow of reinsurance premium being ceded to reinsurers located outside that country or region.

The main disadvantage of a pool is the potential danger of accumulation of risks of a similar nature. There is a high possibility that all or many pool risks might be affected by a single loss event. The resources of the pool members might be insufficient for them to cope with a loss of that nature. The protection of the pool by catastrophe excess of loss reinsurance reduces this danger to a certain extent, as would a separate risk excess of loss protection against large individual risk losses affecting the pool.

Facultative Obligatory Treaty

As the name implies, a facultative obligatory treaty has the characteristics of both individual facultative quota share placements and obligatory proportional treaties. It is an agreement where the ceding company has the *option* to cede a particular risk. Once the ceding company has made its decision, the reinsurer is *obliged* to accept a share of that individual cession. The ceding company is therefore not obliged to make any cessions (as in facultative reinsurance) whilst the reinsurer is not allowed to decline any cessions made (as under an obligatory proportional treaty arrangement). This is the background to the term "facultative obligatory", often abbreviated to "fac oblig".

A facultative obligatory treaty normally applies after a surplus treaty (or programme of surplus treaties). It gives the ceding company an automatic reinsurance facility if the capacity of the underlying surplus treaty or treaties has been exhausted. It also acts as a further surplus treaty, except that the ceding company has no obligation to cede any risks, especially if the ceding company's other proportional reinsurance arrangements offer more beneficial terms.

Advantages and Disadvantages

Advantages for the ceding company are:

(1) Immediate reinsurance after main proportional treaty facilities.

(2) Automatic facility for risks of a specific nature or of irregular occurrence pattern.

Disadvantages for the Reinsurer are:

(1) No control can be exercised over the business ceded.

(2) No flow of business can be guaranteed as under a quota share or surplus treaty.

(3) There is a danger of anti-selection by the ceding company.

A possible advantage to the reinsurer is that a facultative obligatory treaty might enable it to gain a slightly better spread of risks than by just accepting individual facultative cessions. The reinsurer might also be able to establish original premium rates, terms, conditions and exclusions by accepting perhaps one or two selected facultative obligatory treaties in various countries.

The differences between the treaty wording for a facultative obligatory treaty and that for an obligatory quota share or surplus treaty are often slight. It might not be clear whether the ceding company is obliged to cede a share of each risk falling within the terms of the reinsurance (obligatory treaty) or whether it has discretion to make a cession or not (facultative obligatory treaty).

8

Non-Proportional Reinsurances

Non-proportional reinsurance is known as excess of loss reinsurance. An excess of loss contract is an agreement entered into between a reinsured and one or more reinsurers. Please note that we use the word "reinsured" for excess of loss, rather than "ceding company" or "cedant" for proportional reinsurance. Similarly, we refer to "contracts" rather than "treaties" in this method of reinsurance.

Under excess of loss contracts, the reinsurer agrees to indemnify the reinsured for losses that exceed a certain specified monetary amount identified by the reinsured and arising out of a portfolio of risks being protected. The reinsured retains the whole amount up to this identified monetary limit (the deductible) and the reinsurer pays the balance of any loss that exceeds the deductible (up to the identified limit, or layer, of the excess of loss reinsurance). The amounts, or limits of liability, are normally specified in monetary terms (e.g. Excess of Loss) or in terms of a percentage (e.g. Stop Loss).

The basis for assessing the loss can be expressed in various ways, such as:

"each and every loss, each and every risk" e.g. Risk Excess of Loss

"each and every loss occurrence" e.g. Event Excess of Loss (property) "each and every loss" e.g. Risk or Event

"any one accident or occurrence or event" e.g. Excess of Loss (casualty)

"any one year" e.g. Stop Loss, Aggregate Excess of Loss.

There are other terms, but this gives an indication of what descriptions are available.

The excess of loss contract, or agreement, is not concerned with any proportionate share of the original sum insured on any one risk or the sharing claims between ceding company and reinsurer. The reinsurer pays the reinsured only when an original loss has exceeded the monetary limit that has been agreed. In other words, the size of any loss would decide whether an excess of loss contract is affected, not the original policy itself. Excess of loss reinsurance contracts are therefore formed on a different basis from automatic and obligatory proportional treaties. This is why excess of loss reinsurance contracts are not considered to be "treaties" and the term "non-proportional reinsurance" is used.

Nor is the reinsurer directly concerned with the original premium rates being charged by the reinsured as it rates (or charges premium for) excess of loss contracts in a different manner. The premium for an excess of loss reinsurance contract is often expressed as a fixed rate percentage of the whole premium income of the class or classes of business covered. This method represents a convenient way of calculating the reinsurance premium that the reinsurer seeks to obtain for its liability under the contract.

Excess of loss reinsurance often involves a complex form of coverage. Over the past forty years its use has extended to fulfil a very large number of functions, from the reinsurance of individual risks to catastrophe protections for losses arising from natural perils. Due to its ease of administration, excess of loss has largely replaced proportional forms of reinsurance in many classes of business. However it can be a very misunderstood form of reinsurance (for both reinsureds and reinsurers alike) unless both parties are very clear as to what is being reinsured and how the reinsurance has been constructed.

The different functions performed by excess of loss reinsurances can be grouped as follows:

Working (Risk) Excess of Loss

This form of coverage is intended to limit losses that arise on the reinsured's normal day-to-day operations. Insurance companies exist to pay claims and working excess of loss assists the management and planning of their operations. In the context of reinsurance of liabilities to third parties, many excess of loss reinsurance contracts are "working excess of loss". It is comparatively easy to establish the value of a building or a ship if policies of fire and marine insurance are involved. Accordingly, it is possible to reinsure risks of this nature on a proportional basis. It is not so easy to quantify a specified retention on a limit of indemnity covering potential legal liability to a third party, so many liability or casualty accounts are only protected by excess of loss reinsurance.

The "value" of a liability exposure might be established only after a claim had occurred and an award been made by a competent court of jurisdiction. It is only then that the original insured would know whether or not it had bought enough coverage and the insurance company discovered whether or not it had purchased sufficient reinsurance. It is also possible that a number of claims could arise out of the same loss event.

A motor collision might injure a number of people; a

chemical manufacturer's product might poison many people; a hospital might employ a surgeon who incorrectly performs an operation. That is why it is necessary to define what "loss" is being reinsured. Generally that loss recovery would relate to all claims that arise from the same "occurrence", "event" or "source". This subject is discussed in greater detail in Chapter 9.

"Risk excess of loss" reinsurance is also considered to be a "working" cover because the reinsurer often provides protection within the limit of a single identified risk exposure. This form of reinsurance is mainly used for property exposures and is a substitute for proportional reinsurance. This subject is discussed in Chapter 10.

Catastrophe Excess of Loss

This form of coverage is intended to limit or restrict the reinsured's exposure to an aggregation of individual losses arising from one identified event, such as an earthquake, severe windstorm or flood. The basic function of "catastrophe" reinsurance is to provide an important tool to the reinsured's management planning. This type of coverage is described in Chapter 11.

The term "catastrophe" has a double meaning. In journalistic terms, the word "catastrophe" could apply to a very large loss affecting one individual risk or to a large accumulation or aggregation of losses arising from one identified event. Within the insurance and reinsurance industry, "catastrophe excess of loss" reinsurance is generally taken to mean the latter situation, namely a large accumulation or aggregation of losses arising from one identified event. However, some "working" excess of loss reinsurance contracts, particularly those covering losses that arise from an "accident", "event" or "occurrence", perform a dual function. In those situations, the contracts might have an exposure to either a very large single loss or an accumulation of single losses arising from one identified event or cause. The reinsured and reinsurer would identify and rate (establish the cost) of such protections at the formation of the contract.

Stop Loss

This is a form of excess of loss reinsurance that applies to the aggregate of all losses occurring in one annual period. The function of the various forms of "stop loss", "aggregate excess", "excess of loss ratio" and similar is intended to stabilise the reinsured's annual underwriting result. A claim arises under this type of reinsurance if an accumulation of defined losses exceeds the stated deductible during the annual (or other agreed) period of the reinsurance. The coverage is normally expressed in percentage terms. If accumulated losses over a twelve months period exceed a stated percentage of the reinsured's premium income (or equivalent monetary amount), then the stop loss contract would respond up to a further percentage or monetary amount. This type of coverage is explained in Chapter 12.

The following headings appear on excess of reinsurance slips. The details supplied in connection with these headings vary according to whether coverage is for excess of loss, stop loss or aggregate excess of loss. We will discuss the specific requirements in the following chapters.

>   Reinsured and its Location
>   Period and Coverage
>   Type
>   Class or Classes of Business (often includes identified Perils covered)
>   Territorial Scope
>   Limit and Deductible

Reinstatement(s)

Rate

Minimum and Deposit Premiums (and how and when payable)

Brokerage (if applicable)

Warranty (if applicable)

Applicable Law and Jurisdiction

Arbitration

General Conditions

Exclusions (often shown under General Conditions)

Wording

Information

Statistics

Reinsured Under excess of loss reinsurance, there is no proportional cession of risks, premiums, commissions, expenses or claims. The insurance company seeking protection is known as the "reinsured" not the "ceding company". It is important to show the location of the reinsured's head office (or local company, if applicable). Sometimes, local regulations require the reinsured's registered company number to be shown as well.

Period Many excess of loss contracts are concluded for a period of 12 months. Most will be issued on a "losses occurring during basis", but there are other coverages (which we will discuss in later chapters). If two dates are mentioned, e.g. 1st January 2003 to 31st December 2003, the words "both dates inclusive" should be included, as should the phrase "local standard time" if the contract protects the reinsured' operations in a number of different countries. Sometimes original policies are issued at a certain time of day (e.g. 16.00 hours). In order to avoid confusion, such time stipulation should also be included.

Type This normally states "Excess of Loss Reinsurance" and whether it relates to risk, catastrophe or another form. As with surplus treaties, many excess of loss programmes involve a number of consecutive layers, giving the reinsured sufficient vertical coverage. Sometimes the ascending layer number (first, second, third layer etc.) might be shown here.

Class This identifies the class (or classes) of business and the perils to be protected by the excess of loss reinsurance. It should also show whether there are any prior proportional reinsurances ("Reinsured's Net Retained Account etc …") or none ("Reinsured's Gross Account etc …"). Modern usage tends towards listing all classes or branches of insurance covered, and an agreed list of perils covered within each. If a class or peril is not listed, then the excess of loss contract should not respond to any loss arising from that source.

Territorial Scope This identifies the geographic location of the business protected and whether the reinsured requires incidental overseas extensions for any policies it issues. Reinsurers often impose a limitation for North American exposures.

Limit This is the maximum monetary amount that a reinsurer would pay for any one claim if it exceeded the stated excess of loss deductible. It is often known as the "limit of liability".

Deductible This is the fixed monetary amount that the reinsured decides to retain on any one loss. The reinsured would be able to recover amounts above this figure from excess of loss reinsurers. Amounts may be stated in monetary terms or as a percentage of total premium income. The reinsured loss could arise from an individual risk or an accumulation from one identified event, such as a storm or serious motor accident, or the aggregate of all claims arising in a specified period.

Reinstatements If a reinsurer is called upon to pay claims under an excess of loss contract, the amount of cover remaining to the reinsured could be diminished by those payments. It is possible that the total amount of available reinsurance protection is exhausted by those payments. Reinstatement provisions allow the reinsured to automatically reinstate cover, normally by the payment of an additional premium. For example, "2 reinstatements each @ 100% Additional Premium (A.P.)" means that the reinsured has guaranteed coverage for up to three total losses (original cover plus its two reinstatements) in any one annual period, subject to payment of additional premium on the basis shown. The level of reinstatement premium would be negotiated between the parties and could be expressed as pro rata, 25%, 50%, 75%, 100%, 150% A.P. (or another specified amount). All non-marine reinstatements are pro rata as to the amount reinstated, the factors shown above relate to the time feature. Whatever figure is used, they represent the specified percentage of additional premium to be paid by the reinsured if a loss were to affect an excess of loss contract.

A reinstatement premium could therefore be calculated as follows:

> pro rata to the amount of loss reinstated (when the excess of loss limit is only partially exhausted) and pro rata for the period remaining from the date of loss until the end of the contract period (here the time factor is the second "pro rata" mentioned)

> or

> pro rata to the amount of loss reinstated and at 100% of the annual premium for the excess of loss contract (here the time factor is 100% and the full annual premium is used irrespective of number of days cover remaining to end of contract period)

Reinstatements are usually calculated at the time a reinsurance claim is paid. A claim is normally settled after deduction of any applicable reinstatement premium. If a claim is paid before the adjustment premium (see below) is paid, then the reinstatement premium is calculated on the deposit premium (see below). There should also be a subsequent adjustment of the reinstatement premium when the finally adjusted premium is known.

Chapter 11 contains an example of a typical reinstatement clause that would appear in an excess of loss contract wording.

There are various methods of assessing reinstatements. Some contracts pre-pay reinstatement premiums by offering a large premium for an identified maximum number of recoveries from that contract in any one year. For example, the limit of a contract might be $200,000 and the contract premium $2,000,000. This means that a reinsurer would be willing to pay for 10 losses in the contract period. The reinstatement condition could be expressed as "nine free reinstatements" (original loss plus its 9 reinstatements = 10 losses) or "maximum $2,000,000 annual aggregate amount recoverable during contract period = 10 losses).

Some excess of loss reinsurance contracts are still issued on the basis of "unlimited reinstatements" (whether free or paid), so that reinsurance protection is always available. It would be fair to say that this type of coverage has reduced considerably and would only be offered in exceptional circumstances, perhaps as a result of local regulations.

Reinstatements restrict the reinsured's horizontal coverage, or the maximum number of losses it could recover from an excess of loss contract, in any one annual period. As with other aspects of excess of loss reinsurance, the number of reinstatements would be a function of price and the attitude of the reinsuring market at that point in time.

Rate This is the factor a reinsurer applies to the total premium income of all the business in the portfolio to be protected. The result, known as the rate, is the premium the reinsurer would charge for providing excess of loss coverage. It is normally expressed as a fixed percentage figure. Excess of loss reinsurances, whether they are working or catastrophe covers, are accounted for differently from proportional treaties. For proportional treaties, the ceding company remits written or accounted premium received for the class(es) of business ceded less any agreed commissions and expenses. Under excess of loss contracts, the reinsured pays a premium to the reinsurer that has been agreed between them. This can be a fixed rate percentage applied to the total premium generated by the reinsured for the class of business covered or it could vary according to the actual loss experience of the portfolio (subject to minimum and maximum premium limitations). In certain rare cases the reinsurer might quote a flat monetary premium that is not adjustable (see below).

The excess of loss premium is calculated on the actual liability assumed by reinsurers. Reinsurers therefore make no allowance for ceding commission and excess of loss premium is normally quoted "net" or free of any deductions (other than local premium taxes and brokerage, if applicable).

There are different premium bases that accord with the reinsured's chosen method of accounting. Many excess of loss contracts are issued on a losses occurring during basis and would be rated on premiums earned or accounted during the contract period. "Earned" premium follows the "unexpired liability" and "unearned premium" system for proportional reinsurances, whereas "accounted" relates to all financial transactions recorded by the reinsured in an identified period, irrespective of attachment dates of original policies. If excess of loss premiums are based on "written" premiums, then any excess of loss contracts follow the date of inception of the original policies they protect. This coverage is known as "risks attaching" or "policies issued and renewed" or "policies incepting" during an identified contract period.

In brief, there are various definitions for the total premium income for the protected portfolio, such as "Gross Net Written or Earned or Accounted Premium". If the account is subject to prior proportional reinsurance, the definition would be expanded to include the word "Retained" such as "Gross Net Written or Earned or Accounted Retained Premium Income".

Minimum and Deposit (and Adjustment) Premium The reinsurer expects to be paid in advance for its acceptance of liability under an excess of loss contract. Since the reinsured does not know in advance what its final premium income will be, the reinsurer calculates an amount that the reinsured should pay during the contract period. This is known as a "deposit premium". The deposit premium is paid either in one amount at inception of the contract or in quarterly or half yearly instalments, either in advance or in arrears. This would all be by agreement and the amount of deposit premium varies between 80% and 100% of the estimated earning potential for the contract. The deposit premium would then be adjusted at the end of the reinsurance contract period when the reinsured's actual total premium income figure is known. This is known as the "adjustment premium".

When a reinsurer quotes a fixed rate percentage and applies that to the reinsured's estimated total premium income, the reinsurer has calculated what the cover will earn and includes that estimate for its own management purposes. If the reinsured has been optimistic in its assessment of the premium for its portfolio, and the actual total premium falls below its estimate, then the reinsurer might receive insufficient premium for the risk it has accepted. The reinsurer therefore specifies a "minimum premium" for the contract. The minimum premium could be set at the same amount as the deposit premium or it could be set at a different figure. Minimum premium figures also vary between 80% and 100% (or more) of the estimated earning potential for the contract. The minimum premium often acts as a guarantee for reinsurers if the total adjustment premium income is not as favourable as anticipated.

Brokerage This is the agreed amount that reinsurers agree to pay the reinsurance intermediary. It is normally expressed as a percentage figure of the contract premium. Many markets do not allow brokerage to be deducted from any reinstatement premiums payable following a loss, but practices vary.

Warranty This identifies if reinsurers have imposed any special conditions on the operation of the excess of loss contract.

Applicable Law and Jurisdiction Reinsurance is a very international business often involving transactions between insurance and reinsurance companies located not only in different countries, but also within different legal jurisdictions. Following many reinsurer (and insurer) insolvencies and consequent legal problems, many regulators have imposed a requirement that any disputes concerning the subject matter of any reinsurance contract should be conducted in accordance with their own legal system and relevant insurance laws, policy forms and coverages applicable to that country. This effectively protects their national or local policyholders. It is generally accepted that the applicable law and jurisdiction should be that of the country in which the reinsured's head office is located, but the parties could agree to an alternative arrangement. This is particularly the case for many facultative reinsurance placements. It is not unusual to have local laws applying to the original insurance, but (say) English Law applying to the reinsurance. Readers should be aware of this very important aspect of all reinsurance placements, whether facultative, treaty or contract.

Arbitration As legal processes become more expensive, many regulators encourage disputes to be settled by arbitration (or mediation), rather than take the case to a formal court of law. The arbitration clause identifies the process to be followed by the contracting parties and identifies where such arbitration should take place.

Note: Readers should differentiate between the three legal considerations above. The first is the subject matter of the reinsurance, namely the legal form of the original policies themselves. The second is the legal jurisdiction that should be considered for the operation of the reinsurance agreement and the third is the legal (or other) process to be followed in the event of arbitration, mediation or alternative dispute resolution (another form of resolving a contractual argument).

General Conditions This is normally expressed as a list of specific clauses that apply to the excess of loss contract. Often, the clause is well known and used by many markets, so only the title of the clause would be listed. Where the clause is unique, special, or has been amended from any standard version, then the full text of the clause should appear as part of "General Conditions". Certain markets require that the full text of all clauses is included as this makes for transparency between the parties and avoids any potential misunderstandings. A recent development is for the full excess of loss contract wording to be submitted at the time the contract is considered by the reinsurer. This allows the reinsurer to identify any contentious aspects of the agreement and immediately address items of potential conflict.

Exclusions The excess of loss contract might not cover all types of risks of a particular class or branch of business. The reinsured and reinsurer agree an acceptable list of exclusions applicable to that particular excess of loss protection. Certain exclusions are known as "market" exclusions (e.g. War and Civil War and Nuclear Energy Risks) and are imposed in the majority of international insurance and reinsurance markets. A recent new "market" exclusion is Terrorism. Other exclusions would be specific to a country, company or class, and would be identified on a case-by-case basis.

In general, reinsurers are reluctant to cover both original insurances and the reinsured's own account of its inwards reinsurance acceptances. It would not be unusual to see the exclusion of obligatory (proportional) reinsurance treaties, excess of loss reinsurance contracts (including stop loss) and perhaps individual facultative excess of loss acceptances from an excess of loss protection. Facultative quota share acceptances are perhaps not so contentious as the liability, premium, terms and conditions normally follow those of the original policy.

Wording The excess of loss contract wording needs to identify the management of any claims that might arise under the reinsurance agreement. Claims are not settled in account as they are under proportional treaties since periodic accounts are not issued for excess of loss contracts. The deposit premium is settled by one or more specific payments during the contract period and an adjustment is made at the end of the period. Each claim recovery is settled individually as soon as the reinsured has provided proof of loss and requested payment. The provisions for reporting claims to excess of loss reinsurers are many and varied. Although claims tend to be advised on an individual basis, this is not always the case. Under a stop loss contract, for example, the annual aggregation of losses is important. This means that any loss advice is presented at the end of the contract period when all losses amounts are known.

The duty to report potential claims can be quite onerous for "event" excess of loss reinsurance protections covering third party liability claims. For example, the reinsured might be required to advise the reinsurer of all claims where the incurred loss amount is estimated to exceed 75% of the stated contract deductible. In reinsurance, the term "incurred" means the total of paid and outstanding (reserved) elements of an individual claim. It may or may not relate to the excess of loss layer. If it does, we would use the phrase "incurred loss to the layer".

This advice gives the reinsurer advance warning of any major loss that could eventually result in a reinsurance recovery, even though the incurred loss amount does not apparently affect the excess of loss reinsurance cover at that time. Increases in loss amounts are caused by the effects of inflation, movements in currency rates of exchange, an escalation in court awards or changes in court practices, and sometimes by other factors. The Loss Reporting Clause might contain a list of categories involving serious bodily injury. If a claim involves any of these specified categories such as brain damage to an injured third party, then the reinsured is obliged to report the circumstances and details of such claims to reinsurers. This is irrespective of quantum (loss amount) or liability, but the advice provides the reinsurer with an opportunity to establish an outstanding loss reserve for the possibility that the claim might ultimately affect the excess of loss protection.

Developing this important relationship between reinsured and reinsurer, the Loss Reporting Clause could include what is known as a "Claims Co-Operation Clause". The wording of this clause ranges from a simple requirement for the reinsured to co-operate with the reinsurer "as far as is reasonably possible" to an agreement that gives the reinsurer absolute control over the assessment and settlement of any original claim. Finally, some Loss Reporting Clauses do not allow the reinsured to commence any legal action without the prior consent of the reinsurer.

Information and Statistics The reinsured should supply full information on the content of the account and its loss history, preferably for the previous 5 years (or longer for certain classes). The reinsured should highlight any important changes between historic information and the account as constituted for the period under discussion. This information enables the reinsurer to assess and structure the necessary reinsurance requirements, calculate a price and impose acceptable terms, conditions and exclusions.

9

Event Excess of Loss

This chapter describes the group of "working" excess of loss reinsurances that respond to losses arising out of an "accident", "event" or "occurrence". These are "working" covers, because both the reinsured and reinsurer accept that there will be losses that regularly occur and appreciate that this form of reinsurance protects the normal daily exposure for the business covered. Excess of loss deductibles are often relatively low and therefore could be affected by many losses. The coverage could be exposed to any one policy, any one risk or to a minor catastrophe (all as individually defined in the relevant contract terms and conditions).

The operation of this form of reinsurance could best be described in the following example:

A reinsured decides that the amount that it could safely retain in a loss arising from any one event is $200,000. It has assessed its liability and seeks a reinsurance contract where reinsurers would pay all losses in respect of any one event in excess of its selected deductible (or excess of loss retention) of $200,000.

If the reinsured incurred a loss of $300,000 *from the ground up*, it would retain the first $200,000 for its own account and reinsurers would pay the next $100,000. If the loss amounted to $175,000 *from the ground up*, the reinsured would retain that whole amount for its own account. The reinsurer would have nothing to pay as the loss had not exceeded the reinsured's chosen deductible of $200,000. In this form of reinsurance the reinsurer therefore pays all losses in excess of the reinsured's deductible (or retention as it is more usually called), up to the maximum monetary amount of the agreed layer over and above that deductible.

Please note the words "from the ground up", often abbreviated to "f.g.u." We have seen that the loss itself is critical in excess of loss reinsurance. Reinsurers use the phrase "from the ground up" to describe the total loss from zero ("the ground") to its ultimate amount. This loss amount is known as the reinsured's "Net Retained Loss", abbreviated to "N.R.L." This amount is after all recoveries from the reinsured's other reinsurances (normally proportional). The loss amount might also include specialist investigation fees. This combination of N.R.L. and any external fees combine to form the "Ultimate Net Loss" or "U.N.L." for most excess of loss contracts. These three items are fundamental to understanding excess of loss reinsurance. Both N.R.L. and U.N.L. Clauses differ between classes and practices in various markets and whether any prior reinsurances are in force before utilisation of the excess of loss contract or programme.

Reverting to our example, it is usual for an excess of loss reinsurance contract to have an upper monetary limit. This restricts the reinsurer's liability in any one layer so that the reinsurer does not pay any amount above that layer limit. The reinsurer might have agreed only to pay losses up to a further $300,000 in excess of $200,000. If any loss exceeds $500,000, the reinsured would theoretically have to pay its retention of $200,000 plus the balance of any loss above $500,000.

The reinsured might decide that it does not want to retain losses above the $500,000 limit for its own account. It could arrange another excess of loss protection to deal with losses greater than $500,000. In doing so, the reinsured is creating an excess of loss programme of ascending layers of excess of loss coverage.

The reinsured has two layers of excess of loss protection giving it $1,000,000 total coverage from the ground up. The reinsured suffers four losses for the amounts shown below. The subsequent table shows how those losses would be recovered from the programme:

Loss A) $ 300,000 f.g.u.
Loss B) $ 850,000 f.g.u.
Loss C) $ 125,000 f.g.u.
Loss D) $1,500,000 f.g.u.

	Amount exceeding Excess of Loss Programme				$500,000
$1,000,000	2nd Layer Excess of Loss. Reinsurers pay amounts up to maximum limit of this layer = $500,000		$350,000		$500,000
$500,000	2nd Excess Point	————	————	————	————
	1st Layer Excess of Loss. Reinsurers pay amounts up to maximum limit of this layer = $300,000	$100,000	$300,000	NIL	$300,000
$200,000	1st Excess Point	————	————	————	————
	Deductible payable by reinsured = $200,000	$200,000	$200,000	$125,000	$200,000
	Original Loss f.g.u.	$300,000	$850,000	$125,000	$1,500,000
	Loss	A)	B)	C)	D)

In example (A)
    Original f.g.u. loss is $300,000
    Reinsured pays $200,000 (amount of Deductible)
    1st Layer reinsurers pay $100,000 (balance falling under 1st Layer)

In example (B)
    Original f.g.u. loss is $850,000
    Reinsured pays $200,000 (amount of Deductible)
    1st Layer reinsurers pay $300,000 (limit of 1st Layer)
    2nd Layer reinsurers pay $350,000 (balance falling under 2nd Layer)

In example (C)
    Original f.g.u. loss is $125,000
    Reinsured pays $125,000 (amount is below the Deductible)

In example (D)
    Original f.g.u. loss is $1,500,000
    Reinsured pays (1) $200,000 (amount of Deductible)
    Reinsured also pays (2) $500,000 (balance in excess of reinsurance programme limit)
    1st Layer reinsurers pay $300,000 (limit of 1st Layer)
    2nd Layer reinsurers pay $500,000 (limit of 2nd Layer)

On a reinsurance placement slip, the limits and deductibles would be expressed as:

1st Layer   Losses up to $300,000 in excess of $200,000 (abbreviated to $300,000 xs $200,000)

2nd Layer   Losses up to $500,000 xs $500,000 (i.e., the total of the Deductible and the 1st Excess of Loss Layer)

The reinsurance premium could be a flat monetary premium (now quite rare, as we have mentioned) or based upon a fixed percentage rate applied to the total premium income generated by the reinsured for the entire class of business covered. The method of determining the actual premium rate depends on the level of excess of loss coverage. In simple terms, losses are more likely to affect the programme if the level of excess of loss protection is near to the ground (zero). Accordingly, reinsurers would charge a high premium to reflect the expected high frequency of losses. The higher the level of excess of loss coverage (above the ground), frequency diminishes, but severity could be a problem. Many reinsurers now have sophisticated loss probability models to assess the likelihood of a loss of a particular severity or intensity affecting a particular level of excess of loss coverage.

For low (or working) excess of loss layers, reinsurers would often charge a rate of premium based upon the loss experience of prior years (this loss experience is termed the "burning cost" or "loss cost"). The best way to illustrate this method is to consider the following example:

Assume an excess of loss layer for $100,000 xs $100,000. The reinsured's results for the previous 5 years, and on a comparable basis, might be as follows (all figures in $):

Period	Premiums	All Losses	Incurred losses less 100,000 each claim	
			Number	Amount
1999	10,000,000	1,000,000	5	500,000
2000	12,500,000	1,600,000	8	800,000
2001	15,000,000	2,000,000	10	1,000,000
2002	17,500,000	2,500,000	13	1,200,000
2003	20,000,000	3,000,000	15	1,500,000
Totals	75,000,000	10,100,000	51	5,000,000
Est. 2004	22,500,000			

We would calculate the pure burning cost (or pure loss cost or pure loss burden) by dividing the total incurred losses (both paid and outstanding) to the layer by the total premiums for the period, and then multiply the result by 100/1. "Pure" means the actual cost before reinsurers have applied any loading factor to cover their own management and operating expenses.

$$\frac{\text{Incurred Losses to Layer (whole period)}}{\text{Total Premium Income (whole period)}} = \frac{5{,}000{,}000}{75{,}000{,}000} \times \frac{100}{1} = 6.67\%$$

The pure burning cost is often loaded by a factor, sometimes expressed as 100/70, 100/75 or 100/80. This factor attempts to cover the reinsurer's expenses of operation. It includes an allowance for each of the following: fluctuations in future results, profit, safety margin, retrocession costs and any specific target identified by the reinsurer's own general management. If necessary, that result would then be loaded by an amount for brokerage. Let us assume an overall loading factor of 100/75 (excluding brokerage) and develop the rate above from its pure burning cost to a loaded rate.

Pure burning cost over 5 year period		6.67%
Load by 100/75	(6.67% x 100/75)	8.89%
Load by 10% brokerage	(8.89% x 100/90)	9.88%

Reinsurers might ask the reinsured to pay 9.88% of its premium income for the excess of loss contract in the 2004 contract period. The reinsured has estimated that premium income at $22,500,000. The proposed 9.88% rate would produce $2,223,000 in excess of loss premium for 2004. If this account protected legal liabilities, then such a simple calculation would still probably be insufficient.

Please look at the development of the premiums and losses over the period. Between 1999 and 2003, premiums have doubled, but incurred losses to the excess of loss layer have trebled. It might be better for the reinsured to retain more (perhaps $150,000 each loss in this example) in order to reduce the cost of its reinsurance protection. Conversely the value of a $100,000 deductible has effectively halved between 1999 and 2003. In 1999 the $100,000 deductible represented 1% of $10,000,000 premium income. In 2003 the $100,000 deductible represented 0.5% of $20,000,000 premium income. Clearly, the value of the deductible has not been maintained and there would be substantially more losses affecting this much lower level of coverage. Perhaps this explains the apparently high cost in our example.

We have deliberately created the example above to highlight various trends within the account. Our example has nevertheless *not* taken into account such factors as any allowance for Incurred But Not Reported (I.B.N.R.) claims, inflation, or the reliability of the reinsured's estimation of outstanding loss reserves.

Incurred But Not Reported (loss) figures relate to the anticipated development to ultimate settlement of various accounts from the total incurred loss amounts known at a particular point in time. Insurers and reinsurers particularly apply I.B.N.R. factors to accounts involving complicated legal liabilities. It often takes a long time for individual claims to be advised, and then even longer for those claims to be fully settled. Insurers and reinsurers make allowances for developmental I.B.N.R. increases in different ways.

Please refer to the following example. Loss figures for the more recent years have not yet fully developed because not all the losses have been advised (I.B.N.R. losses). For this reason, the loss experience would tend to be presented in a different form. One method, used here, is known as a "chain ladder". This method shows how losses of earlier years might have fully developed. The following shows the usual format of such a development table. We have used the *actual* total loss figures from the table above, not those incurred to the excess of loss layer. We are trying to establish the ultimate development for this account, so we use all losses, from the ground up, and in original currency if necessary. In this example, we have further assumed that total incurred "all loss" figures are those at the end of Year 1 of each period. Once again, all figures are expressed in $.

ALL Losses, not those to XL layer, known in 2003 (bold figures):						
Period	Premium	Year 1	Year 2	Year 3	Year 4	Year 5
1999	10,000,000	1,000,000	1,800,000	1,900,000	2,000,000	**2,000,000**
2000	12,500,000	1,600,000	2,800,000	3,000,000	**3,200,000**	
2001	15,000,000	2,000,000	3,300,000	**3,700,000**		
2002	17,500,000	2,500,000	**4,000,000**			
2003	20,000,000	**3,000,000**				

Total of All Losses at latest known position (in 2003)   **15,900,000**

Development Year 4 to 5   2,000,000   2,000,000 *(1999)*
Development Factor   100%

Development Year 3 to 4   4,900,000   5,200,000 *(1999 & 2000)*
Development Factor   106%

Development Year 2 to 3   7,900,000   8,600,000 *(1999, 2000 & 2001)*
Development Factor   109%

Dev. Year 1 to 2   7,100,000   11,900,000 *(1999, 2000, 2001 & 2002)*
Development Factor   168%

We have totalled all losses according to the year or years indicated in italics. For example, to reconcile the totals for the development between Years 2 and 3, add the three *complete* years in the Year 2 and 3 *columns*. So, in the Year 2 column add 1,800,000 + 2,800,000 + 3,300,000 = 7,900,000, then in the Year 3 column add 1,900,000 + 3,000,000 + 3,700,000 = 8,600,000. We leave the latest year (2002) from this particular calculation as it has no comparable year. All other development comparisons follow a similar pattern.

We would then divide the later total by the earlier total to obtain the development factor. The factor between Years 1 and 2 is therefore 11,900,000/7,1000,000 = 168%.

We could use these development factors to project latest known incurred figures to their estimated ultimate settlement. (We have not shown premium in the next table).

Period	Year 1	Year 2	Year 3	Year 4	Year 5	Total
1999	1,300,000	1,000,000	1,800,000	1,900,000	2,000,000	= 2,000,000
2000	1,600,000	2,800,000	3,000,000	3,200,000	x 100%/1	= 3,200,000
2001	2,000,000	3,300,000	3,700,000	x 106%/1	x 100%/1	= 3,922,000
2002	2,500,000	4,000,000	x 109%/1	x 106%/1	x 100%/1	= 4,621,600
2003	1,500,000	x 168%/1	x 109%/1	x 106%/1	x 100%/1	= 4,852,680
Total of estimated ultimate losses using I.B.N.R. factors shown						= 18,596,280
Total of known losses (in 2003, as per original table above)						= 15,900,000
I.B.N.R. Account Factor 18,596,280/15,900,000						= 117%

The I.B.N.R. factor on this account is the percentage increase between total known losses at the latest year (2003 in our example) and the estimated ultimate loss projection. This I.B.N.R. account factor, 117% (rounded) in this example, would be used in any assessment of the excess of loss contract premium. An example of the rating progression could be:

Pure Burning Cost (from original table)	6.6700%
Add Account I.B.N.R. factor 117% (6.67% x 117%)	7.8039%
Load by reinsurer's expenses (say 140%) (7.8039% x 140%)	10.9255%
Load by brokerage (10% assumed) (10.9255% x 100/90)	12.1394%

Factually, this loaded rate of 12.1394% (compared to the

previous loaded rate of 9.88%) might still be insufficient.

Reinsurers would apply various factors to the original premiums, claims and identify any changes in the account over the observation period (number of years experience available). These factors would include the class of business and its "mix", its geographical spread, and would also reflect the economic environment existing at that time. Inflation (measured by movements in cost of living or wages indices) could also be an important factor in the revaluation process.

Superimposed inflation (also known as social drift) is an additional consideration. This type of inflation is caused by events in society at large – increased court awards and/or changes in court practices, increased costs of health care, increased life expectancy, increased consumer awareness and peoples' expectations in general. Often, this form of inflation is difficult to anticipate.

This "re-casting" of the account would produce a substantially higher pure burning cost (and I.B.N.R. account factor) after all these types of loading or revaluation had been applied. It is perhaps too complicated to develop that theory here, but readers should be aware of this important principle of premium and loss revaluation in the calculation of any excess of loss contract premium. As we have said, this principle is especially critical in the assessment of original accounts involving legal liabilities.

An alternative method of calculating the excess of loss premium rate is to base the premium directly upon the actual incurred loss experience of the contract. Under this method of "experience rating" the reinsurance premium for the 2004 contract year could be based upon the incurred losses affecting the excess of loss reinsurance for that one contract year.

In order to allow for a degree of flexibility, the premium

rate is often expressed in terms of a minimum and a maximum percentage instead of a fixed percentage. These rates are usually set at approximately one half and twice the expected pure burning cost (based on historic and comparable loss experience). If we use our original example (without any revaluation), the minimum rate might be 3.40% and the maximum rate in the region of 13.00%. The full contract rate and premium terms could be expressed as below. We have set the minimum premium at 3.40%, and the deposit premium halfway through the "scale". Please note this is purely an example, and practice would differ between different countries.

Period	1st January 2004 to 31st December 2004, both dates inclusive
Layer	$100,000 xs $ 100,000
Rate	Pure BC plus loading of 100/75
subject to minimum	3.40% Gross Net Accounted Premium Income
and maximum	13.00% Gross Net Accounted Premium Income
Estimated 2004 premium income	$22,500,000
Minimum Premium	$765,000 (3.40% of est. $22,500,000)
Deposit Premium	$1,845,000 (8.20% of est. $22,500,000)
Maximum Premium	$2,925,000 (13.00% of est. $22,500,000)

The actual premium paid by the reinsured for 2004 would be related to the total incurred loss experience for that year. The pure burning cost for incurred losses to the layer would then be loaded by an agreed factor, 100/75 in our example, although other loadings are often used. Readers should be aware that there is no standard loading. Any rate must still fall within the agreed minimum and maximum parameters. Effectively, the minimum rate protects reinsurers and the maximum rate protects the reinsured. Let us look at a number of examples, once again all expressed in $.

A) Actual total premium income 2004   22,500,000
Total incurred losses xs $100,000 in 2004   1,800,000
Pure burning cost (1,800,000/22,500,000) 8.00%
Loaded burning cost (8.00% x 100/75)   10.67%
Premium payable to reinsurers
(22,500,000 x 10.67%)   2,400,750
Less deposit premium   1,845,000
Adjustment premium   555,750

In this example, the reinsured has provided an accurate premium estimate and "loaded" incurred losses have remained within the "scale". The reinsured would pay reinsurers an adjustment premium amounting to the difference between the loaded pure burning cost and the deposit premium. The minimum premium could be ignored in this example.

B) Actual total premium income 2004   18,000,000
Total incurred losses xs $100,000 in 2004   2,400,000
Pure burning cost (2,400,000/18,000,000) 13.33%
Loaded burning cost (13.33% x 100/75) 17.77%
Theoretical premium if maximum
ignored   3,198,600
Actual Premium payable
(18,000,000 x 13.00%)   2,340,000
    (max)
Less deposit premium   1,845,000
Adjustment premium   495,000

In this example, the reinsured has dramatically undestimated its premium income and we have increased incurred losses to 2,400,000. These losses produce a loaded rate of 17.77% that far exceeds the "scale" parameters. If no maximum rate existed, then reinsurers could expect to receive 3,198,600 in premium (18,000,000 x 17.77%). In this example, the agreed maximum rate applies and the adjustment premium payable to 13.00% of the substantially reduced premium income. Although reinsurers would still receive a reasonable adjustment premium, this example clearly shows the loss of earnings potential if there is any inconsistency between estimated and actual premium income figures.

C) Actual total premium income 2004   22,500,000
   Total incurred losses xs $100,000 in 2004   500,000
   Pure burning cost (500,000/22,500,000)   2.22%
   Loaded burning cost (2.22% x 100/75)   2.96%
   Premium payable to reinsurers
   (22,500,000 x 2.96%)   666,000
   Minimum premium applies   765,000
                                              (min)
   Less deposit premium   1,845,000
   Return Adjustment premium
   (payable by reinsurers)   (1,080,000)

In this example, the reinsured has accurately estimated its premium income, but very few losses have affected the account. These losses produce a loaded burning cost of 2.96%, still well below the agreed minimum rate. The reinsured has already paid reinsurers a deposit premium far higher than the actual loaded burning cost for the year in question. In this example, the minimum rate would apply, but reinsurers would have to return the difference between the deposit and minimum premiums.

In all these examples, the final premium for 2004 would only become known early in 2005 when the reinsured had ascertained its actual premium income and incurred loss figures. As with all excess of loss contracts, reinsurers would not be prepared to wait that long for the reinsurance contract premium to be paid to them. They might have to pay losses in the period of their involvement and need suitable consideration, in advance, for their acceptance of liability under any excess of loss contract.

An agreed deposit premium is therefore paid to reinsurers during the course of the contract period. It might be in full at the beginning of the year or in periodic instalments. As we have seen, the deposit premium is usually set at a figure slightly lower than or equal to the expected contract premium (estimated premium income multiplied by fixed rate percent). The deposit premium is adjusted at the end of the year when the actual premium income is known. This might involve the reinsured paying reinsurers an additional premium or receiving a return premium, dependent upon any agreed minimum premium for the contract. In many contracts, the deposit and minimum premiums are the same amount, but serve different purposes. In most excess of loss contracts, there is only one premium adjustment, but there are occasions when annual premium adjustments continue for as long as losses remain unsettled.

For example, if the premium for an excess of loss agreement were based upon incurred loss experience, then the contract wording would provide for interim (annual) premium adjustments to be made until all losses for that contract year were finally settled and the ultimate paid loss experience became available. The contract wording would contain the following example premium clause:

(Example) PREMIUM CLAUSE

The Reinsured shall pay to the Reinsurer premiums at the rate calculated to three decimal places in accordance with the following formula:

All amounts both paid and outstanding in respect of losses occurring during the year being rated and for which the Reinsurer is liable hereunder

_____ x 100/1 x 100/75 =   %

gross net premium income of the Reinsured
in respect of the year being rated.

of the gross net premium income of the Reinsured in respect of the business covered hereunder and accounted for during the period hereon. The term "gross net premium income" shall mean gross premiums (less only cancellations, return premiums, premiums for excluded risks, and premiums paid away for other reinsurances, if any, recoveries under which inure to the benefit of Reinsurers hereon) accruing to the Reinsured from all business falling within the terms of this Agreement.

The Reinsured shall pay to the Reinsurer a Deposit Premium of $ in four equal quarterly instalments at the 1st January, 1st April, 1st July and 1st October of each annual period of this Agreement. This Agreement shall be subject to a Minimum Premium of $ .... for each annual period of this Agreement.

As soon as possible after the end of each annual period of this Agreement, but in any event within three months after the anniversary date, the Reinsured shall supply to the Reinsurer a declaration of its gross net premium income as defined above. If the premium due to the Reinsurer computed on the basis set forth in the first paragraph of this Article exceeds the Minimum and Deposit Premium, the amount in excess thereof shall be paid immediately by the Reinsured to the Reinsurer.

Further calculations of premium shall be made annually in respect of each year until all outstanding claims hereunder have been settled and any additional or return premium due after taking into account any premium previously paid for such year shall be settled in the manner set out above.

Due to lack of credible loss experience, it is often difficult to rate higher layers in the same way as lower layers, as no burning cost experience is available. The reinsurer relies on its own (or market) experience of contracts with similar characteristics and usually charges a fixed percentage rate of gross net premium income, with identified minimum and deposit premiums. Please refer to the definition of "gross net premium income" in the example clause above.

As computer technology improves, various modelling

packages are created to reflect worldwide loss experience of a particular type. These "virtual" loss scenarios assist reinsurers to develop sophisticated excess of loss rating programmes. In simple terms, computer models assess the likely return period of a loss of a particular intensity, magnitude or severity and identify the likelihood of an excess of loss programme being affected at a particular level from the ground ("zero" in reinsurance terms).

Following that assumption a graph could be drawn as follows:

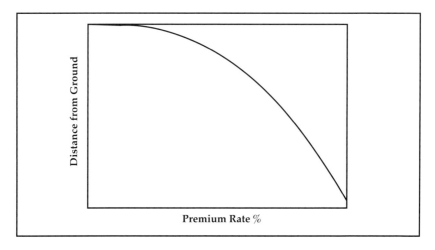

The graph shows that the rate for a particular level of exposure varies according to the slope (or shape) and position of the curve. A reinsurer's own experience of programmes of a similar nature would affect the shape of the curve and any excess of loss rate it would quote.

We could see this in the example below. It shows various curves for possible reinsurance pricing:

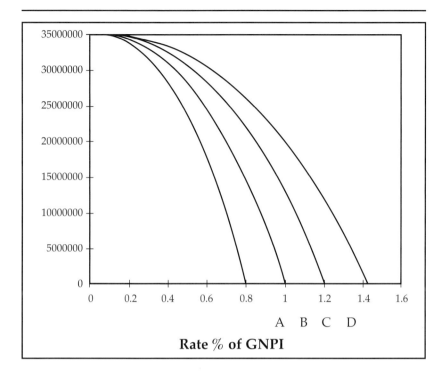

A very steep curve (A) would produce a low excess of loss rate at a particular level. The other curves (B), (C) and (D) would produce higher rates. In this model the premium rate for the layer up to $10,000,000 xs $25,000,000 would range from 0.50% to 0.90%. Please use a ruler to check where the axes are "broken" for each of the four curves.

This method is often used for certain classes of business involving low loss incidence, but high severity. Property catastrophe excess of loss falls into this category, as do motor third party and similar forms of legal liability coverage. The reinsured is able to establish the cost of reinsurance coverage at inception and is able to budget accordingly.

Please remember that the reinsured bears the whole incurred loss up to the monetary amount of the excess of loss deductible. The interests of the reinsured and reinsurer are very different and there is no sharing in the fortunes of the original business.

As we have said, it is often very difficult to define what is meant by the word "accident", "event" or "occurrence" under excess of loss reinsurance programmes.

The details of legal liability "event" excess of loss reinsurance would be submitted to the reinsurer in the form of a slip containing the following information. Once again, fictitious details have been used.

Reinsured:	WXY Insurance Co. of Manchester, England
Period:	Losses occurring during the 12 month period commencing 1st January 2003, local standard time where loss occurs
Type:	Excess of Loss Reinsurance – First Layer
Class of Business:	Business classified by the Reinsured as Motor, Employers' Liability and General Third Party Liability
Territorial Scope:	UK and Republic of Ireland (excluding losses occurring in United States of America and Canada)
Limits:	To pay up to $ 500,000 ultimate net loss each and every loss in excess of $ 500,000 ultimate net loss each and every loss
Rate:	Adjustable at 8.00% Gross Net Premium Income
Minimum & Deposit Premium:	$1,500,000 payable in equal instalments quarterly in advance at 1st January, 1st April, 1st July and 1st September 2003
Reinstatements:	Unlimited free for losses involving motor third party liability, but four free reinstatements in all during the period hereon for all other legal liability classes. Losses arising from motor own damage shall be limited to one free reinstatement during the period heron
Brokerage:	10%
General Conditions:	Ultimate Net Loss Clause Net Retained Lines Clause, if applicable Aggregate Extension Clause

Information:	Stability (Index) Clause in respect of bodily injury losses only. Base date 1st January 2003, wages, all sectors of UK economy. Currency Fluctuation Clause Estimated 2003 gross net premium income: $ 20,000,000 Loss information as attached

Certain new terms have been used on this slip and they need to be explained.

Ultimate Net Loss As we saw in an earlier chapter, this is the total sum incurred in settlement of any claim and is the amount to be set against an excess of loss layer or programme. In addition to the indemnity itself (compensation to the damaged or injured party or parties in an accident), the incurred amount includes loss expenses, loss salvages and any available recoveries on that loss. Also, recoveries due from prior reinsurances (known as inuring reinsurances) would first be deducted to ascertain the incurred amount to an excess of loss programme. Prior reinsurances help define the reinsured's *Net Retained Line* after the deduction of any prior reinsurances protecting the account in question. The reinsured's costs of running its own claims department would not form part of the UNL.

Each and Every Loss The intention of this form of reinsurance is to allow the reinsured to accumulate any and all claims that arise from the same originating cause as one excess of loss recovery. Consequently, a whole series of terms has been created to define the basis for identifying a reinsurance claim.

These can be all amounts paid by the reinsured in respect of "any one loss", "any one accident", "any one event", "any one occurrence" and even "all individual losses arising out of and directly occasioned by one accident or by one occurrence or series thereof arising out of one and the same event or cause". In recent years the scope of liability insurance has extended to cover a wide range of economic loss, property damage or personal injury to third parties. These phrases can therefore find themselves being called upon to respond to a wide variety of claims from:

> a number of people being injured or killed in a serious motor accident;

> a number of people being injured or killed in the collapse of a building. The fault could lie with both the architect and the contractor so that a minimum of two different original insureds would be involved in the same event;

> a number of workers could develop an occupational disease or illness as a result of their exposure to specific working conditions (asbestos mining, coal mining, cotton mills, etc.). If the disease developed as a result of exposure to the same conditions over a period of years, all reinsurances over that period could be called upon to respond on a proportional basis (the "exposure" approach). If the reinsurances had been issued on a "manifestation" basis, only the coverage for the year when the disease was diagnosed would pay the claim;

> a number of consumers could be injured by a defective batch of a particular product. The product might have been manufactured in an earlier year and exported to a number of countries. The DES case in the US established a basis for claiming injury into the next generation because of the genetic damage that drug had caused;

> a number of investors could lose money through receiving bad advice from an accountant. The same advice might have been given over a period of years;

a claimant loses his or her right to a legal action because the lawyer did not issue the writ in time (or did not follow an accepted legal process). In this instance, a failure to do something would constitute the "accident" or "event".

Losses occurring Under excess of loss reinsurance, cover can be provided on the basis of "losses occurring", "risks attaching" (also known as "policies issued and renewed"), "losses discovered or reported" or "claims made".

"Losses occurring" means that all losses that occur during the period of the reinsurance are covered by the contract irrespective of the inception date of the original policy or policies.

"Risks attaching" (or "policies issued and renewed") means that the reinsurance covers only losses occurring on those policies that had been issued or renewed on or after dates falling within the specified period of the reinsurance contract.

"Losses discovered or reported" or **"claims made"** basis means that the reinsurance only covers losses discovered or claims made during the specified period of the reinsurance. This formulation ignores the inception date of the original policy or policies or the date of the occurrence of the loss. This type of cover is often used when it is difficult to pinpoint an exact date of occurrence, e.g. Fidelity Guarantee and Professional Indemnity policies. It has also become popular in recent years as a means of reinsuring "long-tail" insurances. These generally cover liabilities to third parties (such as Products Liability and many forms of Professional Indemnity), where it can take an exceptionally long time for a claim to become apparent and then be advised to the reinsured. The reinsurer benefits since it would no longer be liable once the loss discovery period had expired and the reinsured is assured of protection provided it maintains its reinsurance coverage in force.

Such protections are quite complicated and insurance regulators have imposed disciplines on these types of cover. Two examples are the *retroactive date* provision (the contract responds to losses made during the specified reinsurance period but arising on original policies issued up to an specified number of years *before* the specified reinsurance period had started) and *an additional period for reporting claims* if the original policy (or reinsurance) is cancelled.

Aggregate Extension Clause or Claims Series Clause This clause attempts to address some of the issues that arise in connection with defining "each and every loss" (see the discussion above). These problems do not merely apply to excess of loss reinsurance but extend to the level of the original policy coverage itself.

An original insurance might cover death or bodily injury to third parties resulting from the use or consumption of a product manufactured or distributed by the original insured. This can be covered either as an original policy or as an extension to a general third party liability policy.

A defective batch of medicine might cause harm and many claims received by the insurance company. The medicine might have been manufactured in a number of countries over a number of years. The harmful effects might also arise over a period of years. The loss might be caused by one or more defective batches of the product. Although it is recognised that the medicine caused the injuries, it would be difficult (if not impossible) to identify the event (the consumption of the dose) that caused the actual harm (and therefore the insurance contract period which should respond). Many Products Liability insurances are therefore issued on an "annual aggregate" rather than "per accident" basis. This means that all products claims arising in that policy period are covered within the aggregate limit without the original insured having to identify each claim as a separate "accident". The Aggregate Extension Clause (AEC) or Claims Series Clause responds by treating these "aggregate" claims as if they arose from a single "accident" or "event". A great variety of AEC and Claims Series wordings have been developed over the years and it is always wise to check exactly what extension of cover is being granted. Otherwise it could become very easy for an "event" excess of loss reinsurance to become a stop loss (aggregate excess of loss) without a suitable premium having been paid. Please refer to our comments in Chapter 17 on the modern solution to this problem of an aggregation of losses arising from one identified cause.

Aggregate Extraction Clause This clause should not be confused with the Aggregate *Extension* Clause. In certain circumstances a ceding company or reinsured might write original policies or reinsurances on an aggregate basis. The Aggregate Extraction Clause allows the ceding company/reinsured to isolate (or extract) its incurred loss amount from one identified loss or event (e.g. an individual risk loss or a natural perils storm or earthquake loss) from the *annual* aggregate protection available and include that element of the "extracted loss" within its ultimate net loss. This would allow the ceding company/reinsured to maximise its reinsurance recoveries in such circumstances. Care must be taken when identifying the elements of (say) a stop loss contract that could contribute to a "loss event" situation. The Aggregate Extraction Clause could be used for both large individual risk losses (property or casualty) and natural perils event losses.

Stability or Index Clause Inflation normally has a very serious effect on the results of a direct insurance company. For an excess of loss reinsurer the effect can be even more serious. The inflationary effect on property excess of loss reinsurances is not too onerous because property claims tend to be advised quickly and settled without too much delay. However, reinsurances of legal liability business are vulnerable because of the length of time it takes for claims to become apparent, be advised to either reinsured or reinsurer (or both) and then to be settled. This period is known as the settlement "tail". Often, settlement then only takes place after some form of legal action and many years may have passed from the date of the accident itself. Sometimes, the eventual settlement is a multiple of the original reserve estimate of the original claim purely because of the effect of inflation.

Inflation affects individual claims (known as "vertical" inflation). Over time as monetary values increase, the effective value of any excess of loss deductible might decrease. More claims would affect the diminishing monetary level of that deductible. This form of inflation is known as "horizontal" inflation.

We could summarise the ways by which a reinsurer's liability could be affected by inflation.

(1) **Increase in amount paid for claims** – claims already affecting the XL cover are settled for larger amounts.

(2) **Increase in claims frequency** – claims previously settled for an amount less than the deductible now exceed that monetary amount and affect the XL cover.

In the first case, the reinsured could bear some of the effects of inflation in that it pays the increase in claims up to the deductible. Above that amount, the reinsurer would also bear its part of the inflated claim. In the second case, the whole of the cost of inflation might be borne by the reinsurer. Both situations place an increased burden on the reinsurer who eventually might have to pay more than was contemplated when the excess of loss cover was arranged.

To solve this problem the Stability (also known as Index or Indexation) Clause has been devised to share or apportion the effect of inflation fairly between the reinsured and the reinsurer. This clause therefore appears very often in legal liability and motor third party reinsurances because of the high inflation experienced by most countries in previous years. We concede that worldwide interest rates are relatively low at the time of writing, but who knows what the future might bring?

The following is a specimen of a Stability Clause that might appear in an excess of loss contract wording:

> It is the intention of this Agreement that the retention of the Reinsured and the limit of liability of the Reinsurers shall retain their relative values that exist at the commencement of this Agreement.
>
> In the event of any loss hereunder the retention of the Reinsured and the limit of liability of the Reinsurers shall be adjusted by reference to an Index, as hereinafter defined, for the period embracing the 1st January 20xx, in the manner hereinafter set out. The Index for the period embracing the above mentioned date shall be called the BASE INDEX.
>
> If at the Date of Payment, as defined below, of any loss settlement(s) made under this Reinsurance Agreement, the Index, specified below, has increased by more than 10% (ten per cent) from the BASE INDEX, the retention of the Reinsured and the limit of liability of the Reinsurers shall be adjusted as follows:
>
> In respect of any loss settlement(s) made under this Reinsurance Agreement, the Reinsured shall submit a list of payments comprising such loss settlement(s) showing the Amount(s) of Payment and the Date(s) of Payment. All payments made by the Reinsured in respect of a Bodily Injury claim relating to a Claimant, including the Claimant's legal costs and legal costs incurred by the Reinsured in the defence of a claim, shall be aggregated and the Index used shall be that for the period embracing the Date of Payment, as defined below. However, continuing regular payments and payments in respect of claims where an award of provisional damages and subsequent further damages have been made under the provisions of *(we would identify here the specific legal requirements of the country concerned)* or out of court settlements made under (specified) terms and issued in conjunction therewith shall be treated as if they were separate payments.
>
> The amount of each payment shall be adjusted by means of the following formula:

$$\frac{\text{(Amount of Payment) X (BASE INDEX)}}{\text{Index for the period embracing the Date of Payment}} = \text{Adjusted Payment Value}$$

In respect of all other payments not mentioned above, the "Adjusted Payment Value" shall always be equal to the actual "Amount of Payment".

All Amounts of Payment and Adjusted Payment Values shall be separately totalled and the retention of the Reinsured shall be multiplied by the fraction:-

$$\frac{\text{Total of Amounts of Payment}}{\text{Total of Adjusted Payment Values}}$$

If, however, the Index for the period embracing the Date of Payment is less than the BASE INDEX, the retention of the Reinsured and the limit of liability of the Reinsurers shall remain as stated in this Reinsurance Agreement.

Definitions – the clause would also contain definitions of the index to be used, its date and basis, what happens to losses occurring inside and outside the country concerned and full details of what is meant by the "date of payment".

This clause needs some explanation. The first paragraph is a statement identifying the spirit and intention of the clause. The next two paragraphs indicate what would be used to measure any change or changes in relative monetary values. In this example, there would be no adjustment until any indexation had attained or exceeded 10% at time of payment. The fourth paragraph defines the way in which a *bodily injury* claim would be paid by the reinsurer. Property damage elements of a claim are not normally subject to the Stability Clause, whereas legal (and similar) expenses are. "Paid" claims also include partial payments, continuing "regular" payments and the other (court-driven) awards identified. An example should clarify these paragraphs.

A motor excess of loss reinsurance contract is arranged to cover losses up to $ 500,000 xs $ 500,000 for the 12 months period at 1st January 2003. At inception, the wages index ("base date") is 100.

A claim occurs during 2003 and is initially reserved for $600,000 from the ground up (f.g.u.). It is finally settled in *one payment* in 2010 for $780,000. At the time the loss is settled, the index has increased to 130 (from 100% at start of 2003 to date of settlement in 2010 when the index has increased to 130%).

Using the formula above, the *adjusted payment value* would be:

$$\frac{\$780,000 \times 100\%}{130\%} = \$600,000$$

The reinsured's retention (and the reinsurer's liability) would be apportioned by using the second part of the formula:

$$\text{Reinsured's retention } \$500,000 \times \frac{\$780,000}{\$600,000} = \$650,000$$

The actual claim settlement of $780,000 would be apportioned as follows:

  Reinsured's retention $650,000

  Reinsurer's liability $130,000 ($780,000 − $650,000)

Arithmetically, the 30% increase in the cost of the claim due to the effects of inflation has been fairly apportioned between the reinsured and reinsurer.

Currency Fluctuation Clause Certain specific problems arise under excess of loss reinsurance where the reinsured accepts business (or incurs liability) in a currency different from the main limits of the reinsurance contract or programme.

This problem does not arise under proportional reinsurance where all transactions are shared in relation to the original cession. On the other hand, an excess of loss reinsurance contract containing a fixed monetary deductible and limit of coverage could find itself quite badly affected by currency fluctuations or devaluations.

For example:

>Main excess of loss limits $1,000,000 xs $1,000,000
>
>Rate of exchange at inception (for example) $2.00 = £1.00

A claim for £ 750,000 arises during the reinsurance period, but the rate of exchange rate has moved to $1.60 = £1.00 at that time. The claim is also settled at that later rate of exchange.

Converting £ 750,000 at $ 2.00 = £ 1.00 produces an incurred loss of $ 1,500,000, but there has been a substantial movement in the rate of exchange (80% of that ruling at inception). The Currency Fluctuation Clause is then applied.

Convert main limits to currency limits using rate of exchange at inception:

$ 1,000,000 xs $ 1,000,000 = £ 500,000 xs £ 500,000

Recover £ 750,000 loss from converted limits = £ 750,000 – £ 500,000 = £250,000

Convert XL recovery at *settlement* rate of exchange = £ 250,000 x $ 1.60 = $ 400,000

This actual recovery equates to 80% of the theoretical recovery and follows the actual movement in rates of exchange.

The Currency Fluctuation Clause was designed to apportion the effects of these currency movements fairly between the reinsured and reinsurer and uses principles similar to those found in the Stability Clause. A typical clause might read as follows:

> In respect of losses in a currency other than that in which the monetary limits of the Agreement are stated, the liability of the Reinsurer shall be calculated as follows:
>
> (1) The retention of the Reinsured and the liability of the Reinsurer as expressed in this Agreement shall be converted into the currency concerned at the rate of exchange ruling at the inception date of this Agreement in accordance with the attached currency list

and

(2) The balance of any loss payment in excess of the Reinsured's retention shall be converted from the currency in which the loss was settled into the main currency stated in this Agreement at the rate or average rates of exchange as used by the Reinsured and ruling on the date or dates of settlement of the loss by the Reinsured.

Reinstatement We have explored the principle of reinstatements in an earlier chapter. Until recently, many excess of loss reinsurance programmes covering business such as Motor & General Third Party were issued on the basis of "unlimited free" reinstatements. This meant that excess of loss cover would be reinstated automatically following a loss, but without payment of an additional premium. It also gave the reinsured a theoretically unlimited number of excess of loss recoveries in any one annual period.

At the time of writing, many legal liability programmes are now subject to limited (normally free) reinstatement conditions, other than for legal liability classes involving original policies issued for an unlimited amount. Private motor insurance in the United Kingdom is a prime example. There is a legal requirement that UK private motor policies must be issued for an unlimited amount for third party bodily injury and a minimum of GBP 250,000 for third party property damage. Excess of loss reinstatement restrictions for such original unlimited policy coverage might change in the future and readers should be aware of any developments in their own markets.

Excess of loss reinsurance of many other classes of business would normally be subject to limited reinstatements. This might involve the payment of an additional premium, but would depend upon any agreement made between reinsured and reinsurer. The placement slip should state if the coverage is intended to be restricted by way of an annual aggregate limitation (of losses recoverable from the contract) or is subject to a specified number of reinstatements, whether paid or free.

10

Risk Excess of Loss

Because of adverse underwriting results of many proportional treaties (in all parts of the world) and subsequent contraction in proportional reinsurance capacity, many original insurance companies have had to increase the levels of retention they keep on single risks.

This has caused them to retain most of their small to medium sized risks so that any proportional treaties only cover larger-sized risks. Consequently, these insurance companies have had to retain far more of their exposures than was perhaps justified by their financial strength or underwriting results and have had to purchase "per risk" excess of loss reinsurance to protect that increased level of retention.

The example in Chapter 6 showed how cessions would be made to a 30 line surplus treaty. If, by way of a further example based on those figures, the surplus treaty reinsurers had decided to reduce the capacity of the treaty from 30 lines to 15 lines, the insurer would have had to increase its retention from $ 10,000 any one risk to $ 20,000 any one risk in order to retain the same automatic underwriting capacity.

However the insurance company might not be happy to retain $ 20,000 on an any one risk basis. In order to maintain a maximum net retention of $ 10,000, that insurance company could arrange a "per risk" excess of loss reinsurance for losses up to $ 10,000 xs $ 10,000.

"Per risk" excess of loss reinsurance need not operate merely as an addition to (or as a replacement of) proportional reinsurance. It is often used as a valuable form of "working" reinsurance protection for many property or similar "first party" classes of insurance.

The premium for a "per risk" excess of loss reinsurance is not based upon the proportional "sharing" principle of original premium, expenses and claims. The rating is normally based upon two methods:

1. Actual incurred loss experience to excess of loss layer or programme for prior years.

2. Potential exposure to an excess of loss layer or programme

The historic incurred loss experience is not always a useful guide. Well-structured "per risk" excess of loss reinsurances should not be affected by many individual claims in any one contract period. This avoids "dollar swapping" and heavy administration unless there are specific reasons for doing so. The intention of excess of loss rating is that, over time, the reinsurer should cover its claims costs plus profit, brokerage and a reserve for catastrophe or unusual fluctuations. By using the term "well-structured", we mean that the deductible should be set at a level that would exclude smaller losses. It is generally accepted that a "per risk" excess of loss retention should be a *minimum* of 10% of the reinsured's gross acceptance (after proportional cessions) on any one individual risk.

Present day reinsurers tend to use both the "experience" and "exposure" methods when rating the same "per risk" account. The "exposure" method is based upon the "risk profile" for the portfolio of business being reinsured.

Chapter 9 explained how reinsurers use graphs to calculate their exposure to loss at different levels of deductible. A similar graph of loss exposures is used for rating "per risk" excess of loss reinsurance contracts and programmes.

These graphs are based upon statistical analyses of loss distribution. The distribution of losses is uneven in that the number of losses at the lower end of a sum insured range is often larger than the losses affecting the top end of the sum insured range. Thus, if we set the deductible at (say) 50% of the maximum sum insured (EML or PML), it might follow that most of the claims would be below that 50% deductible. Therefore the cost of the layer for 50% xs 50% of the maximum sum insured would be much less than 50% of the original premium for the risk. The cost of financing losses (the risk premium) could well be at a level of 20% or less of the original risk premium. The following is an example of such a graph.

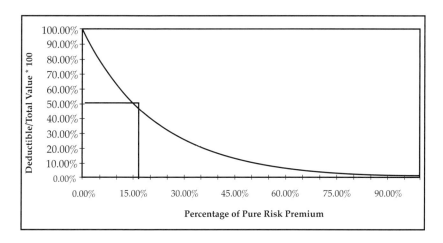

The shape of the curve would be affected by such factors as the type of risk being covered, area or location of risk, occupation, construction, EML or PML calculations and the original deductions allowed by the reinsured. Reinsurers tend to use the net risk premium (original premium less original acquisition costs) when assessing their "exposure" rate. Loadings would be added according to the reinsurer's underwriting guidelines.

The table used in Chapter 6 to illustrate proportional cessions to different levels of surplus treaty reinsurance is an example of a "risk profile". The following profile is based upon those figures. The figures shown originally as sum insured limits have been expressed in different sum insured "bands". Please note that a risk only appears once in its respective "size" sum insured band.

No of Risks	Band ($) $	Average value of risk	Aggregate Value	Aggregate Premium
1,050	0 – 10,000	5,000	5,250,000	105,000
2,300	10,001 – 25,000	17,500	40,250,000	575,000
1,222	25,001 – 50,000	37,500	45,825,000	611,000
580	50,001 – 90,000	70,000	40,600,000	522,000
150	90,001 – 150,000	120,000	18,000,000	225,000
100	150,001 – 200,000	175,000	17,500,000	150,000
60	200,001 – 1,000,000	600,000	36,000,000	450,000
40	1,000,001 – 1,500,000	1,250,000	50,000,000	450,000
20	1,500,001 – 2,000,000	1,750,000	35,000,000	200,000
10	2,000,001 – 2,500,000	2,250,000	22,500,000	125,000
5	2,500,001 – 2,750,000	2,625,000	13,125,000	27,500
1	2,750,001 – 2,900,000	2,825,000	2,825,000	2,900

It is then possible to construct a table of the risk excess of loss premium for particular layers of coverage above an excess of loss deductible of $ 100,000. We have used slightly different scale values from the graph above in calculating the reinsurer's premium percentage amounts.

Band	Average value of risk	Deductible/ Average X 100	Aggregate Premium	Reinsurer's % of Prem	Reinsurer's Agg Prem
1	5,000	below deductible	105,000	0	0
2	17,500	below deductible	575,000	0	0
3	37,500	below deductible	611,000	0	0
4	70,000	below deductible	522,000	0	0
5	120,000	83%	225,000	15%	33,750
6	175,000	57%	150,000	45%	67,500
7	600,000	17%	450,000	55%	247,500
8	1,250,000	8%	450,000	70%	315,000
9	1,750,000	6%	200,000	75%	150,000
10	2,250,000	4%	125,000	80%	100,000
11	2,625,000	4%	27,500	80%	22,000
12	2,825,000	4%	2,900	80%	2,320
	Total				938,070

The amount of $ 938,070 represents 27.24% of the total premium income of $ 3,443,400. This is the *pure risk premium* or estimated exposure cost. This pure risk premium then needs to be loaded by a margin to allow for the reinsurer's own administration costs and an element for profit. As mentioned, reinsurers would also add a contingency reserve to allow for fluctuations in loss experience and brokerage (if applicable). This premium is then expressed as a fixed percentage rate of the reinsured's total estimated gross net premium income for the protected business. As with other forms of excess of loss, it would be subject to reinstatement limitations and minimum and deposit premiums.

It should be noted that the "exposure" rating method produces an excess of loss cost for unlimited coverage – in other words, there is technically no restriction as to the *number* of losses recoverable from a contract or programme in any one reinsurance period. Reinsurers therefore discount the cost for restricting the number of reinstatements they are prepared to offer within a contract period.

Similar to other forms of reinsurance, this method of coverage has its specific uses and there might be occasions when it would not be the most appropriate form of cover. Some advantages and disadvantages could be listed as follows:

Advantages

"Per risk" excess of loss reinsurance provides an alternative to proportional reinsurance, especially when the market for proportional reinsurance is restricted.

The reinsured might find that the cost of its "per risk" reinsurance protection is lower because it is not paying away premium on a proportional basis.

Disadvantages

The reinsured pays the whole of the loss up to the monetary amount of the deductible. This is known as being in a "first loss" situation. The reinsured might find itself with insufficient cover if the reinsurance does not provide adequate reinstatements.

The reinsurance premium is effectively "net" premium so that the reinsurer does not contribute towards the acquisition costs of the original business.

The details of a "per risk" excess of loss reinsurance would be submitted to the reinsurer on a placement slip containing the following information (fictitious details have again been filled in as an example):

Reinsured:	PQR Insurance Co, Melbourne, Victoria, Australia
Period:	Losses occurring during the 12 month period at 1st July 2003
Type:	Risk Excess of Loss Reinsurance

Class of Business:	Business written by the Reinsured and classed as Fire and Allied Perils, including the perils of earthquake, storm and hail, but excluding flood
Territorial Limits:	Commonwealth of Australia
Limits:	To pay up to $500,000 ultimate net loss each and every loss, each and every risk in excess of $500,000 ultimate net loss each and every loss, each and every risk
Reinstatement:	Six (6) full reinstatements, each at 100% additional premium as to time, pro rata to amount reinstated only
Event Limitation:	Maximum recovery any one event $1,500,000
Rate:	0.75% of Gross Net Premium Income
Minimum & Deposit Premium:	$135,000 payable quarterly in advance
Brokerage:	10%
General Conditions:	Ultimate Net Loss Clause Net Retained Lines Clause Run-Off Clause at 50% of premium hereon Losses to be taken in chronological order of the date of their loss occurrence Definition of "any one risk" as per Reinsured's Underwriting Guidelines
Information:	Estimated 2003/2004 gross net premium income: $20,000,000 No known or reported losses exceeding $500,000 Largest loss ever was in 2001: $405,000 (100% and f.g.u.). Cause: fire, suspected electrical fault

Once again, there are certain terms used above that are specific to Per Risk Excess of Loss reinsurances. We explain these below, although they are not in the order of the placement slip:

Ultimate Net Loss This is the total sum incurred by the reinsured in settlement of losses. As we mentioned previously, the incurred loss amount usually includes loss expenses, salvages and recoveries (including recoveries from other reinsurance treaties or contracts that inure to the benefit of the per risk excess of loss cover).

Where risk excess of loss is the primary type of reinsurance protection, reference to prior reinsurance recoveries is redundant. In contrast, where an individual facultative placement, surplus or quota share treaty operate to provide the first "slice" of reinsurance protection, then clearly recoveries due under those priority reinsurance should be taken into account in the computation of any excess of claim.

Net Retained Lines This emphasises the importance of deducting prior reinsurances in arriving at the reinsured's net retained loss for setting against the excess of loss protection.

Each and Every Loss, Each and Every Risk The excess of loss cover provides for the reinsured to determine what is one risk. This is shown under General Conditions as "Definition of 'any one risk' as per Reinsured's Underwriting Guidelines".

It could involve one building or a group of buildings on a single site or location, or single building or group of buildings at a series of different locations (known as a "schedule" of insurances). The reinsured has the right to decide what it considers to represent a single risk. It is normal for the reinsured to agree any definition with reinsurers, preferably at contract formation stage. This should avoid any problems if a loss occurred that was not within the terms of the agreed "any one risk" definition. If this happened, the reinsured would not be able to make a full recovery.

Please note that there is no standard definition of "any one risk". If the reinsured uses an underwriting mechanism such as accepting business on an EML or PML (or other) basis, then such assessments would also have to be discussed with reinsurers at the formation stage of any excess of loss contract.

Run-Off Clause This contract is on a "losses occurring during" basis. This means that whilst the reinsurance coverage is for an identified 12 months period, it would protect original policies coming into force before and during that period and liability under those policies would potentially continue after the reinsurance period had ended.

Reinsurers recognise this potential loss of coverage (normally if the reinsurance contract is cancelled) and offer the reinsured coverage for a further 12 months. This covers the so-called "run off" of unexpired liability of the protected account and in force at date of cancellation. Reinsurers would charge an additional premium for the coverage. In this example, we have used a pre-agreed contractual figure of 50% of the current year's reinsurance premium. The run-off terms would be agreed individually and it is normal for the clause to be invoked (utilised) before the end of the current 12 months period has ended.

Reinstatements Since risk excess of loss contracts are "working" in that they are expected to involve an identified loss incidence, there must be an adequate number of reinstatements available to the reinsured, certainly sufficient to cover the number of claims anticipated in any one annual period. There are various methods of expressing reinstatements, but reinstatements tend to be a function of price. In our example, we have used paid reinstatements and have given the reinsured annual coverage for a maximum of 7 (seven) losses (original loss plus its 6 (six) reinstatements).

This could equally be expressed as a "maximum annual aggregate limit of losses recoverable hereon of $ 3,500,000". Instead of triggering an additional premium as and when losses occurred and paying reinstatement premiums when the losses were subsequently settled, reinsurers could charge that entire contract premium "up front" or in full and in advance.

This would mean that the reinsured would have to pay $1,050,000, but know that total annual excess of loss coverage for $ 3,500,000 was available. This method also shows the contract rate on line, 30% in this instance (premium divided by liability).

Another method of expressing the reinstatement condition would be to charge the full contract premium in advance ($1,050,000, as above), but offer reinstatements as "six full and free reinstatements". As with the second example, all that reinsurers have done is to request the full contract premium in advance, rather than receive it as a function of paid losses to their excess of loss coverage.

It is sometimes possible to purchase "backup" coverage. This type of contract operates after exhaustion of all reinstatements under the original reinsurance coverage. If there had been an unexpectedly high number of losses in a particular contract period, then the reinsured could find itself without automatic cover as all its reinstatements (under the original contract) had been exhausted.

Event Limitation As its name implies, "per risk" excess of loss is a form of reinsurance designed to protect losses that affect a single identified risk. Each loss should result from a fortuitous event involving a specific site or location. Per risk excess of loss reinsurance is not intended to provide catastrophe reinsurance against (say) the same windstorm damaging a number of separate risks in a particular area.

In the early 1970's, many "per risk" excess of loss reinsurers discovered that if a catastrophe loss occurred, then their "per risk" contracts had to pay many multiples of their maximum "per risk" liability under those contracts. Since the concept of replacing proportional reinsurance by "per risk" excess of loss was in its infancy, many reinsurers did not restrict coverage by limiting reinstatements and consequently suffered extensive losses as the excess of loss premiums they charged were often quite low.

Initially, limited reinstatements (as described above) were introduced and this restriction was further refined at certain levels of "per risk" coverage where there was an identified exposure to natural perils. This imposition is known as an "event limit". It has the effect of restricting the recovery of "per risk" losses involved in an identified natural perils event from the "per risk" excess of loss contract.

Please note that each risk loss would first have to affect the "per risk" layer, but the sum of those incurred loss amounts (to the layer) must not exceed the stated "event" limitation. The reinsured would be able to add all losses within its retention (own net retained losses) in that natural perils event, plus any "per risk" elements unrecovered from the risk excess of loss contract and set the total amount against any catastrophe excess of loss coverage it had purchased. We review catastrophe excess of loss reinsurance in Chapter 11.

Losses to be taken in Chronological Order of the Date of their Loss Occurrence It is relatively easy to place losses into a chronological order by the date of their occurrence. Settlement patterns do not necessarily follow that chronological order and often present problems if certain reinstatements are free and subsequent reinstatements are subject to the payment of an additional premium. As an example, reinstatements could involve a mixture of free and paid, perhaps two free, plus two further reinstatements each at 25% additional premium, then four more, each at 50% additional premium. This shows that there is no "standard" method.

Reinsurers recognise this aspect and many "per risk" contracts contain this "losses to be taken ..." provision to avoid any misunderstandings.

11

Catastrophe Excess of Loss

Catastrophe excess of loss contracts protect the reinsured against the risk of accumulation or aggregation in the event of a catastrophe. In reinsurance terms, we would normally describe a catastrophe as an event involving natural perils, perhaps an earthquake, cyclone or flood. Recent events have shown that a catastrophe might also involve man-made perils.

Such a natural perils event would destroy or damage a large number of risks. Many governments consider the perils to be fundamental and possibly uninsurable as their effects are often so severe and cause incalculable damage to national economies.

When considered individually, the reinsured's acceptance of, and chosen retention on, each of its insured risks might be reasonable. If, however, several buildings in one particular area or location (and all insured by that reinsured) suffered a loss from one identified event, then the reinsured's accumulation or aggregation in that event could reach a very high monetary amount, and certainly more than the reinsured would retain on an "any one risk" basis.

In Chapter 6, the discussion on multiple surplus treaties contained a table of cessions to a surplus treaty. The reinsured's total accumulation of net retained sums insured is $219,900,000 producing a retained premium income of $2,115,000. The table is as follows:

Number of Risks	Retention per risk	Accumulation
1,050	$10,000	$10,500,000
2,300	$20,500	$57,500,000
1,222	$50,000	$61,100,000
580	$90,000	$52,200,000
150	$100,000	$15,000,000
100	$100,000	$10,000,000
60	$100,000	$6,000,000
40	$100,000	$4,000,000
20	$100,000	$2,000,000
10	$100,000	$1,000,000
5	$100,000	$500,000
1	$100,000	$100,000
	Total Accumulation	$219,900,000

Although the reinsured's retention is no more than $100,000 on a single risk, it is clear that it has a considerable exposure should any disaster occur which affects a number of risks. In the unusual event of a cyclone causing up to 100% damage to the area involved (as actually happened in Cyclone "Tracy" in Darwin, Australia in December 1974), then the total amount to be paid by the reinsured would be considerable. Hence the need for catastrophe excess of loss protection.

The specific considerations that apply to the placing (and acceptance) of catastrophe excess of loss reinsurance programmes relate mainly to:

Exposure The amount of coverage that the reinsured needs to buy is dependent upon what is available at a price (the market capacity) and the reinsured's estimation of its aggregate net retained exposure.

The calculation of the aggregate net retained exposure is the first and most important step in the design of an adequate catastrophe reinsurance programme. It is only after that calculation has been made that it is possible to consider what part of the exposure would be harmed by a natural peril. In the past only superficial attention was paid to the design of a proper catastrophe reinsurance programme. This probably reflected an extended period during which there were very few natural disasters of any magnitude. Events of the past fifteen to twenty years have contained an exceptional number of Earthquakes, Hurricanes, Cyclones, Floods, etc. in *all* parts of the world. The storm of October 1987 in the UK was considered, at that time, to be a "once-in-a-three-hundred-year" occurrence. Then, in January and February 1990, came 90A, 90C, 90D and 90G (though only 90A and 90G caused major damage).

Any serious research on weather patterns in the UK, for example, would have shown that natural disasters have always occurred regularly with large loss of life and much damage to property. In the past not much property was insured and then generally for relatively low insured values. The same would have been true for most countries until quite recent times. The only uncertainty is when such disasters might occur.

In the intervening period there have been a staggering number of catastrophe losses. We have shown a selection below:

1991	Typhoon Mireille (Japan)
1992	Hurricane Andrew (United States and Bahamas)
1993	Blizzards and severe snowstorms (United States, Mexico and Canada)
1994	Northridge Earthquake (United States)
1995	Kobe Earthquake (Japan)
1998	Typhoon Vicki (Japan and Philippines)
1998	Hurricane Georges (United States and Caribbean)
1999	Hurricane Floyd (United States and Bahamas)
1999	Typhoon Bart (Japan)
1999	Storm Anatol (Western and Northern Europe)

1999	Storm Lothar (France, Switzerland and other European countries)
1999	Storm Martin (France, Germany, Switzerland and other European countries)
2001	Tropical Storm Allison (United States)
2001	World Trade Centre, New York City, terrorist attack
2002	Central European Floods (Czech Republic, Germany, Austria and other countries)

This list of losses (and there are many more we could have included) shows that as society develops, so do insured values. Demand for housing possibly exceeds supply and values increase. Pressure to build new homes has perhaps contributed to the size of the losses themselves. There is hardly a country in the world that has not seen a dramatic increase in the number of new homes being built. The problem is perhaps *where* those homes have been constructed. Flood-plains, reclaimed (drained) land, refilled (waste or mining) land have all been used to provide housing, but are obviously vulnerable if a flood or other "natural perils" event loss occurs.

There have also been tremendous advances in geographical, geological and meteorological studies over the last fifteen years and computer technology has developed to a similar extent.

These developments have been brought together to form impressive computer models. The content of an account is "mapped" and various weather (and other) data applied to that model. The weather data would provide information on the so-called "return period" of a particular type of loss (earthquake, storm, flood) of a particular severity, magnitude or intensity affecting the insured account. The *return period* is an estimate of the probability of a loss of an identified size affecting a particular country, area or location. This converts, in simple terms, to the frequency of an expected loss to an excess of loss (XL) contract. Reinsurers use expressions such as "rate on line" or "payback" to express the relationship between the XL contract premium and limit of liability for a layer. "Rate on line" is the XL layer premium divided by the limit of liability for the layer and the result expressed as a percentage and "payback" is the limit of liability for the layer divided by the XL layer premium and the result expressed in years. We explore some examples later in this Chapter.

Such has been the advance in computer technology that many rating agencies now expect all insurance companies to show that they have "modelled" their catastrophe exposures and purchased sufficient catastrophe excess of loss reinsurance. As a reminder, rating agencies previously concentrated on the ability of a company to repay any money it borrowed (debt rating). It did not matter whether the company was connected with insurance or reinsurance. Over time, the various rating agencies have developed assessment techniques specific to the insurance and reinsurance industry. In addition to assessing a company's ability to repay its borrowings, rating agencies also assess the "claim-paying" ability of both insurance and reinsurance companies.

An important tool within this assessment is therefore the use of computer modelling techniques. At the same time, there is a convergence in international accounting standards in the preparation and content of a company's annual report and accounts. This means that, in time, standard accounting procedures should lead to a fair financial comparison of insurance and reinsurance companies operating anywhere in the world. This emphasises the importance that regulators and other interested parties attach to the claims-paying ability of an insurance or reinsurance company and the rating assigned to that company.

A number of years ago a standard form of reporting lines

or classes business was created to help identify where any insured risks were physically located. This system is known as CRESTA (**C**atastrophe **R**isk **E**valuating and **S**tandardizing **T**arget **A**ccumulations) and is chaired in alternative years by Munich Reinsurance Company and Swiss Reinsurance Company, the two companies instrumental in its formation. There is hardly a country in the world where CRESTA "zones" have not been identified. It implies that any insurance or reinsurance company, operating anywhere in the world, must allocate its exposures in accordance with identified CRESTA zones. This enables all insurers and reinsurers to control their own aggregations on the same basis, since control of accumulations is fundamental to the concept of catastrophe excess of loss reinsurance.

If we based the total net retained sum insured aggregate on the example earlier in this Chapter, we might find that the account is exposed to four zones. In order to illustrate the concept of catastrophe excess of loss reinsurance more accurately, we have multiplied the net retained sums insured by a notional factor of 10 and then simplified the amount. This represents an amount of $2,200,000,000 at risk. We could allocate those exposures to their respective zones:

North Zone	40% of $2,200,000,000	=	$880,000,000
East Zone	20% of $2,200,000,000	=	$440,000,000
South Zone	20% of $2,200,000,000	=	$440,000,000
West Zone	20% of $2,200,000,000	=	$440,000,000

Under normal circumstances, a reinsured would not be able, nor need, to protect the full net retained sum insured amount at risk. The likelihood of a loss totally destroying the full sum insured in any one zone is very remote (although it could happen), so an assessment is made of the true probability of a loss of a particular intensity or magnitude occurring. We could then reduce the total net retained sum insured to a more quantifiable figure for the purchase of any catastrophe excess of loss programme. One method used is that known as "Probable Maximum Loss" or PML. In simple terms, this shows the level of coverage required in any one identified zone. Using notional PML estimates by zone, we could reduce the total net retained sums insured to the following optimum PML purchase indications:

North Zone	$880,000,000	x	10% PML	=	$88,000,000
East Zone	$440,000,000	x	5% PML	=	$22,000,000
South Zone	$440,000,000	x	6% PML	=	$26,400,000
West Zone	$440,000,000	x	10% PML	=	$44,000,000

Using a purely notional net retained premium income of $50,000,000 for this account, we could begin to structure the catastrophe excess of loss programme. The question is: do we start from the bottom or from the top ?

Given that we used an incremental factor of 10 for the net retained aggregates, we could assume that the reinsured's maximum net retention after proportional reinsurance is now a larger figure of $1,000,000 (rather than $100,000).

The upper end of the catastrophe excess of loss programme should be close to $90,000,000, as it represents the reinsured's largest single exposure by individual zone. This would allow the reinsured to "grow" its account over the 12 months period of the programme. We must mention that our example also assumes that only one zone could be affected by a loss event. If two or more zones could be affected, then different considerations would apply and higher programme coverage should be purchased.

Deductible The lower end of the programme, namely the catastrophe excess of loss deductible, is a different consideration. It is generally accepted that a catastrophe retention should fall between 5% and 10% of the reinsured's gross net retained premium income. In our example, we have a premium income figure of $50,000,000, revealing that the deductible should lie within a range of $2,500,000 and $5,000,000.

We have identified that in reinsurance terms a catastrophe implies two or more original risks should be involved in the same event. To guarantee this situation, reinsurers use a contractual condition known as the "Two Original Risk Warranty". Sometimes a placement slip contains this condition, on other occasions the catastrophe deductible is clearly larger than one maximum per risk retention. Even at $2,500,000, the programme deductible would comply with that "two original risk warranty" condition as the reinsured's maximum per risk retention is a maximum of $1,000,000, so two or more risks would certainly have to be involved to produce a loss to any catastrophe programme.

Reinsurers would also use historic loss experience to set the level of the deductible and market conditions and availability of reinsurance capacity at that time would be just as important.

We will use $2,500,000 for our programme deductible and then divide the optimum purchase of $90,000,000 into various layers that will form the catastrophe excess of loss programme.

Limits

1st Layer   Up to $7,500,000 ultimate net loss each and every loss in excess of
$2,500,000 ultimate net loss each and every loss

2nd Layer   Up to $15,000,000 ultimate net loss each and every loss in excess of
$10,000,000 ultimate net loss each and every loss

3rd Layer   Up to $25,000,000 ultimate net loss each and every loss in excess of
$25,000,000 ultimate net loss each and every loss

4th Layer   Up to $40,000,000 ultimate net loss each and every loss in excess of
$50,000,000 ultimate net loss each and every loss

Please remember that catastrophe reinsurance does not merely apply to properties exposed to natural perils. There is, for example, a large market for Personal Accident reinsurance on a catastrophe basis. After a reinsured has made cessions to its proportional treaties, it would still be exposed to a large loss if a number of original insureds travelled together on one aircraft and that aircraft subsequently crashed. The excess of loss deductible would be set at a level where a number of insured lives would need to be involved in the same accident. This is known as a "per life" warranty and is similar in its operation to that used in property. An example might be "three or more original lives to be involved in a loss event before any recovery hereunder".

Premium As we have seen, excess of loss reinsurance premium is almost always expressed as a fixed percentage rate of the reinsured's gross net retained premium income. The premium for the higher layers of coverage could be on a simple "flat" premium basis and non-adjustable, but such usage now tends to be quite rare.

Let us illustrate the "rate on line" and "payback" principles we mentioned earlier. Using the reinsured's gross net retained premium income of $50,000,000, we might have programme pricing as follows:

Layer Limit	Layer % Rate	Earns	Rate on Line	Payback
$ 7,500,000	3.00%	$1,500,000	20%	5 years
$15,000,000	3.60%	$1,800,000	12%	8.33 years
$25,000,000	2.50%	$1,250,000	5%	20 years
$40,000,000	1.60%	$ 800,000	2%	50 years
Total Programme				
$87,500,000	10.70%	$5,350,000	6.11%	16.36 years

As we have seen, reinsurers use "rate on line" and "payback" to identify how long it would take to recover a total loss from a particular excess of loss contract. This assumes that the layer premium remains the same and the reinsurer continues to write the business for the whole period ! Such pricing ignores brokerage and administration costs.

These concepts are not very scientific but they do enable a quick and simple comparison to be made between similar levels of catastrophe reinsurance. They can also draw attention to the inadequate programme premium rates sometimes charged for catastrophe reinsurance protections. For example, a rate on line of 0.2% would imply a "payback" of 500 years. If reinsurers charged such a low premium, it would be indicative that the estimated loss probability to a particular layer is very remote. Readers should be aware that reinsurers often charge a minimum rate on line (or payback) in order to justify acceptance of an individual catastrophe excess of loss layer.

Reinstatement As we explored in earlier Chapters, if a loss has been paid under a catastrophe excess of loss contract, then the amount of cover left for the remainder of the reinsurance period is reduced by the amount of the loss paid. Obviously, the reinsured does not anticipate that it would be exposed to more than one disaster in a year. In the period from 1988 until now, and especially in 1999, historic events have shown that it can and does happen.

It is essential therefore that the full liability should be reinstated following a loss, otherwise the reinsured could find that it had inadequate catastrophe protection if a further catastrophe were to occur in the same annual period. This could have a serious effect on its claims-paying ability and shareholders and/or policyholders might ask difficult questions of the reinsured's board of management.

Reinsurers recognise this fact and incorporate an automatic reinstatement feature into their pricing of a catastrophe excess of loss layers and programmes. A typical reinstatement condition would read:

One full and automatic reinstatement at 100% additional premium as to time, pro rata as to amount reinstated only.

Nowadays, reinsurers are reluctant to offer more than one automatic reinstatement for catastrophe excess of loss programmes. This could be due to restrictions imposed by their own retrocessionaires, or a reluctance to expose their assets to an adverse (or unexpected) series of loss events in any one annual period. The usual clause contained in many contract wordings provides for the reinsured to pay an additional premium to reinstate any portion of the liability exhausted by a loss. A typical clause also limits the amount payable by the reinsurer in any one year to (say) two times the original limit of liability:

Reinstatement Clause

> In the event of loss or losses occurring under this Agreement, it is hereby mutually agreed to reinstate this Agreement to its full amount from the time of the occurrence of such loss or losses until expiry of this Agreement subject to the payment of an additional premium of 100% of the final adjusted premium hereunder, to be provisionally calculated on the basis of the deposit premium. The foregoing additional premium is in respect of a total loss, lesser amounts shall be calculated in proportion that the amount reinstated bears to the total limit of liability hereon. Such additional premium shall be paid by the Reinsured when any loss or losses arising hereunder are settled, but nevertheless Reinsurers shall never be liable for more than the amount stated in the Limits Clause in respect of each and every Loss Occurrence (as defined) nor more than twice this amount in all, representing one full reinstatement only of the above limit of indemnity in any one annual period.
>
> Losses shall be considered in chronological order by date of their loss occurrence but this shall not preclude the Reinsured from making provisional collections in respect of losses that may ultimately not be recoverable hereon.

There is little value in attempting to discuss the possible advantages and disadvantages of catastrophe protection on an excess of loss basis since this is generally the only form of reinsurance available for this purpose. Certain other mechanisms, such as derivatives and futures, have been developed in recent years but these have not come into widespread use. An alternative would be to arrange stop loss coverage, covering, for example, a domestic building and contents portfolio against weather losses. The very attractiveness to a reinsured of such a comprehensive coverage is counterbalanced by the reluctance of reinsurers to offer such protection.

Sometimes catastrophe excess of loss reinsurance is purchased to protect what is known as the "common account" of the reinsured and its proportional reinsurers. This means that the net retained account is the total of the reinsured and those proportional reinsurers. In such event, the deductible and limit are applied to the gross loss and the excess of loss premium and claims recoveries are apportioned according to the shares in the treaty. Care should be taken to amend the Ultimate Net Loss and Net Retained Lines Clauses by the addition of the phrase "amended to allow for proportional reinsurers".

The details of a catastrophe contract would be submitted to reinsurers on a placement slip giving the following information (as always, fictitious details have been used):

Reinsured and Location:	ALORS Insurance Company, Paris, France
Period:	Losses occurring during the period of 12 months at 1st January 2003, local standard time at the place where the loss occurs
Type:	Catastrophe Excess of Loss Reinsurance
Class of Business:	In respect of the Reinsured's net retention of Fire and Allied Perils risks (as identified) and accepted by the Reinsured in their Head Office in Paris and in accordance with list of

	named perils mutually agreed between the Reinsured and Reinsurer hereon
Territorial Scope:	Metropolitan France
Limits:	To pay up to Euro 25,000,000 ultimate net loss each and every loss occurrence in excess of Euro 25,000,000 ultimate net loss each and every loss occurrence
Reinstatement:	One full reinstatement at 100% additional premium as to time, pro-rata as to amount reinstated only
Premium Rate:	Adjustable at 2.50% of the Reinsured's Gross Net Retained Premium Income accounted for during the period hereon
Deposit Premium:	Euro 1,000,000 payable in two equal instalments half-yearly in advance
Minimum Premium:	Euro 1,250,000
Brokerage:	10%
Law and Jurisdiction:	This reinsurance shall be subject to French law and practice
Arbitration:	ARIAS Arbitration Clause Seat of Arbitration: Paris, France
General Conditions:	Ultimate Net Loss Clause Net Retained Lines Clause Excess of Loss Reinsurance Exclusion Clause Definition of Loss Occurrence, including Hours Clause Extended Expiration Clause General and other specific exclusions as per agreed list
Information:	Estimated 2003 Gross Net Retained Premium Income: Euro 50,000,000
	No losses exceeding Euro 25,000,000
	Largest loss occurred in 1999 – Euro 22,500,000 (converted from FFcs), for 100% f.g.u.
	Reinsured's Maximum Retention any one Risk Euro 2,500,000

It is usual for the terms and conditions of the reinsurance contract to be set out in a formal contract wording. Wordings for catastrophe reinsurances will be similar to that discussed in Chapter 17 but with specific amendments. The terms that need to be examined in more detail are as follows:

Ultimate Net Loss Clause This defines the basis on which the reinsurer would pay any loss. As in other forms of excess of loss reinsurance, the incurred loss amount is calculated on the total sum actually paid by the Reinsured in settlement of losses including loss expenses, loss salvages and recoveries including recoveries from treaties (or other reinsurances) inuring to the benefit of the catastrophe excess of loss cover. As the coverage is intended to apply only to the reinsured's net retention after the operation of those other reinsurances (e.g. Surplus, Quota Share, Risk Excess) the ***Net Retained Lines*** clause would make it clear that the catastrophe reinsurance should apply only to those net retained amounts. To this would be added the ***Other Reinsurers*** clause which states that the catastrophe reinsurer's liability would not increase if the retained amount becomes greater because the reinsured could not make recoveries from other reinsurers on the coverages which operate in priority. Insolvency of a reinsurer is often a cause for non-collection. Many reinsureds now include an Insolvency Clause to protect themselves against this eventuality. We should also point out that many UNL clauses also allow the reinsured to state that underlying reinsurances (that is, lower layers of the same programme) are for the sole benefit of the reinsured and would be disregarded when recovering any loss from upper layers of that programme.

Definition of Loss Occurrence, including Hours, Clause The definition of the "loss event" can give rise to considerable problems. It is often difficult to identify when a storm starts or where and when it ends, particularly when it is closely followed by another storm that causes further damage. An earthquake can give rise to aftershocks that cause damage to already weakened structures. Where the reinsurance covers losses arising from the effects of a severe winter, it is often difficult to decide whether damage was caused by falling snow, freezing conditions or ice and/or snow melting in the subsequent thaw. These difficulties are addressed by the inclusion of an "Hours Clause" in the contract wording. This defines how certain perils are considered to give rise to a claim under the reinsurance. A typical clause would state:

DEFINITION OF LOSS OCCURRENCE

The words "Loss Occurrence" shall mean all individual losses arising out of and directly occasioned by one catastrophe. However, the duration and extent of any "Loss Occurrence" so defined shall be limited to:

(a)   72 consecutive hours as regards hurricane, typhoon, windstorm, rainstorm, hailstorm and/or tornado;

(b)   72 consecutive hours as regards earthquake, seaquake, tidal wave and/or volcanic eruption;

(c)   72 consecutive hours and within the limits of any one city, town or village as regards riots, civil commotions and malicious damage

(d)   72 consecutive hours as regards any "Loss Occurrence" which includes individual loss or losses from any of the perils mentioned in (a), (b) and (c) above;

(e)   168 consecutive hours for any "Loss Occurrence" of whatsoever nature which does not include individual loss or losses from any of the perils mentioned in(a), (b) and (c) above

and no individual loss from whatever insured peril, which occurs outside these periods or areas, shall be included in that "Loss Occurrence".

The Reinsured may choose the date and time when any such period of consecutive hours commences and if any catastrophe is of greater duration than the above periods the Reinsured may divide that catastrophe into two or more "Loss Occurrences" provided no two periods overlap and provided no period commences earlier than the date and time of the happening of the first recorded individual loss to the Reinsured in that catastrophe.

The last paragraph is important as it allows the reinsured to choose the time period where most damage has been caused if the catastrophe is of greater duration than the stated time limits. However, it is possible for the event to generate more than one loss period, and therefore allow the reinsured to recover two excess of loss claims if the event causes enough damage (and sufficient reinstatement coverage is available and subject, of course, to separate deductibles being applied for each such claim). The loss periods must be successive and must not overlap. Readers should be nevertheless be aware that some reinsurers are attempting to restrict reinstatement clauses by not allowing reinstatement in the same event.

Extended Expiration This clause is a logical continuation of the Hours Clause. It could happen that a catastrophe occurs on say 30th December, and the period of 72 or 168 hours would then extend into the following year. If, for example, the contract had been cancelled at 31st December, then only 48 hours would be covered. This important clause provides cover for the whole period of the loss irrespective of whether or not the agreement terminated during the event covered.

EXTENDED EXPIRATION CLAUSE

> If this Agreement should expire or be terminated while a Loss Occurrence covered by this Agreement is in progress, it is understood and agreed that subject to the other conditions of this Agreement, the Reinsurers hereon are responsible as if the entire loss or damage had occurred prior to the expiration or termination of this Agreement, provided that no part of that Loss Occurrence is claimed against any renewal or replacement of this Agreement.

Named Perils Following successive years of costly catastrophic events, and in anticipation of major computer problems at the change from 1999 to 2000 ("Y2K"), many reinsurers imposed a condition to restrict excess of loss coverage only to losses that were caused by identified perils, and for which they had been able to calculate a suitable premium.

This had the effect of concentrating minds and possibly stopped the inclusion of "free" coverage for smaller accounts from those reinsurances. Readers should be aware of developments and practices in their own markets, but remember a simple phrase "everything has its price". Similarly, reinsurers might want to exclude a particular class or line of business. They might be willing to delete or amend that exclusion in return for payment of a suitable additional premium.

12

Stop Loss and Aggregate Excess of Loss

Stop Loss

Stop Loss reinsurance, also known as Excess of Loss Ratio, limits the aggregate amount that the reinsured could lose on a given class of business in an identified annual period. The amount is normally related to the reinsured's annual gross net retained premium income for the class of business in question and is expressed as a percentage of that income, subject to minimum and maximum monetary amounts. The reinsurer is not liable for any losses until the percentage loss ratio for the year exceeds the agreed percentage of premiums. Thereafter the reinsurer is responsible for all losses, great or small, until the limit of liability of the reinsurance is reached. The reinsurer's limit is also expressed in the form of a percentage loss ratio, once again subject to minimum and maximum criteria.

Stop loss contracts are the reinsured's "last line of (reinsurance) defence", so the gross net retained premium is often identified as gross net *absolute* retained premium income. Normally the premium would be the premium earned or accounted during the period. The word "absolute" implies that the reinsured is allowed to deduct the cost of all other reinsurances it has purchased before arriving at the Stop Loss contract.

Stop loss covers are often used as the principal form of reinsurance protection for specialist portfolios of business, such as crop insurance. It is difficult to establish what is "one risk" for a crop portfolio and what is one "event" that might cause a loss. Growing and standing crops are especially prone to damage from hail, severe cold weather such as frost, cyclones or typhoons. There are three stages in the life-cycle of any crop, planting (whether as seeds or seedlings), the growing period to full plant size and then the time when the crop is standing, or ready to be harvested. Many national economies still depend on agriculture and protecting harvest yields would be critical to that country's population. Crops are therefore a valuable commodity and should be protected against different weather perils. These problems make it difficult to use other types of reinsurance, other than, perhaps, Quota Share reinsurance.

A typical stop loss cover would be expressed as:

> To pay the amount in excess of an 80% loss ratio up to 120% loss ratio.

This may also be expressed slightly differently as:

> To pay the amount in excess of an 80% loss ratio up to a further 40% loss ratio.

It is often the practice for the reinsured to retain for its own account a proportion of the amount reinsured (say 10%). The cover would then be expressed as:

> To pay 90% of all losses in excess of 80% loss ratio up to 90% of a further 40% loss ratio.

As we saw in proportional reinsurance, both the term for "earned premium" and "loss ratio" would also be defined in the contract wording. An example might be as follows:

Earned Premiums shall mean the incoming Premium Reserve for unexpired risks plus Premiums Written during the annual period of this Agreement less the outgoing Premium Reserve for unexpired risks.

(Pure) Incurred Losses shall mean the total of Losses Paid during the period of this Agreement plus the outgoing Outstanding Loss Reserve less the incoming Outstanding Loss Reserve.

(Pure) Incurred Loss Ratio shall mean the percentage result of dividing (Pure) Incurred Losses (as defined) by Earned Premium (as defined).

A further safeguard for the reinsurer would be to fix a monetary limit at which its liability would stop even if the maximum loss ratio was not reached. This would prevent the reinsurer's liability being increased beyond what was expected due to the reinsured writing too much premium income.

An example should explain the reasoning.

The following stop loss cover is given to a reinsured that estimates that its premium income will be $10,000,000.

> To pay 90% of all losses in excess of a 110% loss ratio subject to a minimum amount of $8,800,000, *whichever is the greater*, up to 90% of a further 40% loss ratio, subject to a maximum of 90% of $4,800,000, *whichever is the lesser*.

Using those limits, the reinsurer calculates that its maximum monetary exposure under that agreement should be $3,800,000, being 90% of $4,000,000 (i.e. 40% of $10,000,000). By allowing a "tolerance margin", the reinsurer's maximum limit of liability would be restricted to $4,320,000, being 90% of $4,800,000.

We have used a tolerance margin here of *minus* 20% for the reinsured and *plus* 20% for the reinsurer.

Deductible $10,000,000 x 80% x 110% = $8,800,000, whichever is the greater
Limit $10,000,000 x 120% x 40% = $4,800,000, whichever is the lesser

If the losses during the year totalled $15,000,000 and the

final premium income amounted to $12,000,000, then the reinsurer's losses would be calculated as follows:

Losses = $15,000,000 (approximately 125% loss ratio)
Deductible = $12,000,000 x 110% = $13,200,000
Amount recoverable = $15,000,000 − $13,200,000 = $1,800,000 (15% of income)
Reinsurers would pay 90% of $1,800,000 = $1,620,000.

In this example, the final premium income is at the upper end of the 20% tolerance margin and should show why the deductible is qualified by "whichever is the greater". Even if the reinsured had written more than $12,000,000 in income, the opposite qualification, "whichever is the lesser", on the limit would come into effect and protect reinsurers.

As its name implies, a stop loss is to "stop" a reinsured from having too large a loss. Stop loss protections must nevertheless *not* guarantee the reinsured a profit. The deductible should be set at a sufficiently high level to ensure that the reinsured has truly made a loss before the cover operates. Developing this theory, true stop loss contracts should not suffer a total loss from either one risk retention or one catastrophe retention.

This being the case, the reinsured would normally provide a list of all its prior reinsurances, both proportional and excess of loss, to reinsurers. The stop loss would normally contain a warranty that all those reinsurances remain in force during the period of the stop loss and even if they were to be exhausted, that "as if" recoveries would be made before interesting the stop loss. This is implied when the words "or so deemed" are used.

The details of the stop loss contract would be submitted to the reinsurer on a placement slip that would contain the following information (fictitious details have been filled in as an example):

Reinsured and Location:	KLM Insurance Co., Madrid, Spain
Period:	12 months at 1st January 2003
Type:	Stop Loss Reinsurance
Class of Business:	To cover the Reinsured's acceptances of hail business written in Spain, including its Spanish interests overseas
Territorial Limits:	Spain and Spanish interests abroad (essentially The Canary Islands)
Limits:	To pay 90% of all losses in excess of 110% Loss Ratio up to a further 90% of 40% Loss Ratio, provided always that the Reinsurer shall not be liable for more than 90% of Euros 24,000,000 in any one annual period
Premium Rate:	90% of 4.80% of Reinsured's Gross Net Retained Earned Premium Income
Minimum and Deposit Premium:	90% of Euros 2,400,000 payable in full at 1st April 2003
Warranty:	10% of all losses retained net and unreinsured by Reinsured
Warranty:	Reinsured's Proportional, Risk and Catastrophe Excess of Loss Programmes maintained in force during period hereon, or so deemed
Brokerage:	10%
Information:	Estimated 2003 Gross Net Retained Earned Premium Income: Euros 50,000,000
Statistics:	(Usually attached for past 10 years or more)

Aggregate Excess of Loss

An aggregate excess of loss reinsurance works on the same principle as stop loss but instead of expressing the deductible and limits as percentages of the annual premiums, they are stated as actual monetary amounts. Thus, the reinsurance might cover annual losses in excess of $3,000,000 *in the aggregate* up to a further $2,000,000 *in the aggregate*. The reinsured would pay all losses up to $3,000,000 in the aggregate during the annual contract period and the reinsurer would pay all losses over $3,000,000 but not more than a further $2,000,000 *in the aggregate* during the annual contract period. Any amount in excess of $5,000,000 would therefore revert to the reinsured.

A reinsurer must be extremely careful in giving such a cover. If, in the above example, the reinsurer gave cover based on an estimated premium income of $2,500,000, and the reinsured actually wrote $4,000,000 of premium, then the monetary value of the aggregate deductible of $3,000,000 would no longer represent a loss ratio of 120%, but a far lower one, a 75% loss ratio. The reinsured could now be guaranteed a profit (and actually abuse the trust of its reinsurer).

A reinsurer would receive details on a placement slip that would give the following (fictitious) details:

Reinsured and Location:	GER Insurance Company, Auckland, New Zealand
Period:	12 months at 1st January 2003 in respect of the Reinsured's 2003 Year of Account
Type:	Aggregate Excess of Loss
Class of Business:	To cover the Reinsured's net retention on all risks classified by the Reinsured as Domestic Property
Territorial Limits:	New Zealand, including incidental extensions
Limits:	To pay up to $10,000,000 in the aggregate of all losses falling under their 2003 Year of Account in excess of $12,500,000 in the aggregate of all losses falling under their 2003 Year of Account

	Reinsurers hereon shall not be liable if the Reinsured's final Gross Net Retained Premium Income accounted for during the period hereon exceeds 125% of the amount estimated at inception
Premium Rate:	8.33% of Gross Net Retained Premium Income accounted for by the Reinsured during the period hereon
Minimum & Deposit Premium:	$1,000,000 payable in full at 1st April 2003
Brokerage:	10%
Information:	Estimated 2003 Gross Net Retained Premium Income (accounted) $12,000,000
Statistics:	(Usually attached for the past 5 years or more)

13

Reinsurance Planning – Basic Principles

This chapter is devoted to the planning of a typical reinsurance programme and should enable the reader to understand the principles involved in choosing one type of treaty or contract rather than another. The guiding principle should be to keep a reinsurance programme as simple as possible. The cost of administration of a complicated programme can often outweigh the apparent benefits. Furthermore, there are no hard and fast rules that can be applied. Differences sometimes arise between the design of a programme and what is ultimately placed. The final placement tends to be the result of a certain degree of bargaining that takes place between insurer and reinsurer.

However, a number of factors need to be taken into consideration when preparing a reinsurance programme. These factors are listed below and are reviewed in detail in the course of this chapter.

1. Paid-up capital and free reserves
2. Risk-based capital
3. Size and structure of the portfolio
4. Frequency and size of losses
5. Geographical location of operations
6. Management, underwriting and claims capabilities
7. Future marketing plans
8. Investment and liquidity policy

9. Reinsurance philosophy
10. Reciprocal exchanges
11. State of the reinsurance market.

Paid-Up Capital and Free Reserves (also known as Total Free Assets)

The financial strength of the insurance company is the first important factor that needs to be considered when designing a reinsurance programme. There are few insurance companies in the world that are able to dispense entirely with the need to buy reinsurance protection. However, it is a general rule that the newer or the smaller the insurance company, the more reinsurance it would need to purchase against large loss events, whether in the form of a single, large risk or an accumulation of losses arising from one natural perils event. In either case, such a loss event could be catastrophic to the planned results of that insurance company.

When regulatory bodies look at the viability of an insurance company in a particular market, they look at its margin of solvency. This tends to be expressed as the ratio between capital and free reserves on the one hand and net premium on the other (i.e. the premium net of reinsurance cessions. Some authorities base the solvency test on gross figures and make a separate assessment for reinsurances). Certain countries establish minimum ratios below which they would consider an insurance company to be insolvent. These legal minimum levels are often some way below what is considered to be commercially acceptable in various insurance markets.

By providing reinsurance capacity, the reinsurer, in effect, adds the strength of its own capital and reserves to those of the reinsured company and thus allows the latter to accept large risks that it would otherwise be unable to accept without increasing its own capital. For example, a quota share treaty might be arranged that would reduce the net premium of an insurance company and therefore the ratio between its capital and free reserves and its retained premium income. (Please refer to the example in Chapter 1). Consequently, the insurance company gains a measure of relief from its financial obligations.

Conversely, and as a general rule, the higher the paid-up capital and free reserves the larger the retention of the insurance company would be.

Risk-Based Capital

Readers should be aware that regulators in many parts of the world are now considering alternative methods of measuring an insurance company's solvency. This is perhaps a result of convergence in international accounting standards and the increasingly global nature and multi-national ownership of insurance and reinsurance companies.

The concept of risk-based capital involves complicated mathematical models (which are not discussed here). These computer models seek to identify the largest risk and catastrophe exposures accepted by an insurance company on a gross and net basis and the ultimate financial effects on the insurance company's capital base. Different loss scenarios are set against all its reinsurance protections in force. After identifying potential reinsurance recoveries, the computer model would calculate the effect on that insurance company's retained account and whether its assets would be protected or damaged by its original gross acceptance philosophy and its planned reinsurance protections. Obviously, if the model revealed that its planned reinsurance protections would not be beneficial, then such reinsurance programmes would have to be re-designed. As we have mentioned, rating agencies also use this methodology in assessing the financial strength of many insurance and reinsurance companies.

Readers should be aware of developments in their own markets.

Size and Structure of the Portfolio

Having decided what the wishes of management are, the next step in the preparation of any reinsurance programme is a thorough study or analysis of the insurance company's total insurance portfolio and the constitution of various classes of business within it. In other words, if motor were the predominant class, say 60% of the entire 100% insurance premium written by the insurance company, and property represented only 25% of 100%, then the insurance company might perhaps place a greater emphasis on any reinsurance protections for its motor account. The so-called "mix" of business is therefore another important consideration in designing suitable reinsurance protections.

In property, marine and aviation classes a typical portfolio consists of a large number of small and medium-sized risks and a small number of very large risks, whether the size of risk is measured in terms of sum insured or an identified limit of indemnity or liability.

An example of such a small portfolio would be:

Range of sums insured per risk ($)	Number of risks	Cumulative Number	Cumulative percentage of total number of risks
0 – 10,000	10,508	10,508	18.02
10,001 – 20,000	23,066	33,574	57.58
20,001 – 30,000	12,220	45,794	78.54
30,001 – 40,000	5,895	51,689	88.65

40,001 – 50,000	2,562	54,251	93.06
50,001 – 60,000	1,607	55,858	95.80
60,001 – 70,000	995	56,853	97.51
70,001 – 80,000	504	57,357	98.37
80,001 – 90,000	360	57,717	98.99
90,001 – 100,000	208	57,925	99.35
100,001 – 110,000	151	58,076	99.61
110,001 – 120,000	75	58,151	99.73
120,001 – 130,000	53	58,204	99.83
130,001 – 140,000	39	58,243	99.89
140,001 – 150,000	24	58,267	99.93
150,001 – 160,000	19	58,286	99.97
160,001 – 170,000	10	58,296	99.98
170,001 – 180,000	6	58,302	99.99
180,001 – 190,000	3	58,305	100.00
190,001 – 200,000	1	58,306	100.00

A graph could be plotted using sums insured as the horizontal axis and cumulative percentages of risks as the vertical axis. The following graph shows the shape of the relationship.

Portfolio Profile of 58,306 Risks Ranging From $0 to $200,000

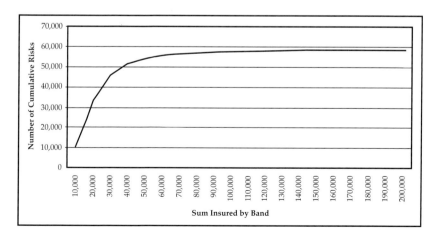

The portfolio profile determines what type of reinsurance is most suitable for that portfolio.

In this example, quota share reinsurance would not be suitable. The insurance company would be giving away a large proportion of its premium on its many small risks in order to obtain coverage for the same percentage of the few large risks.

A surplus treaty would be more suitable. As approximately 90% of the risks are of less than $40,000 in value, the maximum per risk retention could be set at this limit. This would mean that all risks of less than $40,000 would be retained for the insurance company's own net account and those amounts above this figure would be ceded to a surplus treaty after that maximum $40,000 per risk retention.

Sometimes a combined quota share and surplus treaty could be arranged, so that the bulk of the medium risks could be placed easily and cheaply by the quota share element, leaving only the small proportion of the larger risks to be reinsured by the surplus element.

Interestingly, the loss distribution (losses by cumulative amount within identified sum insured bands) for property and other first party insurances often follows the shape of the portfolio profile.

The distribution of risks and losses do not follow the same pattern for legal liability insurances. For example, in many countries the legal minimum insurance requirement for motor third party bodily injury might be unlimited, or subject to very large limits of indemnity. The risk profile would therefore be a horizontal line (or infinity if the account is unlimited), and there would be many losses tracking the horizontal axis, but relatively few tracking the full extent of the vertical axis.

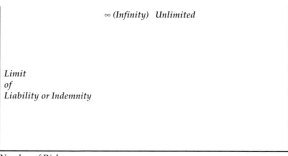

In this case quota share or surplus reinsurance would not be suitable as the reinsured would still retain a proportion of an unlimited amount. In these circumstances, it would be normal to use excess of loss reinsurance.

For general third party insurances, the profile is again different because most individuals or corporations buy policies for limits of indemnity in accordance with their own requirements. The profile could be identified in "blocks" of indemnity limits according to the various occupations involved. The profiles might look as follows:

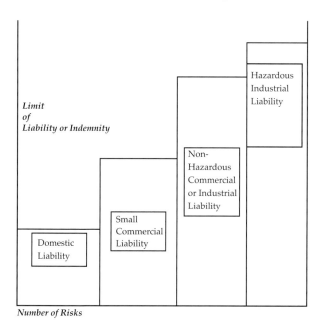

A quota share or surplus treaty could be used in this example. Even though most risks involve high limits of indemnity, it would be possible to identify a monetary retention and allocate premium, liability and subsequent losses on a proportional basis. However, as a general rule, reinsurers are not keen to provide proportional facilities for legal liability business. Exceptions are made where experience in a particular territory is good or where the reinsured is small or in the early stages of its development. Nowadays, it is more usual to reinsure business covering legal liabilities to third parties on an excess of loss basis.

Frequency and Size of Losses

It should be reasonably obvious that a reinsurance programme must take into consideration the anticipated loss pattern of the portfolio and its past or historic results.

Frequency and size of losses are important in deciding the level of retention and type of reinsurance programme.

If the loss experience involves small losses by size but they are large by number, rather than large losses but small by number, then the insurance company might be better advised to arrange a quota share treaty. This might not be feasible in practice as reinsurers might not be willing to give such coverage. It is important to note that at the time of writing, many reinsurers are reviewing all natural perils exposures covered by proportional reinsurance treaties, whether quota share or surplus.

By the very nature of their construction, quota share treaties cover many small risks and these tend to involve domestic (householder's or personal lines) accounts. A large catastrophe exposure therefore exists in many quota share treaties and it is this exposure aspect that reinsurers are seeking to restrict. Please refer to our comments on Cession and Event Limits in the earlier chapters on proportional treaties. Readers should be aware of developments in their own markets.

If the reinsured's loss experience showed that it had relatively large losses but these were relatively few by number (low loss incidence), then it could consider using a surplus treaty. It would choose a matrix of retentions (underwriting table of limits or guidelines) to follow its actual loss pattern and maximise its retained premium income.

If losses occurred principally on very large risks but were still very small in number, then that might be indicative of the superior quality of the reinsured's underwriting capabilities. The reinsured might prefer to arrange individual facultative reinsurances on those very large risks to balance its overall portfolio. Alternatively, the reinsured could purchase just a risk excess of loss programme (protecting its entire underwriting capacity) and dispense with all forms of proportional reinsurance. These choices show that there is no "standard" reinsurance programme or combination of different methods of reinsurance – only that which is best for the reinsured at a particular point in time.

Geographical Location of Operations

It is important that the programme should be suited to the country where the insurance company operates, since the geographical, political and legislative environments affect the characteristics of the portfolio and the perils to which the business is exposed.

A reinsured has to identify those perils that cause problems in the geographic area under review. For example, for the perils of earthquake, typhoon and volcanic eruption, the accumulation of sums insured in any one zone or area must be determined. We saw this previously when we discussed

CRESTA zones and the identification of a probable maximum loss or P.M.L. for those areas and zones. Based on that information, the reinsured has to decide how much catastrophe excess of loss cover should be purchased to protect its net retained account. Other questions that need to be considered are:

> Is there compulsory insurance? If so, what are the required limits?

> Are there any compulsory cessions to a local reinsurer?

These points need to be considered carefully, as they all affect the way in which any reinsurance programme would be designed.

Management, Underwriting and Claims Capabilities

The above may be considered as subjective, since they describe the environment in which the insurance company operates. Having considered these aspects, the next step in the preparation of the reinsurance programme is to pose the question: "What does the general management want to achieve during the year (or years) to come?"

It is very important to discover and understand the philosophy of the reinsured's general management. The philosophy could change if the General Manager or Managing Director were to retire or leave the insurance company.

If the reinsured's aim is to retain as much premium as possible (in order to achieve its planned growth potential) then retentions would have to be set at a high level. Excess of loss would perhaps be preferred to quota share.

If the reinsured's aim is to achieve a better "bottom line" or ultimate financial result, irrespective of the size of its net retained premiums, then a totally different reinsurance programme would be needed.

The management's confidence in the ability of its underwriters of a particular class of business could also affect the way in which the reinsurance programme would be designed. Greater use of facultative reinsurance might be recommended so as to make use of the reinsurer's expertise. At the time of writing, it is probably fair to say that facultative excess of loss is now preferred to facultative quota share placements.

The importance of suitably qualified claims managers and loss assessors has become very important over recent years. Establishing correct loss reserves, conducting successful settlement negotiations and then comparing ultimate loss settlement patterns to original loss reserves are critical to the successful structure and placement of many reinsurance programmes. As regulators, consumer groups and rating agencies take a far greater interest in an insurance company's ability to administer its claims portfolio correctly, so has the importance of the entire claims function. Many insurance companies now use actuarial techniques to price original insurance products, monitor existing loss reserves and calculate the development of known incurred losses to their ultimate anticipated settlement figure (Incurred But Not Reported or I.B.N.R. development).

Most insurance companies are also committed to reducing administrative expenses. The reinsurance department's contribution towards that aim might be to replace complicated surplus treaties that are expensive to administer with a combination of risk and facultative excess of loss. On the other hand, the loss of ceding commission (and its beneficial contribution to the ceding company's operating costs) could be a determining factor in deciding whether or not to make the change to excess of loss reinsurance.

Future Marketing Plans

Looking at past results helps to adjust the thinking on what should be done. But it is insufficient just to look at past results when arranging a reinsurance programme. One has to consult with individuals in underwriting, claims, actuarial and marketing to see what plans they have for expansion and then align those to the general and financial management of the insurance company. What are their expected loss ratios? What are the expected sizes of individual losses and the expected frequency of those losses? No portfolio of business is static. It would be important to discover whether and how the structure of the portfolio would change during the ensuing year. More underwriting capacity might be needed to cope with the acquisition of another insurance company's portfolio or for the opening of a new branch or the launching of a new product.

Investment and Liquidity Policy

Cash flow produced by business written has become very important in view of the marginal underwriting results of many insurance companies. This has been compounded by the low investment potential available in worldwide financial markets. If the type of business written produces a high cash flow, the insurance company could theoretically carry a higher retention than it would for a similar portfolio with a lower cash flow. Otherwise, it would pass some of that cash flow to its reinsurers. Liquidity also affects the fixing of cash loss limits. If the insurance company holds large cash funds and short-term money deposit investments, it is said to have a high "liquidity". It is therefore able to have a high retention and high cash loss limit. If funds are invested in longer term securities then the retention would be lower.

Over the years, many regulators have established

guidelines for the investment of insurance funds. In the main, an insurance company must have an acceptable balance of cash deposits, equities (shares in publicly quoted companies), short, medium and long-term securities or bonds and properties it owns. Many regulators insist that the majority of insurance funds are held in liquid form, or that those funds are realisable at a very short period of notice.

Reinsurance Philosophy

An insurance company whose reinsurers have suffered abnormal losses from writing its business in the past should (theoretically) allow those reinsurers to recoup some of their losses. This means that the insurance company has to answer the following questions:

> Should it look at its reinsurance as a long term equalisation fund?
>
> Should it seek to make a quick profit from its reinsurers?
>
> How does it view continuity or a long-term relationship with its reinsurers?
>
> Should it place its business through brokers or directly with reinsurers?
>
> What is the price to pay for good quality reinsurance security (their claims-paying ability and rating)?

Reciprocal Exchanges

A reciprocal exchange involves the swapping of similar portfolios of business, often using the same reinsurance method, between insurance companies operating in different countries. Although reciprocal exchanges are no longer used as much as they were in the past, there are still valid reasons why an insurance company might decide to enter into a reciprocal exchange. It might have a low retention that allows it to cede more small risks to its reinsurers and attract the reinsurer's business in reciprocity or it might decide to arrange a limited quota share for reciprocal purposes and use surplus reinsurance above the quota share limit.

The following are some questions that need to be considered:

> Is the time right for considering a reciprocal exchange?
>
> How are the markets performing in the countries or regions where it wants to exchange business?
>
> Is its own business of sufficient good quality to encourage reciprocity?
>
> Is the insurance company looking at the security of its reciprocal reinsurers or only at their business?
>
> Are premium and outstanding loss reserve deposits to be waived?

State of the Reinsurance Market

Whatever plans are developed by an insurance company, they must be acceptable to potential reinsurers. The insurance company must therefore remain in touch with the realities of the state of the reinsuring market. How receptive would the market be to the reinsurance plans proposed by the insurance company? Is the availability of proportional reinsurance declining? Is the excess of loss market "tough" at present? Is the insurance company prepared to cancel participations of local reinsurers who are perhaps too demanding? How would this affect its standing in the local insurance community?

These are some of the general factors that could affect an insurance company's whole reinsurance programme. We have shown below some of the specific factors that also need to be considered in determining the terms and conditions of the various types of reinsurance, but we have not commented on all of them again.

PROPORTIONAL TREATIES

1. **Balance**
2. **Acquisition Costs**
3. **Treaty Experience**
4. **Cash Flow** (already discussed)
5. **Reciprocal Exchanges** (already discussed)

It is tempting to suggest that a proportional treaty should have as high a limit of exposure for any one risk as possible. However, this limit should be compared to the estimated premium ceded to that treaty. We saw previously that this ratio is termed the "balance" of the treaty. A ratio of 20:1 (liability to premium) would indicate a poor balance and a ratio of 1:1 a good balance. It is normal to expect that a quota share treaty should have a better balance than a surplus or facultative/obligatory treaty. A typical quota share relationship might be $200,000 maximum treaty liability any one risk compared to a ceded income of $4,000,000 to the treaty. The balance would be expressed as 0.05 to 1.00, or 20% exposure under the treaty (ceded premium divided by treaty liability).

The (exchange) commission payable by the reinsurer to a ceding company is meant to represent a contribution towards the commission or brokerage paid by the latter to acquire the business and to cover the management expenses incurred by the ceding company in its administration of that business. A profit commission is normally paid in addition as a reward to the ceding company if reinsurers make above average profits on the treaty.

However determining the level of commission is not simple. It is perhaps the most contentious area in the negotiation of the terms and conditions of many proportional treaties.

When proportional treaties offered reinsurers a consistent profit, this was certainly the main factor used to determine the level of commission. However, poor results of proportional treaties over many years have caused the level of commissions to be assessed in a far more critical manner. A reinsurer would pay commission that could be justified solely by the quality of the treaty results. Since the combination of fixed rates of commission and separate profit commission is difficult to administer, many treaties are now subject to sliding scales of commission. This system is of immediate effect for both ceding company and reinsurer and simplifies administration for both parties, and any broker involved.

EXCESS OF LOSS CONTRACTS

Some factors to be considered in fixing premium rates to be applied to excess of loss reinsurances include:

1. **Past Experience**
2. **Changes in Past Experience**
3. **Revaluation of Account to Present Day Values**
4. **Loadings for Catastrophe (and Other) Exposures**
5. **Type of Business**
6. **Cost of Reinsurance (including allowance for Brokerage, if applicable)**
7. **Profit Margin and Use of Reinsurer's Capital**
8. **Continuity**

The insurance company would normally prepare statistics showing premium income and original losses (i.e. for 100% incurred amounts "from the ground up" and without application of reinsurance deductibles) for each reinsurance period.

These statistics would be used to calculate the pure burning cost. We have seen that this is the basis of rating for many layers of excess of loss reinsurance, especially where there is a credible loss experience. Other considerations must also be applied to the pure burning cost before arriving at the final excess of loss premium rate. Certain considerations need to be made.

Do the loss figures represent the probable final cost of each claim? Do past results conform to results normally expected for that type or class of business? If they differ from "market" statistics, what are the reasons? What was the value at the start of the observation period (the number of years historic experience available) to the value today?

To what extent do changes in the portfolio change the pattern of the past results? How would inflation have affected the result? To what extent have fluctuations in currency affected the results? To what extent have fluctuations in premium income affected the results? Do we have details of original premium increases and decreases over the observation period? What would have been the effect of one extraordinary claim on the results? What would be the effect of an unforeseen deterioration on the results?

What is the likelihood of a catastrophe affecting the cover? What are the catastrophe exposures by different peril? What loading should be incorporated into the calculation of the excess of loss premium rate for such an eventuality?

What is the general market experience of the type of business covered? What effect would a change in legislation, court practices or regulatory discount factors have on the type of business covered? (Some countries suggest that large court awards are settled partially in cash and partially in the form of an annuity. The annuity would guarantee an income for the life expectancy of the injured claimant. The discount factor is the accepted method of calculating what needs to be deposited to produce sufficient income from such an annuity. This is also known as the "time value of money").

The reinsurer would add its own administration costs to the pure burning cost and would build in a profit margin (identified by its management) for the use of the reinsurer's own capital. The reinsurer might also include a safety margin or security loading in certain circumstances. If the business were to be placed through a broker, then the reinsurer would include an allowance for brokerage. It would also assess the likelihood of its retaining the business over a long-term period to offset any losses it might have incurred through past associations with that reinsured.

14

Reinsurance Planning – Practical Application

The basic principles of reinsurance planning have been explained in the preceding chapter. This chapter shows, by way of a practical example, how those basic principles should be applied.

An insurance company requests its broker or reinsurer to assist in the preparation of its reinsurance programme. It gives both parties the following information:

Name of Company	Woodman Insurance Company Limited
Shareholders' Paid-Up Capital	$65,000,000
Free Reserves	$35,000,000
Total Free Assets	$100,000,000 (*total of shareholders's paid-up capital and its free reserves*)
Area of Operation	Mauritius
Type of Business written	Fire and Allied Perils, Motor (all classes), Workmens' Compensation and/or Employers' Liability (as applicable) and other Miscellaneous Accident classes (coverages and perils for *all* classes would be agreed between reinsured and reinsurer – see individual information sections)

Information on relevant laws applicable to the classes of business written	(a)	Motor insurance is compulsory and legal liability is unlimited for all third party bodily injury (private and commercial TPBI) and private third party property damage (TPPD)
	(b)	Workmens' Compensation and/or Employers' Liability Laws provides for a statutory minimum limit of $10,000,000 at common law

Management Philosophy

The insurance company wishes to maximise the size of its net retained portfolio, but without unduly exposing its capital base. It recognises the validity of purchasing various reinsurance programmes for all the various classes of business in its portfolio. This would assist the insurance company in achieving its management objectives and at the same time protect its original policyholders and shareholders. The insurance company therefore wants its various reinsurance programmes to provide both the best effects and positive financial results on its various net retained accounts. The ability of the Woodman's general management, underwriting, claims, accounting and actuarial staff is first-class.

Gross Portfolio (all figures expressed in $)

1. *Fire & Allied Perils*

(a) Estimated 2003 Gross Original Premium Income   42,500,000

(b) Historic Gross Original Premium Income figures:
        199829,850,000

1999	31,150,000
2000	34,500,000
2001	36,950,000
2002	39,900,000

(c) Results for the class show an average loss ratio of 65% over the last 5 years

(d) Average commission paid to agents is 20%

(e) Administration expenses are 8%

(f) Distribution of gross risks (figures for 100% as at 30th November 2002):

Gross Sum Insured Bands From	To	No. of Risks	Aggregate Net Sum Insured	Average Sum Inured	Band Premium
0	100,000	34,780	2,805,200,000	80,656	13,718,200
100,001	200,000	12,650	2,067,500,000	163,439	8,597,000
200,001	300,000	1,805	499,275,000	276,607	1,557,955
300,001	400,000	1,005	371,700,000	369,851	1,223,010
400,001	500,000	1,090	499,500,000	458,257	1,439,550
500,001	750,000	1,600	1,114,400,000	696,500	2,699,200
750,001	1,000,000	990	866,100,000	874,848	1,948,860
1,000,001	2,000,000	1,090	1,888,000,000	1,732,110	3,880,000
2,000,001	5,000,000	525	2,100,000,000	4,000,000	3,780,000
5,000,001	10,000,000	45	369,000,000	8,200,000	627,300
10,000,001	and above	15	187,500,000	12,500,000	281,250
	Total	55,595	12,768,175,000	229,664	39,752,325

(g) Cyclone is the major catastrophe hazard and is automatically included with standard FLEXA perils. Both private and commercial policies include the special peril of cyclone

(h) Largest loss per risk   900,000 (1998, 100% f.g.u. and for net retained account)

(i) Largest loss per event   10,000,000 (1999, 100% f.g.u. and for net retained account)

2. **Motor** *(Entire Account)*

(a) Estimated 2003 Gross Original Premium Income   100,000,000

(b) Historic Gross Original Premium Income figures (please note that reinsurers would normally require information for at least 7 years):

1998	60,000,000
1999	70,000,000
2000	75,000,000
2001	80,000,000
2002	90,000,000

(c) Average commission paid to agents is 15%

(d) Administration expenses are 8%

(e) Legal and Other Limits of Indemnity

Private and Commercial Motor TPBI	Unlimited
Private Motor TPPD	Unlimited
Commercial Motor TPPD	5,000,000 (rarely 10,000,000)
Maximum Private Own Damage	100,000 (first party, per vehicle)
Maximum Commercial Own Damage	500,000 (first party, per vehicle)
Maximum Accumulation any one Dealer	1,000,000 (average less than 500,000)
Maximum cyclone exposure in Port Louis	5,000,000 (postcode or zipcode basis)

(f) Loss experience – see comments in section

3. ***Workmens' Compensation & Employers' Liability***

(a) Estimated 2003 Gross Original Premium Income   25,000,000

(b) Historic Gross Original Premium Income figures (as with Motor, reinsurers would normally require information for at least 7 years):

1998	15,000,000
1999	16,000,000
2000	17,500,000
2001	18,000,000
2002	20,000,000

(c) Average commission paid to agents is 15%
(d) Administration expenses are 8%
(e) Maximum Limit Per Insured Per Occurrence 10,000,000 (including costs)
(f) Loss experience – see comments in section

4. *Miscellaneous Accident and General Third Party Liability*

(a) Estimated 2003 Gross Original Premium Income   50,000,000

(b) Historic Gross Original Premium Income figures (as with Motor, reinsurers would normally require information for at least 7 years):

Year	Amount
1998	34,000,000
1999	37,500,000
2000	40,000,000
2001	44,000,000
2002	48,000,000

(c) Main classes written and portfolio breakdown as follows (estimated for 2003)

(i)	General Third Party Liability	30,000,000
(ii)	Personal Accident Group	9,500,000
(iii)	Personal Accident Individual	2,500,000
(iv)	Theft/Burglary/Plate Glass	1,500,000
(v)	Contractors' All Risks	6,500,000
	Total	50,000,000

(d) Average commission paid to agents is 15%
(e) Administration expenses are 8%
(f) Loss experience – see comments in section
(g) Maximum Underwriting Limits:
   (i) General Third Party   5,000,000 per occurrence or event and/or in all in the aggregate in any one policy period plus costs, limited to an additional maximum limit 10% of indemnity
   (ii) Contractors' All Risks   2,000,000 per event (third party liability section only)

(iii)	Personal Accident	500,000 per person (group or individual)
(iv)	Personal Accident	1,000,000 per event (group known accumulation)
(v)	Theft/Burglary	500,000 per event
(vi)	Plate Glass	200,000 per event
(vii)	Professional Indemnity	Not written by the Reinsured

THE PROPOSED REINSURANCE PROGRAMMES

Fire and Allied Perils

The analysis of the gross portfolio produces the following risk profile and the graph would be as follows:

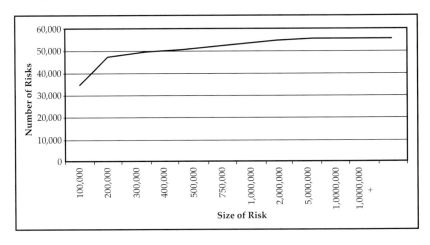

On the basis of their experience over the years, insurance companies and reinsurers have evolved a set of "rules of thumb" for determining retention levels, especially for property and property-related classes. These could be summarised as follows:

1. **Technical**

a) The maximum gross retention for the best types of property risk lies between 1% and 3% of the *gross original premium income*. By "gross retention", we mean the insurance company's own retention after using its surplus treaties. There are certain variations according to the constitution of the property account. A typical "mix" might involve, domestic, agricultural, commercial and industrial business.

b) An unbalanced portfolio, perhaps containing mainly large and complicated industrial risks, should have a retention towards the lower end of the scale rather than the upper end.

c) Similarly, portfolios with a high frequency of losses should have retentions at the lower end of the scale.

2. **Financial**

a) The same maximum gross retention, again for the best type of risk, lies between 0.5% and 1.5% of the total of the insurance company's paid-up shareholders' capital and free reserves combined (i.e. its total free assets).

b) An insurance company with high liquidity or good cash-flow should have retentions at the upper end of the scale.

c) The calculation of both property risk and catastrophe excess of loss retentions is slightly different. As a general "rule of thumb", the level for a risk excess of loss retention lies between 2% – 4% of *gross net premium income* or a minimum of 10% of the monetary amount of the insurance company's own gross retention. The level of retention for catastrophe excess of loss lies between 5% – 10% of gross net premium income. In this way, any catastrophe excess of loss programme must clearly involve two or more original risks. This structure would automatically comply with the implied "Two Original Risk Warranty" for many catastrophe programmes.

"Gross net premium income" means the insurance company's net retained premium income after cessions to prior proportional treaties (normally surplus and facultative quota share, and sometimes quota share treaties as well). Readers should also be aware that the cost of risk excess of loss protections should be deducted from the gross net premium income for calculating any catastrophe excess of loss premiums.

Let us identify the possible parameters for our insurance company, the Woodman.

Base	Amount Involved	Parameters Low	High	Monetary Amount Low	High
Free Assets	100,000,000	0.50%	1.50%	500,000	1,500,000
Gross Income	42,500,000	1.00%	3.00%	425,000	1,275,000

As shown in our graphical representation, the portfolio seems to be well balanced and the loss ratio is reasonable. In this example, a maximum gross retention of 1,000,000 might be acceptable. This retention level is in the middle of the "assets" range and towards the top end of the "income" range. It would also be easy for the Woodman to design a table of limits using 1,000,000 as a maximum gross retention. For ease of this example, we shall also assume that all risks are accepted on a full-value, sum insured basis.

If the Woodman were to analyse its gross account, there is one important question to answer. What is the largest sum insured within its portfolio? The average (within the band 10,000,001 sum insured and above) is 12,500,000, so this amount would be a reasonable indication of the surplus capacity required.

Using a maximum gross retention of 1,000,000 sum insured, this would mean that the Woodman would need 11.5 lines of surplus capacity to cover its average sum insured of 12,500,000. Since only 15 risks are greater than 10,000,000 sum insured, the Woodman might be advised to place those risks on a facultative quota share basis and restrict its surplus capacity to 9 lines of a maximum of 1,000,000 sum insured. We have shown the surplus treaty details in the example slip below.

How should the surplus commission be calculated? As we have seen, the purpose of commission payable to an insurance (or ceding) company is to cover its administration expenses and original agents' commissions. In this example, a minimum commission of 32% would be justified, being 20% original costs, 8% own expenses and 4% overriding commission. In practice, the commission level would depend on the historic results of the treaty. If we add that suggested commission figure of 32% to the average loss ratio of 65%, namely 97%, reinsurers might consider the resultant margin of 3% to be too thin. In all probability, reinsurers would suggest a sliding scale of commission, rather than a combination of fixed commission plus profit commission. We shall nevertheless use 32% as the commission rate, but not allow a profit commission in recognition of these apparently "tight" terms. Clearly, if brokerage were involved, then reinsurers would probably reduce commission and/or brokerage – or possibly both !

The placement slip might be as follows:

Reinsured:	Woodman Insurance Company Limited, Port Louis, Mauritius
Type of Treaty:	Surplus Treaty
Class of Business:	Fire and Allied Perils, including Cyclone
Territorial Limits:	Mauritius and its dependencies
Period:	Continuous agreement at 1st January 2003, subject to 3 months notice of cancellation at 31st December in any year

Maximum Limit per line:	$1,000,000 sum insured any one risk
Number of lines:	9
Maximum Limit hereon:	$9,000,000 sum insured any one risk
Cession Limits:	North Zone $2,275,000,000 sum insured
	South Zone $1,225,000,000 sum insured
Event Limits:	North Zone $70,000,000 sum insured
	South Zone $37,500,000 sum insured
Rate:	Original Gross Rate
Fire Brigade Charges:	3% on Original Gross Premium
Commission:	32% on Original Gross Premium
Profit Commission:	Nil
Premium Reserve Deposit:	None (40% in event of cancellation)
Loss Reserve Deposit:	None (100% in event of cancellation)
Interest:	To be agreed, in event of cancellation only
Portfolio Assumption/ Withdrawal:	Premium 35%
	Outstanding Losses 90%
Cash Loss/Loss Advice Limit:	$300,000 for 100% of treaty
Bordereaux:	None (premiums or claims)
Accounts:	Quarterly
Accounts Settlement Period:	30 days for preparation, 15 days for agreement, plus further 15 days for settlement
Estimated Ceded Premium Income:	$6,000,000 for 100% to treaty
Statistics:	As seen by reinsurers hereon

Please note that we have used purely notional North and South Zones in this example and our estimates of both cession and event limits are also purely notional. We have included them to offer a fair reflection of market practice at the time of writing, even though they seem very high!

The Woodman now has to consider the excess of loss

protections for its own net retained account. After surplus cessions and facultative quota share placements, its net retained profile might look like this:

Net Retained Sums Insured From	To	No. of Risks	Aggregate Net Sum Insured	Average Sum Inured	Band Premium
0	100,000	34,780	2,805,200,000	80,656	13,718,200
100,001	200,000	12,650	2,067,500,000	163,439	8,597,000
200,001	300,000	1,805	499,275,000	276,607	1,557,955
300,001	400,000	1,005	371,700,000	369,851	1,223,010
400,001	500,000	1,090	499,500,000	458,257	1,439,550
500,001	750,000	1,600	1,114,400,000	696,500	2,699,200
750,00	1,000,000	2,665	2,541,100,000	953,508	5,237,860
	Total	55,595	9,898,675,000	178,050	34,472,775

Readers should note that gross total sum insured aggregates and premium income have been reduced to the retained amounts shown above. This table shows the effect of the Woodman's proportional cessions. Let us first consider what risk excess of loss protection the Woodman should purchase and then a catastrophe excess of loss programme.

Dependent upon loss experience (which is not supplied here) the Woodman might decide to purchase two layers of risk excess of loss protection to protect its maximum gross retention of 1,000,000 sum insured. Looking at the profile above, the vast majority of risks lie within a maximum 200,000 sum insured. Logically, that would be a reasonable "break point" in the net risk profile. Rather than purchase one layer, the Woodman could buy two layers, the first up to 500,000, and then a second from 500,000 up to 1,000,000. Although the percentage value of the Woodman's 200,000 risk excess of loss retention is well below the suggested parameters (between 2% – 4% of gross net premium income), it is still equivalent to 20% of the Woodman's maximum own gross retention in this example. This would be an acceptable level for many reinsurers.

Reinstatements would depend upon the Woodman's historic loss experience at both levels and we have shown a suggested placement slip below.

Reinsured:	Woodman Insurance Company Limited, Port Louis, Mauritius
Period:	Losses occurring during the 12 month period at 1st January 2003, local standard time at place of loss
Type:	Risk Excess of Loss Reinsurance
Class of Business:	Business written and retained by the Reinsured and classed by the Reinsured as Fire and Allied Perils, including Cyclone
Territorial Limits:	Mauritius and its dependencies
Limits:	*Section One – First Layer* To pay up to $300,000 ultimate net loss each and every loss, each and every risk in excess of $200,000 ultimate net loss each and every loss, each and every risk *Section Two – Second Layer* To pay up to $500,000 ultimate net loss each and every loss, each and every risk in excess of $500,000 ultimate net loss each and every loss, each and every risk
Reinstatement:	*Section One – First Layer* Annual aggregate limit of $2,100,000 of losses recoverable hereon *Section Two – Second Layer* Two full and automatic reinstatements, each at 100% additional premium as to time, pro rata as to amount reinstated only
Event Limitation:	*Section One – First Layer only* Maximum recovery any one event $1,000,000
Rate:	*Section One – First Layer* 2.30% of Gross Net Retained Premium Income accounted for during the period hereon

Minimum and Deposit Premium:	*Section Two – Second Layer* 0.20% of Gross Net Retained Premium Income accounted for during the period hereon *Section One – First Layer* $675,000 payable in full at inception *Section Two – Second Layer* $58,500 payable in full at inception
Brokerage:	10%
General Conditions:	Ultimate Net Loss Clause
	Net Retained Lines Clause
	Run-Off Clause at 50% of premium hereon
	Losses to be taken in chronological order of the date of their loss occurrence
	Definition of "any one risk" as per Reinsured's Underwriting Guidelines
Information:	Estimated 2003 Gross Net Retained Premium Income: $36,500,000
	Reinsured's Maximum Gross Retention:
	$1,000,000 Sum Insured (scaled down as per Reinsured's Table of Underwriting Limits)
	Largest individual risk loss was in 1998: $900,000 (100% net retained and f.g.u.) – Fire

The Woodman has succeeded in protecting its risk exposure, but now needs to consider how to restrict its exposure to the very real threat of a cyclone affecting its net retained account. If we looked at the total net retained sum insured aggregates above (9,900,000,000), the Woodman would be advised to allocate those sums insured to their correct zones and then reduce those total sums insured at risk to a realistic disaster assessment. We saw in the surplus treaty that two (fictitious) zones – North and South – exist.

If the Woodman completed that exercise, it might find that a sensible probable maximum loss (PML) estimate would amount to 55,000,000 of its net retained sums insured at risk in either zone. (We have assumed that any cyclone loss could not affect both zones at the same time). This purchase would equate to 150% of the Woodman's net retained premium income. Although we have not mentioned this measure before, it is often a useful indication of a reinsured's total catastrophe excess of loss purchase. As an indication, 200% is a reasonable catastrophe purchase "mark", but circumstances obviously differ throughout the world.

Reverting to our example, we know that the largest cyclone loss occurred in 1999 and amounted to 10,000,0000 from the ground up. (We have not applied any revaluation factors to this loss).

Using the parameters, the Woodman's catastrophe retention could lie between 1,825,000 and 3,650,000. Dependent upon other event loss experience, the Woodman might be able to purchase catastrophe coverage in excess of 2,000,000 (clearly well above its risk excess of loss retention), but market circumstances and reinsurers' views would be important to the Woodman's ultimate choice of catastrophe retention. If we accept 2,000,000 as the retention, what should be the extent of the first layer? Here, reinsurers would probably use the largest known loss, 10,000,000, to identify the initial extent of their coverage. The first layer would therefore be 8,000,000 xs 2,000,000 and would cover the largest known loss, albeit on an unindexed (not revalued) basis.

A possible structure and pricing indication (based upon a gross net retained premium income of 36,500,000) for the remainder of the programme might be as follows:

Layer	Limit & Deductible	XL Rate	Earns	Rate on Line
1st Cat XL	8,000,000 xs 2,000,000	4.40%	1,606,000	20.01%
2nd Cat XL	15,000,000 xs 10,000,000	3.70%	1,350,050	9.01%
3rd Cat XL	30,000,000 xs 25,000,000	1.65%	602,250	2.01%
Total	53,000,000 xs 2,000,000	9.75%	3,558,750	6.71%

Whilst 55,000,000 might be sufficient coverage at the start of the period, it would be sensible to allow for an additional amount. This would enable the Woodman to "grow" its account during the 12 months period of the reinsurance contract. Perhaps 60,000,000 would be sufficient in this example, but there would be a nominal change to the premium reinsurers would charge. We have shown below an example placement slip (for the first layer only) of the Woodman's suggested catastrophe excess of loss programme.

The only other protection that the Woodman could consider would be a stop loss on its absolute net retained account. We have not made any proposals here, but readers should be able to identify the progression from studying the Woodman's example property account we have used. The original gross account is protected by surplus and facultative quota share reinsurance. That protection gives the Woodman its underwriting capacity.

That leaves the Woodman with a maximum own gross retention upon which it purchases two layers of risk excess of loss. Those layers give the Woodman protection against the size and number of individual losses affecting its net retained account. After risk excess of loss, the Woodman then purchases three layers of catastrophe excess of loss. That gives the Woodman protection against the aggregation of losses arising from a natural perils loss event. Any stop loss protection would follow *all* those prior reinsurances. Please note that these are only examples, but are still representative of what might happen.

Reinsured:	Woodman Insurance Company Limited, Port Louis, Mauritius
Period:	Losses occurring during the 12 month period at 1st January 2003, local standard time at place of loss
Type:	Catastrophe Excess of Loss Reinsurance – First Layer
Class of Business:	Business written and retained by the Reinsured and classed by the Reinsured as Fire and Allied Perils, including Cyclone
Territorial Limits:	Mauritius and its dependencies
Limits:	To pay up to $8,000,000 ultimate net loss each and every loss occurrence in excess of $2,000,000 ultimate net loss each and every loss occurrence
Reinstatement:	One full and automatic reinstatement at 100% additional premium as to time, pro rata as to amount reinstated only
Rate:	4.40% of Gross Net Retained Premium Income accounted for during the period hereon
Minimum & Deposit Premium:	$1,285,000 payable in full at inception
Brokerage:	10%
General Conditions:	Ultimate Net Loss Clause Net Retained Lines Clause Definition of Loss Occurrence, including 72 Hours Clause – Cyclone Extended Expiration Clause
Information:	Estimated 2003 Gross Net Retained Premium Income: $36,500,000 Reinsured's has in force Risk Excess of Loss protections as follows: $300,000 xs $200,000 (6 reinstatements), also subject to $1,000,000 event limit $500,000 xs $500,000 (2 reinstatements) Largest cyclone loss was in 1999: $10,000,000 (100% net retained and f.g.u.)

Motor, Workmens' Compensation, Employers' Liability and General Third Party Liability

In many countries of the world, coverage for legal liability arising from Motor Third Party Bodily Injury (TPBI) and Motor Third Party Property Damage (TPPD) is unlimited, especially for private motor insurances. Commercial motor insurances are similarly unlimited for TPBI but are often restricted to a specified monetary amount for TPPD. As we have discussed, it is therefore not possible to construct a risk profile for a motor portfolio issued on an unlimited basis.

There is often a further regulatory requirement that insurance companies authorised to write motor business are themselves protected by a vertically unlimited reinsurance programme, and wherever possible, offering horizontally unlimited coverage within all layers of the programme as well. Thus excess of loss is the best method of effecting that reinsurance protection. In many countries, motor third party insurance is also compulsory and offers licensed insurance companies a guaranteed income stream. The calculation of an excess of loss retention tends not to follow the method described for property. Market forces tend to decide the retention level and "set" liability excess of loss programmes are often created for a particular country, its legal system and legal minimum motor third party requirements.

As with Motor Third Party Liability, many countries have specific legislation to protect all employees. There are two basic systems: Workmens' Compensation and Employers' Liability. The former uses a set scale of benefits to recompense individuals and would be subject to legally identified minimum/maximum limits. Employers' Liability systems tend to be based on common law, where individual cases are decided on their individual circumstances. Despite that, various common law jurisdictions often identify minimum legal requirements that licensed Employers' Liability insurance companies should offer as insurance protection.

There is often no legal requirement to purchase General Third Party (or Public Liability) insurance. As society becomes ever more consumer-driven, and legislation enacted to protect the consumer, many corporate entities are effectively forced to purchase legal liability coverage against the possibility of that organisation being sued for creating, operating, using, suggesting, designing a product or service that causes actual bodily injury or physical damage to a third party. Clearly, the level of indemnity purchased would depend upon the perceived "degree of endangerment" in the product, service or usage involved.

It is generally accepted that excess of loss reinsurance is the best method to protect both Employers' Liability and General Third Party (GTP), although proportional reinsurance is still used in some countries for Workmens' Compensation and GTP. We shall use excess of loss here.

At the time of writing, many insurance companies have decided to combine their various legal liability accounts within one overall excess of loss reinsurance protection. This facilitates their administration and offers a combined protection against the situation where motor, employers' liability, general third party and possibly personal accident might be involved in one accident. (Please refer to the "each and every loss" section in Chapter 9 for a definition of "each and every accident").

As we have mentioned, there tends to be a typical structure for combined liability programmes. The first step is to set the level of the Woodman's deductible. If the reinsurances were on a proportional basis, the retention could be set at approximately 1% of its total free assets. That would produce an excess of loss retention of 1,000,000. However, on an excess of loss basis, the retention should be lower as the insurance company would retain all losses below the deductible for its own account rather than merely a proportion as it would under that method of reinsurance. Reverting to our "market" scenario, the Woodman would probably retain 500,000 as its excess of loss deductible and build its combined liability programme as follows.

Layer	Limit & Deductible	Coverage
First	500,000 xs 500,000	All, no exposure for individual vehicles
Second	1,000,000 xs 1,000,000	All, no exposure for individual vehicles
Third	3,000,000 xs 2,000,000	See below
Fourth	5,000,000 xs 5,000,000	See below
Fifth	15,000,000 xs 10,000,000	See below
Sixth	Unlimited xs 25,000,000	See below

We need to make some immediate comments on the inclusion of the three main classes.

Motor (Entire Account)

If we look at the actual exposures included within the phrase "Motor – Entire Account", we would realise that we have first party, third party and possibly other coverages within a comprehensive motor policy. As reinsurance exists to protect the insurance company against larger losses, then we could probably ignore specialist coverages such as personal accident, legal defence costs and theft from a vehicle. The following are the real exposures within such programmes:

(i) first party coverage: value of any one vehicle, private or commercial
(ii) first party coverage: value of maximum known accumulation any one location
(iii) first party coverage: value of maximum known accumulation any one zone

| (iv) | third party coverage: | legal requirement for TPBI, private and commercial |
| (v) | third party coverage: | legal requirement for TPPD, private and commercial |

If we look at the layering above, we would see that we could ignore (i) as no private vehicle would expose the Woodman's 500,000 retention, and the maximum hull value for single commercial vehicles is 500,000. Technically, no exposure exists, but readers should consider the effect of any increases in the commercial vehicle limit.

In (ii), the maximum limit any one dealer is 1,000,000, so that limit exposes only the first layer of this programme. Readers should consider the importance of identifying any dealer's address. Two dealers might have neighbouring show garages and both are insured by the Woodman. There would clearly be an aggregation potential, hence the next consideration.

In (iii), the Woodman has identified its maximum exposure on a zonal basis, 5,000,000. Thus, the maximum "own damage" limit would fully expose just the first three layers of the programme to natural perils. Reinsurers are often reluctant to cover first and third party loss potential within the same programme. At present, they make exceptions for limited motor own or first party damage within combined liability programmes, but only in countries where a comprehensive motor policy includes such first party coverage. Reinsurers would normally restrict reinstatement of losses arising from a natural perils event to one free reinstatement. Such natural perils loss would also be subject to an Event Hours Clause (as in property catastrophe programmes).

In many countries, motor first party insurances are purchased separately from compulsory motor legal liability policies. Separate reinsurances would therefore be purchased for motor own property damage, either as "stand-alone" covers, or perhaps included within property catastrophe programmes.

Items (iv) and (v) are the main reason for the excess of loss protection, but readers should be aware that exposure for commercial vehicle TPPD is also restricted to just the first three layers of the programme.

In effect, the programme goes in "steps" of coverage, with the lower levels exposed to all sections, but the higher levels exposed to an ever-decreasing number of sections.

Workmens' Compensation and Employers' Liability

This is relatively straightforward in our example as the statutory legal limit is 10,000,000, *inclusive* of legal costs. This would mean that just the first four layers of the programme would be exposed to a *single* loss occurrence. As society demands more than the legal limit of cover, facultative excess of loss reinsurance is sometimes used for certain larger original insureds. These original insureds often require limits of 15,000,000, 20,000,000, 25,000,000 or even higher.

Our example excess of loss programme would probably exclude such "excess" policies (in other words, "excess" of the statutory figure and therefore *additional* to such legal limit), as they would operate after the main policy and effectively make that main policy "first loss". Readers should once again be aware of the legal requirements and practices in their own markets.

General Third Party Liability and Contractors' All Risks (Third Party Section)

The policy limits for General Third Party are unusual in that an original policy is often issued on both an "occurrence" basis for "normal" events, but "in all and in the annual aggregate" if products liability is involved.

This gives reinsurers a problem as to how they should cover losses on an aggregate basis. We have discussed the problem of Aggregate Extension and Claims Series clauses elsewhere in two sections of this book, but hope that readers appreciate the importance of considering *"what would happen if ..."* and therefore identify suitable contractual conditions to counter the potential problem of an aggregation of losses arising from one source or cause.

Similar to the risk profile shown in the property section, General Third Party exposures also fall into various bands of indemnity. Obvious divisions would be personal liability (arising from householders' policies), small commercial, medium and large commercial and industrial, and then complicated industrial operations involving hazardous or dangerous processes. Reinsurers would assess their liability by layer on such exposures and charge premiums accordingly throughout the excess of loss programme. This book is aimed at the beginner and we have chosen not to identify such methodology here.

More importantly, in this example the maximum limit any one policy is 5,000,000 *plus* a legal costs factor equivalent to an additional 10% of the limit of indemnity. In this instance, exposure on a single policy creeps into the fourth layer. Historically, many policies were issued *inclusive* of legal costs, thus making the exposure a little more transparent and upper layers of the programme exposed to what is known as a "clash" of policies. As always, readers should be aware of practices in their own markets. Furthermore, some General Third Party policies are also issued on an "excess" basis and please refer to our comments contained in the Employers' Liability section.

As far as Contractors' All Risks (CAR) is concerned, a typical original policy includes both first party (material damage) and third party (legal liability) sections. As we hope we have made clear, reinsurers are increasingly reluctant to cover first and third party when not strictly necessary, so we would suggest that market practice is moving towards including all forms of third party coverage within the same programme. This naturally would include the third party section of CAR policies, and Erection All Risks (EAR) policies if they were involved.

In this example, the Woodman has a maximum exposure of 2,000,000, so just the first two layers of this programme would be exposed to a single loss occurrence.

We have shown below a typical placement slip for a combined liability excess of loss programme. Once again, we have only used the details for the first layer.

Reinsured:	Woodman Insurance Company Limited, Port Louis, Mauritius
Period:	Losses occurring during the 12 month period commencing 1st January 2003, local standard time where loss occurs
Type:	Excess of Loss Reinsurance – First Layer
Class of Business:	Business classified by the Reinsured as Motor, Workmens' Compensation and/or Employers' Liability, General Third Party Liability (including Products Liability), and Third Party Liability Sections of Contractors' All Risks Policies
Territorial Scope:	Mauritius and its dependencies (excluding absolutely losses occurring in the United States of America and Canada)
Limits:	To pay up to $500,000 ultimate net loss each and every accident in excess of $500,000 ultimate net loss each and every accident (as defined)
Rate:	Adjustable at 4.95% of Total Gross Net Premium Income accounted for during the period hereon for all classes covered hereunder

Minimum & Deposit Premium:	$7,200,000 payable in equal instalments quarterly in advance at 1st January, 1st April, 1st July and 1st September 2003
Reinstatements:	Unlimited free for losses involving motor third party liability, but four free reinstatements in all during the period hereon for all other legal liability classes. Losses arising from motor own damage shall be limited to one free reinstatement during the period heron
Brokerage:	10%
General Conditions:	Ultimate Net Loss Clause
	Net Retained Lines Clause, if applicable
	Aggregate Extension Clause
	Stability (Index) Clause in respect of bodily injury losses only. Base date 1st January 2003, wages, all sectors of Mauritius economy
	Definition of "Each and Every Accident", including Hours Clause for Motor Own Damage losses
	Currency Fluctuation Clause
Information:	Estimated 2003 Gross Net Premium Income:

Motor (Entire Account)	$100,000,000
Employers' Liability	$25,000,000
General Third Party	$30,000,000
CAR Third Party	$6,500,000
Total	$161,500,000

Limits and loss information as seen by reinsurers hereon

We have deliberately not used loss experience to identify the pricing of this programme. Please refer to Chapter 9 for a brief description of the "burning cost" method of rating. It is perhaps more important in a book of this nature to identify the principles behind the construction of a particular programme, rather than the costing of that programme. We hope that readers will agree with our philosophy.

We could attempt to identify the pricing for the upper layers of this example programme, but again have chosen not to do so. In a real situation, pricing would obviously depend on the historic loss experience involved, the projected loss incidence and many other factors. Using our suggested price for this first layer (just under 8,000,000 premium for 500,000 maximum indemnity any one loss, or just under 16 losses), readers will see that loss incidence is certainly increasing, and reinsurers are charging prices accordingly. We nevertheless hope that we have conveyed the important concepts involved.

Remaining Miscellaneous Accident Classes

Having removed the legal liability classes from this main section, we are left with personal accident and the odd forms of first party coverage, theft, burglary and plate glass.

The personal accident account could be protected by a "stand-alone" excess of loss programme as there is sufficient premium income involved. The Woodman would have to decide whether to purchase risk coverage (i.e. within a life), or just some form of catastrophe protection (i.e. in excess of a stated number of lives). If the Woodman were to analyse its account, it might find that a "normal" exposure, or number of insured individuals travelling on one conveyance, might be a maximum of six people. Reinsurers would assess this exposure and might offer catastrophe excess of loss in excess of 3 lives up to a further 7 lives. This would cover the Woodman's maximum known accumulation, and offer the insurance company coverage for *unknown* exposures in any accident.

For the very small theft, burglary and plate glass classes, the Woodman might be able to include those small elements within its property risk and catastrophe excess of loss programmes, providing it would be willing to declare premium income (for reinsurers to charge a rate) and exposures (for reinsurers to quantify their potential liability). Historically, such accident classes – even though they are forms of first party coverage – were often included "for free" within combined liability programmes. As we have mentioned, reinsurers are now reluctant to allow this to happen.

Readers will note that the Woodman "does not accept Professional Indemnity business". This is a very specialist class and is not the subject matter of a beginner's guide. For those wishing to develop a better knowledge of that class, please refer to specialist publications.

There are now relatively few countries where proportional reinsurance is used to protect miscellaneous accident accounts, but they still exist and provide a valuable reinsurance facility for the insurance companies involved. Due to the ongoing difficulties of arranging proportional reinsurances, there has been a tendency to replace proportional treaties by excess of loss for the reasons that we have identified – small premium, small limits, high administration costs.

In concluding this chapter, we would repeat some basic reinsurance principles. Excess of loss is the most suitable method of reinsurance to protect portfolios of business that are similar (or homogeneous) both as to the type of risk and exposures involved.

There are definite **advantages** for insurance companies if they adopt excess of loss:

(1) Excess of loss reinsurance does not involve an allocation or apportionment of individual risks. Often, very little information is required and accounting is relatively straightforward.

Consequently, this further reduces administration costs. Deposit premiums are normally paid annually, half-yearly or quarterly and an adjustment is made once a year (subject to minimum premium considerations, as we have seen). This assists the insurance company in its budgetary planning.

(2) The insurance company does not share its premiums proportionally with its reinsurer. The mechanics of excess of loss reinsurance allows an insurance company to retain larger, disproportionate, premium amounts and to invest those premiums for a longer term. The enhanced investment income should flow directly to the insurance company's own balance sheet.

There are also certain **disadvantages** for insurance companies such as

(1) Cost of the excess of loss protection (layer or programme). A reinsurer would normally charge a premium sufficient to cover anticipated claims plus a loading to cover all forms of expenses. The reinsurer would also recognise any exposure to losses potentially larger than the average amount indicated within any historic information. The reinsurer would also factor an allowance for incurred but not reported losses, and the possibility of inflation affecting a particular portfolio of losses. Any excess of loss deductible would have to be high enough to encompass all these considerations, but the insurance company might disagree totally with the views of its reinsurer(s). A high retention would reduce excess of loss costs, but an insurance company must consider the next point in (2) below.

(2) An insurance company would have to pay all losses below the stated monetary deductible. In certain years those losses might be so numerous as to place

a severe strain on the liquidity of the insurance company. If the retention were too high, then the strain on the insurance company would be even greater, as it might be affected by both size of individual losses and an increased incidence of losses.

(3) An insurance company has to maintain unearned premium reserves for unexpired risks for all business within its net retained account. If the reinsurance programme is arranged on an excess of loss basis, the net retained account would be much larger. This might put a further strain on the insurance company as it would have to finance that unearned premium reserve solely from its own resources. This would be different if proportional reinsurers were involved, as they would contribute to such financing strain.

15

Basic Contract Wordings

The negotiation, transaction and administration of reinsurance agreements are evidenced by large amounts of paper: placement slips, cover notes, wordings, closings, accounts, claims advices, reports, etc. The previous chapters contained examples of the "slip" method of placing a reinsurance whereby an offer of the coverage is made to a prospective reinsurer in summary form (on a slip, by facsimile and nowadays by e-mail). This is not the only method of offer and acceptance used. Contracts can be concluded by facsimile, telephone, jottings on the back of an envelope or, as is more usual today, completion of proposal forms and detailed questionnaires.

Whatever method is used for the offer and acceptance of a reinsurance, the terms and conditions agreed between the contracting parties need to be evidenced in a formal contract wording. In the past a reinsurance treaty could be evidenced by a simple exchange of correspondence between the ceding company and reinsurer. Some of these arrangements continued unaltered for many years. Reinsurance has become much more complicated in recent years and has found itself in the unwanted spotlight of the legal fraternity.

It must never be forgotten that a reinsurance contract wording is a record of a formal, legal contract intended to have legal consequences. Great care therefore needs to be exercised in drafting and checking a contract wording to ensure that it properly and clearly expresses the intentions of the contracting parties.

The following paragraphs outline the various provisions usually found in facultative, treaty and excess of loss contract wordings.

FACULTATIVE REINSURANCES

The cost of administration of facultative reinsurance prevents any time being spent on the drafting of complicated contract wordings. The wordings, therefore, tend to be quite simple. Where the facultative reinsurance is on a proportional basis, the documentation often consists of a simple "guarantee" policy wording. (The word "guarantee" was used in days gone by when offices exchanged facultative quota share business quite freely between themselves. Over time, guarantee business became facultative quota share reinsurance in the sense we understand it today). The guarantee sets out the names of the reinsuring parties, the percentage being reinsured and the ceding commission allowed (a copy of the original insurance policy might also be attached). Facultative reinsurance on an excess of loss basis tends to be more complicated since the reinsurance protection placed is not directly related to a proportional share of the original coverage and non-identical terms are agreed. A formal wording is usually avoided by the issuance of what is known as a "slip policy".

Proportional facultative (quota share) placements often contain what is known as a "Full Reinsurance Clause". This clause is intended to link the reinsurance to the original insurance. It might not always be appropriate for the type of reinsurance that has been placed, but the following is a modern example of this type of clause:

Proportional Facultative Reinsurance Clause

In consideration of the premium charged, and subject to the terms and conditions of this contract as set out in the slip and its attachments and/or applicable endorsements, this contract reinsures the reinsured's interest in payments made within the terms and conditions of the original policy.

Unless otherwise stated in this contract the reinsured:

a) shall retain during the period of this contract at least the retention(s), subject to any proportional and/or excess of loss treaty reinsurance, on the identical subject matter and perils and in identically the same proportions(s) as stated in this contract. In the event of the retentions(s) and/or proportion(s) being less, the reinsurer's liability will be correspondingly proportionately reduced.

b) warrants that the premium paid to the reinsurer for this contract is calculated at the same gross rate as the original policy for the identical subject matter and perils and in the same proportions reinsured, less only those deductions stated.

In the event of inconsistencies between the original policy and this contract, this contract shall prevail.

If the reinsured shall make a claim knowing the same to be false or fraudulent as regards amount or otherwise, this contract shall become void and all claims hereunder shall be forfeited.

This clause places an emphasis on the transparency in the relationship between the insurance company and its reinsurer. A contentious area has always been that of claims, whether in their reporting, negotiation or settlement. Reinsurers often include various special clauses to control this important aspect of their contractual arrangements. We have shown below three such clauses.

Claims Notification Clause

Notwithstanding anything to the contrary contained in this contract, it is a condition precedent to reinsurer's liability under this contract that:

a) the reinsured shall give to the reinsurer(s) written notice as soon as reasonably practicable of any claim made against the reinsured in respect of business reinsured hereunder or of its being notified of any circumstances which could give rise to such a claim

b) the reinsured shall furnish the reinsurer(s) with all information known to the reinsured in respect of all claims or possible claims notified in accordance with a) above and shall thereafter keep the reinsurer(s) fully informed as regards all developments relating thereto as soon as reasonably practicable.

Claims Co-Operation Clause

The clause is the same as above but a new section c) is added.

c) the reinsured shall co-operate with the reinsurer(s) and any other person or persons designated by the reinsurer(s) in the investigation, adjustment and settlement of such notified to the reinsurer(s) as previously mentioned.

Claims Control Clause

The clause is the same as the preamble and sections a) and b) of the Claims Notification Clause, but sections c) and d) are as shown below.

c) the reinsurers shall have the right at any time to appoint adjusters and/or representatives to act on their behalf to control all investigations, adjustments and settlements in connection with any claim notified to the reinsurer(s) as previously mentioned.

d) the reinsured shall co-operate with the reinsurer(s) and any other person or persons designated by the reinsurer(s) in the investigation, adjustment and settlement of such claim.

Readers should also be aware of various clauses used in facultative reinsurance to identify the respective obligations in the settlement of premiums and the penalties for non-payment. We have not identified any examples here, but readers should be aware of the normal practices and clauses in their own markets.

Our final example in this section is to shown a modern example of a non-proportional or excess of loss facultative reinsurance clause.

Non-Proportional Facultative Reinsurance Clause

In consideration of the premium charged, and subject to the terms and conditions of this contract as set out in the slip and its attachments and/or endorsements applicable thereto, this contract reinsures the reinsured's interest in those payments made within the terms and conditions of the original policy exceeding the excess amount as set out in the slip up to the limit as set out in the slip.

In the event of inconsistencies between the original policy and this contract, this contract shall prevail.

If the reinsured shall make a claim knowing the same to be false or fraudulent as regards amount or otherwise, this contract shall become void and all claims hereunder shall be forfeited.

PROPORTIONAL TREATIES

Treaty wordings are signed agreements that evidence the terms of the contract of reinsurance made between the parties, i.e. the reinsured (the ceding company) and the reinsurer. The various terms and conditions that apply are contained in "Articles". Wordings are generally signed in duplicate with each party retaining a signed original copy for its records.

Treaty wordings vary so much between companies, countries, types of business, etc., that it is not possible to show standard wordings here. However, over the years, there have been moves towards standardisation of some clauses. There is no fixed order in which the Articles (i.e. individual sections of the contract wording) appear, though the Recital (or Preamble) Clause tends to appear at the beginning and the Signature Clause appears at the end. There is also no consistent practice over where the information that is specific to the contract should appear. Some companies draft wordings that consist of a set of standard clauses together with a schedule listing the details of the reinsurance. Others include the specific information in the body of the wording itself.

Sometimes it may seem that a number of the clauses that appear in contract wordings do not have an immediate usefulness and that they are included "because we always put one of those in a wording". However, the clauses appearing in a wording do fulfil important functions within the overall agreement between the ceding company (the reinsured) and the reinsurer. These clauses could be grouped by the function that they perform. In this chapter we have used the following groupings to clarify what a specific clause is supposed to do in the overall terms of the agreement:

1. The Parties to the Contract
2. The Business Covered
3. The Basis of the Reinsurance and the Limits
4. Premiums and Accounts
5. Claims
6. Inception and Termination
7. Housekeeping
8. Disputes

The following Articles usually appear in a Treaty Wording, whether the wording applies to a Quota Share, a Surplus or a Facultative Obligatory reinsurance. The clauses are as follows:

1. The Parties to the Contract

Recital Clause This Clause defines the parties to the treaty, the ceding company and the reinsurer. It should also show the ceding company's head office and country of domicile, and sometimes the ceding company's national company number.

Signature This Clause provides for the wording to be signed in duplicate by the authorised representatives of the ceding company and the reinsurer.

2. The Business Covered

Business Covered This Article should contain a number of paragraphs describing the class(es) of business covered, the territorial scope of the treaty and those risks which are excluded from the reinsurance.

Exclusions A treaty wording may contain very few or very many exclusions. These would depend upon the type of business, the size and capability of the ceding company, the results of negotiations between the parties. The exclusions might apply to specific risks or groups of risk, types of business or types of peril. Wordings normally exclude War and Nuclear Perils, and nowadays emphasise the exclusion of all forms of Terrorist Acts, whether arising from physical, biological or nuclear attacks.

Self-Insurance Many ceding companies invest their assets in property, which they then insure themselves. This clause allows the ceding company to reinsure their coverage of such property.

Change of Underwriting Policy All changes in the usual underwriting practice of the ceding company pertaining to the agreement should be notified to the reinsurer before they are implemented. The Article is intended as a protection for the reinsurer to prevent the ceding company from increasing its retention (and possibly the amount ceded per line) or writing types or categories of risk that it would not previously have insured.

3. The Basis of the Reinsurance and the Limits

Reinsurance Cession This Article would provide for the ceding company to cede and the reinsurer to accept, by way of reinsurance, a share of the business covered by the treaty. For Quota Share treaties the ceding company's retention and the treaty capacity would be expressed in percentages; for Surplus treaties the capacity would usually be expressed in terms of "lines" (multiples of the ceding company's chosen retention). The treaty capacity might also be subject to a monetary limit or utilisation restriction, dependent upon the classes or categories covered.

Any One Risk The wording would usually allow the reinsured full discretion to decide what is "one risk" for the purposes of the reinsurance. Readers should be aware that there is no standard definition of "any one risk". Individual negotiations would identify particular definitions.

Event Limit The treaty capacity is based upon a limit for "any one risk". Where the business is exposed to natural perils, there may be an "any one event" limit in addition to the risk limit to restrict the reinsurer's exposure to an accumulation of losses arising from an identified catastrophic exposure.

Cession Limit If the treaty is exposed to natural perils, reinsurers might impose a restriction on the amount of natural perils exposures to be ceded to the treaty. As we mentioned previously, the Cession and Event Limit Clauses could be imposed together or individually. Care should be taken to identify how both the Event and Cession Limit Clauses should operate in the situation that either (or both) are exceeded at the date of any natural perils event loss affecting the treaty.

Attachment of Liability This article states when the liability of the reinsurer commences so that there can be no argument if a loss should arise before any bordereaux or accounts have been sent.

4. Premiums and Accounts

Premium This article defines the basis upon which premium is to be ceded. The two most common methods are O.G.R. (original gross premiums less return premiums and cancellations) and O.N.R. (original gross premiums less all original and profit commissions, returns and cancellations). Premiums for excluded risks should also be omitted from the computation. Reinsurance premiums would also be excluded where another reinsurance agreement operates in priority to the treaty.

Commission The commission may be at a fixed rate or on a sliding scale. If on a sliding scale, a table showing the method of calculating the sliding scale of commission would be included in the treaty wording, as would the provisional rate of commission (see Chapter 4 above). Commission can be calculated on O.G.R. or O.N.R. Readers should be aware that commission is normally calculated on written premiums unless specified otherwise. In certain countries, it is also normal practice to cede fire perils at one rate of commission and (say) earthquake perils at a lower (or different) rate of commission.

Profit Commission The profit commission and the basis for calculation are sometimes set out in a separate Article. Readers should be aware that the profit commission is often an "agreement within an agreement". The terms might differ from the actual accounting of the treaty. As with **Commission** above, some profit commission statements might exclude all premiums (and losses) relating to ceded policies exposed to particular natural perils (such as earthquake).

Accounts Premiums, paid losses, commissions, premium and loss reserve deposits (and any interest agreed) and premium and outstanding loss portfolio transfer movements tend to be transacted in treaty accounting statements. These could be issued to the reinsurer at quarterly or half-yearly (and sometimes annual) intervals. The article generally states a time limit for submission of the accounts, often within 30 days of the end of the quarter. The accounts need to be confirmed by the reinsurer and the balance is then paid, both within identified time parameters. Special allowance might need to be made for any cash loss payments (please see below) that might have arisen in a particular quarter.

Currency Clause Where the reinsurance applies to business conducted in a number of currencies, the wording needs to indicate the way in which rates of exchange should be applied for the purpose of calculation of any amounts due in those foreign currencies. This is necessary because rates of exchange often fluctuate so much within short periods that a definite rule is needed to avoid possible disputes later on.

Errors and Omissions This article provides for any errors or omissions to be corrected as soon as they have been discovered (by the ceding company). This is intended to apply to rectification of minor errors, such as the mis-cession or mis-allocation of a particular risk. Any re-allocation should be made before any loss has occurred – reinsurers would probably be a little unhappy if such a re-casting happened after a loss !

Premium Reserve Deposits Where the treaty provides for the retention of premium reserve deposits, the clause would set out the basis for calculation of the deposit, the rate of interest to be allowed and the procedure for releasing the deposit (generally in the corresponding treaty account of the following year). If there is no provision for the retention of a premium reserve deposit, then this clause should not appear in the treaty wording. Readers should also be aware that premium reserve deposits are sometimes withheld in accounts some three years after inception. Given that most original policies are issued for 12 months (plus an agreed "odd-time" period of 3 or 6 months), we would argue that most original liability should have expired (and therefore the premium fully earned) by the end of the second treaty year, thus negating the retention of reserves in accounts for the third treaty year.

(Outstanding) Loss Reserve Deposits Where the treaty provides for the retention of loss reserve deposits for known outstanding losses, the clause would set out the basis for calculation of the deposit, the rate of interest to be allowed and the procedure for releasing the deposit (generally in the corresponding treaty account of the following year). If there is no provision for the retention of a loss reserve deposit, then this clause should not appear in the treaty wording. Readers should be aware of the importance of releasing the previous reserve amount and retaining the new amount advised – otherwise, there could be an over-reserving of outstanding losses and an adverse effect on total incurred losses.

Bordereaux Where the treaty provides for premium bordereaux to be submitted a suitable clause would appear in or near to the **Accounts** clause. Where the treaty provides for claims bordereaux, a suitable clause would appear in the **Claims** Clause.

5. Claims

(Provisional) Claims (or Loss) Advice Limit There are many different clauses dealing with the advice of potential treaty claims to the reinsurer. Some of these do not require the ceding company to give the reinsurer any prior advice of claims that might affect the treaty. Other wordings might require prompt advice of large losses (sometimes considered to be those which are likely to exceed the **Cash Loss** limit – see below). It is not unusual for such "provisional loss advices" to give details of both individual risks and possible aggregations for an identified natural perils event loss, such as a flood, storm or earthquake. Care should also be taken in the level of provisional loss advice – too low and the treaty would be overburdened by administration; too high, there might be unwanted surprises in store for reinsurers. It is generally accepted that a range of between 2.5% to 5% of the treaty limit (or income ceded to the treaty) would be a sufficient level.

Cash Loss Limit This clause sets out the limit (usually for 100% of the treaty) where the ceding company would require special cash settlements from the reinsurer without waiting for the usual quarterly or half-yearly accounts. As with the **Provisional Claims Advice** clause, care should be taken in establishing a correct level suitable for a particular treaty. The clause allows the ceding company to recover an abnormally large paid loss outside of the usual periodic treaty accounts, but readers should be aware of the actions required to account the refund of a cash loss settlement in a subsequent periodic treaty account. The item should appear as a special identified refund, with the paid amount (for that special loss) included in the paid loss entry for that same periodic account.

Outstanding Losses The claims clause often contains a provision requiring the ceding company to provide an estimate of outstanding losses at the end of the treaty year (or with each periodic account). This enables the reinsurer to monitor the performance of the treaty. The estimate might be a simple total of known outstanding losses to the treaty or it might be accompanied by a schedule giving details of large losses (individually by risk and by identified natural perils event).

Follow the Fortunes This clause is considered to be fundamental to the operation of proportional reinsurance as this method is based upon a true sharing of risks, premiums, commissions, expenses and losses between the ceding company and reinsurer. It states that it is the intention of the agreement that the reinsurer is bound by the ceding company in all matters falling within the agreement and follows its fortunes whatever happens (provided it is covered by the treaty). Readers should nevertheless be aware that the concept of follow the fortunes has been placed under severe pressure in recent years. This has led to many reinsurers questioning the inclusion of this clause.

6. Inception and Termination

Inception/Termination Most treaties incept at the beginning of the ceding company's financial year. In many countries and for many companies this would be 1st January. There are notable exceptions. For example, treaties covering Australian business tend to incept at 1st July while Japanese reinsurances tend to incept at 1st April. Some treaties are for a fixed 12 months term. However, most proportional treaties are concluded on a continuous basis and it is usual to allow for termination at the anniversary (renewal) date, subject to prior written notice having been given (usually 3 months or 90 days). This allows both contracting parties to review terms, conditions and levels of participation.

Special Cancellation (also known as **Sudden Death**) This clause allows for the treaty to be terminated immediately on the happening of certain specified events. These include war breaking out between the countries of the two parties, the contract being declared illegal, one party becoming insolvent or bankrupt, or not being able to fulfil its contractual obligations. The clause provides for *either* party to give immediate notice of termination to the other and would also identify what happens to unexpired risks (and unearned premium) and outstanding losses. Readers should be aware that many Special Cancellation clauses now contain a "downgrading of security" provision. This means that if a *reinsurer's* claims-paying ability is reduced by specified rating agencies, then the ceding company has the option to cancel that reinsurer's participation, often from the date of such downgrading. Many clauses stipulate that the cancellation option rests solely with the ceding company, hence our emphasis. This apparently one-sided option is in contrast to the more standard provisions mentioned above.

Premium and (Outstanding) Loss Portfolio Transfers If the treaty provides for a premium portfolio assumption and/or withdrawal then a suitable clause would be included in the treaty wording. It should set out the basis for calculation of the portfolio transfer and how transfers would be made in the periodic treaty accounts. In some cases portfolio transfers could be exercised only at the option of the ceding company. Where the treaty is on a "clean-cut" basis, premium portfolio transfers are automatic at the end of each treaty year so that the reinsurer would only be liable for the earned premium exposures in that year ("earned" could be defined as unearned premiums for the unexpired liability from the *previous* period plus written premiums for the *current* period less unearned premiums for the unexpired liability from the *current* period). The assumption and/or withdrawal of outstanding loss portfolios is a separate issue and also needs to be specifically identified within the wording. Since loss portfolio transfers are often based upon estimates of known outstanding losses, the wording might allow for the loss portfolio figure to be adjusted after a number of years in the knowledge of actual loss settlements. This is sometimes applied to contentious large losses (individual risk or event), where both premium (for the risk or event involved) and the loss settlements themselves are monitored separately from the normal treaty accounts.

Care should be taken for a brand new treaty. There would be no incoming premium or outstanding loss portfolio transfers as the account would only start from the inception date of that new treaty. This often leads to what is known as the "financing strain" for the first few years of the treaty. The "strain" would last until the levels of both ceded premium and outstanding losses had stabilised.

Readers should be aware that many "clean-cut" treaties provide for premium and loss portfolio transfers to be made at (say) 35% and 90% respectively, but the profit commission shows an unexpired premium transfer at 40% and outstanding losses at 100%. This emphasises our contention that sometimes a profit commission is an "agreement within an agreement".

7. Housekeeping

These clauses regulate activities that do not relate purely to what is covered, what premium is paid and how claim recoveries should be made.

Inspection of Records This article allows the reinsurer, or an authorised representative, to inspect the records of the ceding company relevant to transactions under the treaty. With the abolition of bordereaux, the reinsurer often receives little or no detail of what has been ceded and this provision allows it to conduct a reinsurance audit, if it so desires. Such audits are often helpful to both parties.

Alterations This article allows for amendments to be made during the period of the reinsurance. These are made by mutual agreement, by exchange of correspondence or by issuing a formal addendum. It is important that alterations are agreed in writing between the parties. This should avoid disputes that might arise at some later stage.

Intermediary Where a broker is involved in placing the treaty, this article should be included in the wording to allow for correspondence and all transactions between the parties to be routed through the broker.

8. Disputes

Applicable Law This relatively new article identifies the law applicable to the subject matter of the reinsurance treaty and the law applicable to the *operation* of the reinsurance treaty itself. It could also identify the legal jurisdiction for any arbitration proceedings. It has tended to replace the older **Jurisdiction** Clause (see below).

Jurisdiction Reinsurances are often transacted between parties in different countries with different systems of law. It is useful for the parties to agree on what system of law should apply to the reinsurance agreement. That could be the legal system of their own country or that of another country.

Arbitration This article provides for a procedure to be adopted for resolving disputes that might arise between the parties. This used to be a relatively informal procedure and was intended to be an alternative to instituting legal action. Sadly, numerous disputes concerning various reinsurance transactions have caused this clause to take greater precedence. Many wordings refer to ARIAS, an internationally recognised arbitration panel as being an acceptable provider for the resolution of contractual disputes. Many clauses would also identify where any arbitration should take place and the legal system to be used.

Chapter 16 contains an example of a Fire & Allied Perils Surplus treaty wording and discusses some of these clauses in further detail.

NON-PROPORTIONAL or EXCESS OF LOSS CONTRACTS

Non-proportional reinsurance contracts are also set out in wordings which evidence the terms of the contract of reinsurance made between the parties, namely the reinsured and the reinsurer. They are also generally signed in duplicate with each party retaining a signed original copy for their own records, although many brokers (if involved) prefer to use individual schedules for both contract limits and signing pages, as this simplifies administration.

The applicable terms and conditions are also contained in various "Articles". However, unlike proportional reinsurance, there are specific articles that appear in the wording for one form of excess of loss reinsurance but not in another (examples are the "Hours Clause" that only appear in wordings for property catastrophe excess of loss reinsurance and the "Stability (or Index) Clause" that only appears in excess of loss reinsurances covering legal liability business).

In this section we have used the same groupings we used in the section above on proportional treaties to clarify what a specific clause is supposed to do in the overall terms of the excess of loss reinsurance contract.

1. The Parties to the Contract
2. The Business Covered
3. The Basis of the Reinsurance and the Limits
4. Premiums and Accounts
5. Claims
6. Inception and Termination
7. Housekeeping
8. Disputes

1. The Parties to the Contract

Recital (or Preamble) Clause This clause defines the parties to the contract, the reinsured and the reinsurer. This clause would almost certainly contain a reference to the fact that "each reinsurer accepts liability only for its own participation and not for other reinsurers" (on that same contract).

Signature This clause provides for the wording to be signed in duplicate by the authorised representatives of the reinsured and the reinsurer.

2. The Business Covered

Business Covered This article would contain a number of paragraphs describing the class or classes of business covered, the territorial scope of the coverage and (often) those risks excluded from the reinsurance protection.

Exclusions A reinsurance wording may contain very few or very many exclusions. These would depend upon the type of business, the size and capability of the reinsured, the results of negotiations between the parties. The exclusions could apply to specific risks or groups of risk, types of business or types of peril. War, Nuclear Perils and more recently, Terrorism, are exclusions commonly found in contract wordings. Many agreements also exclude the reinsured's acceptance of inwards proportional reinsurance treaties (often referred to as "obligatory treaties"), excess of loss *insurances* and excess of loss and stop loss *reinsurance* contracts. The reinsured's acceptance of facultative reinsurances often causes problems. Facultative proportional acceptances could perhaps be considered less contentious than facultative excess of loss acceptances. Readers should be aware of practices within their own market.

Change in Law Reinsurances covering legal liability to others are susceptible to changes in the law after the reinsurance has been agreed. The level of benefits might be increased, court practices might change or additional legal obligations might be imposed upon original insureds. These changes could have a disproportionate effect upon the liability of the reinsurer. Some versions of this clause allow the parties to re-negotiate the terms of the contract. Other clauses provide for the change in law (or practice) to be ignored in calculating the liability of the reinsurer, especially if an acceptable renegotiation of terms proves difficult to achieve during the currency of that particular agreement.

Change of Underwriting Policy All changes in the usual underwriting practice of the reinsured that relate to the agreement should be notified to the reinsurer *before* they are implemented. The article is intended as a protection for the reinsurer to prevent the reinsured from increasing its normal underwriting limits or writing types of risk that it would not previously have insured.

3. The Basis of the Reinsurance and the Limits

Definition of Loss This clause varies according to the type of excess of loss reinsurance involved. For stop loss reinsurance, the cover would apply to aggregate losses that arise during the stated period. For risk excess of loss reinsurances, coverage might be on an "each and every loss, each and every risk" basis. For legal liability contracts the definition might be "each and every accident or loss or occurrence or series of accidents or series of losses or series of occurrences arising out of any one event". The wording would usually allow the reinsured discretion to decide what is "any one risk" for the purposes of the reinsurance (but please refer to the comments made earlier in this chapter). For reinsurances on a "catastrophe" or "event" basis the parties need to define clearly the circumstances that would trigger a claim under the reinsurance contract or programme.

Limits The amount of the deductible and the reinsurer's limit of liability would be expressed in terms of 100% of the reinsurance contract. As explained above, the limits might be expressed in terms of "aggregate loss any one year", "each and every loss, each and every risk", "any one accident/loss/occurrence", etc. Risk excess of loss reinsurances are usually subject to a further limitation for losses arising out of one natural perils event. In other words, there might be a potential recovery from the risk excess of loss contract of 10 "normal" (separate and individual) losses in an annual period. If a natural perils event loss were to occur involving a number of risks (that all affected the risk excess of loss layer), then reinsurers might impose a maximum recovery of 5 risk losses in that event. Catastrophe reinsurers would assess the benefit to themselves of such risk excess of loss protections.

As we explained in a previous chapter, many excess of loss reinsurances would be further subject to an aggregate limitation of losses recoverable during the contract period. This would be equivalent to the original limit plus the agreed number of reinstatements allowed. Rarely would a reinstatement feature be included in stop loss reinsurances.

Aggregate Extension (or Claims Series) This clause is used in reinsurances covering losses arising out of one "event" or "occurrence" and allows reinsurance coverage to apply to original policies issued themselves on an "aggregate" basis. Effectively, the reinsurance allows aggregate losses that occur during the period of the policy to be the "event" for the purposes of the reinsurance. There is a further requirement that all such losses are directly caused by, or directly attributable to, one proximate cause. This enables the reinsured, for example, to cover Products Liability losses under a reinsurance covering General Third Party Business. Products Liability policies (whether issued on their own or as extensions to General Third Party policies) are usually issued on an aggregate basis. Please refer to our comments in Chapter 9 on the differences between this clause and the *Aggregate Extraction Clause*.

Hours This clause appears in property (and other) catastrophe excess of loss reinsurances and provides a method for identifying the geographic extent and duration of a particular catastrophic event giving rise to a claim. It sets out both the maximum period and area for which the specified event could be considered to be "one loss". An example of this clause appears in Chapter 11.

Extended Expiration This clause appears in property (and other) catastrophe excess of loss reinsurances and normally follows immediately after the Hours Clause. If a natural perils event (as defined in the Hours Clause) starts in one reinsurance contract period and runs over into the next period, then the clause states that the whole event loss should be recovered from the contract period in which the loss started, even though the first contract period would have terminated during the allowed period of hours for that natural perils event. The clause further states that no loss (or part of the loss) might be claimed from any renewal or replacement of the original agreement. An example of this clause appears in Chapter 11.

Ultimate Net Loss This is one of the most important articles for all types of excess of loss reinsurance. It defines what would be included as part of the loss recoveries under the reinsurance. The "ultimate net loss" might include costs of litigation and loss adjustment expenses incurred by the reinsured, but it seldom includes the reinsured's own office or administration expenses. The loss payable under the agreement would be calculated after all possible deductions have been made. This means that there needs to be a provision for interim settlements to be assessed before the final "ultimate net loss" amount has been ascertained. The clause should contain a provision for recoveries from all other reinsurances (normally prior proportional), and then salvages and similar recoveries. These should be credited to the reinsurer to reflect its true loss settlement under the excess of loss agreement. Where excess of loss reinsurances are for the common account of the reinsured and its proportional reinsurers, the ultimate net loss clause would need to be amended accordingly. Readers should be aware of the laws applicable to the insolvency of the reinsured in their own country and what would happen to balances due to or from reinsurers. Although not part of the UNL clause, many agreements now contain an **Insolvency Clause.** This identifies what would happen in the event of the reinsured becoming insolvent. The clause often directly follows the UNL clause.

Net Retained Lines This is the second most important clause for many types of excess of loss reinsurance. The clause sometimes appears as a subsidiary part of the UNL clause and provides for the excess of loss reinsurance to apply to the reinsured's retention after priority reinsurances (normally proportional). Where catastrophe reinsurance is involved, the reinsured might have quota share and/or surplus and/or facultative reinsurance in place so that the excess of reinsurance applies to the accumulation of the reinsured's net retentions. Where the excess of loss reinsurance is itself the priority reinsurance (often known as the "gross line"), this clause should not be used. For example, if such a clause were to appear in the wordings for both risk and catastrophe excess of loss protections on the same account, then it might be confusing as to which coverage operated in priority. (Technically, risk excess of loss pays in priority to any catastrophe programme). To avoid any misunderstanding, many NRL clauses contain a statement to the effect that "the reinsured has other excess of loss reinsurances in force, recoveries under which are for the sole benefit of the reinsured" and should not be taken into account in establishing the NRL (and UNL) for the excess of loss contract in question. Where excess of loss reinsurances are for the common account of the reinsured and its proportional reinsurers, the net retained lines clause would need to be amended accordingly (as we saw in the UNL clause above).

Other Reinsurers If the reinsurance does apply to the reinsured's retention, then the reinsurer should have the benefit of recoveries from any priority protections, i.e. the reinsured would not be able to treat its retention as having increased if it were unable to recover necessary amounts from reinsurers on those protections.

Extra Contractual Obligations (ECO) This clause appears in contracts covering, in any way, US third party legal liability (or casualty) business. It is possible, in that country, for courts of competent jurisdiction to award punitive (or exemplary) damages against original insureds and their insurers who deliberately avoid or delay paying claims to third parties. Depending on the wording of the clause, such damages might be covered by, or excluded from, the excess of loss reinsurance.

Awards in Excess of Policy Limits and Costs in Addition to Policy Limits These are two relatively new clauses. The first seeks to identify what would happen under the reinsurance if a court of competent jurisdiction awarded an amount greater than the original insured's policy limit or limit of indemnity. The second clause is similar, but seeks to identify what would happen under the reinsurance if a competent court decided to award an original insured compensation equivalent to the policy limit of indemnity plus an amount for costs, even though that original policy was issued on a "costs inclusive" basis.

4. Premiums and Accounts

Premium This article defines the basis upon which the reinsurance premium is to be calculated. The most common method is a fixed percentage figure to be applied to the reinsured's total premium income for the account in question. Historically, many high-level contracts attracted a "flat" rate premium. This was expressed as a specified monetary amount with no adjustment feature. We would suggest that such cases are nowadays in the minority. The percentage rate would be applied to the "written" premium income (original gross premiums less returns and cancellations in respect of business incepting or renewing during the period) or "earned" premium (original gross premiums less returns and cancellations and after adjustment for incoming and outgoing unearned premiums). Another method is to use "accounted" premium, or all premium accounted for by the reinsured during the period, irrespective of attachment dates of original policies.

Premiums for excluded risks and the cost of prior or inuring reinsurances should also be omitted from the computation. Where the premium adjustment is made on an "experience" or "burning cost" basis, the method of calculation would be set out in the wording, as would the number of years' adjustment for contracts on a "written" premium basis (often specified as "first adjustment at 24 months from inception, final adjustment at 36 months"). Many contracts use the phrase "gross net premium income". The phrase "net" in this case means the reinsured's original gross premium, less all the deductions shown above, but *includes* the reinsured's original acquisition costs.

Minimum and Deposit Premium Where a deposit premium is charged, the clause would set out the amount, the date(s) on which it is to be paid and when the adjustment should be made (normally "as soon as possible after expiry of the contract"). The deposit premium could also be the same amount as any identified minimum premium, or set at an amount different to the minimum premium. Readers should be aware of the different effects of the deposit premium (an advance payment during the currency of the contract period) and the minimum premium (a guarantee for the reinsurer should the actual premium be under-estimated and the anticipated adjustment figure not be attained).

Accounts No treaty accounts are prepared for excess of loss reinsurances. The deposit premium is paid at the stated date(s) and the adjustment premium is calculated when the reinsured's final premium income figures become available. The adjustment would be subject to any minimum premium stipulation. Loss settlements (and paid reinstatement conditions, if applicable) would be made by separate statements of account.

Reinstatements The reinstatement clause in the contract wording sets out the terms on which the cover would be reinstated to its full value following a loss. The clause would also set out the basis of the premium calculation, i.e. whether reinstatements should be calculated pro-rata as to both time and amount or pro rata to amount only (and subject to the identified *time* stipulation, 100%, 50% or another figure). Since risk excess of loss contracts are of a "working" nature, the applicable number of reinstatements should be adequate for the number of claims expected to arise. In modern practice, "catastrophe" reinsurance contracts usually allow for only one reinstatement. Recently, reinsurers have also imposed limited (and often free) reinstatement conditions on excess of loss reinsurances covering motor, general third party and other legal liability business. Coverage is therefore reinstated automatically without payment of an additional premium up to the agreed number of reinstatements. If such legal liability programmes are "multi-class", then it is not unusual to see a number of reinstatements identified for each class or type of legal liability covered by the programme.

5. Claims

Claims Advice (or Loss Reporting) There is an increased requirement for the reinsured to advise potential claims to the reinsurer as soon as possible. The reinsured is also required to supply the reinsurer with full details of any loss that would or might affect a particular level of cover. This requirement has arisen because of the steady escalation in the cost of claims, particularly those involving legal liabilities, from the time the loss first becomes known to the date when the claim is finally settled.

These requirements vary from the need to advise to the reinsurer as soon as possible of all losses that might involve the excess of loss reinsurance to advising all losses which might exceed a stated percentage of the deductible through to advising specified injuries or incidents immediately, even though no loss estimate (or quantum of damage) had been established.

We could say that the simplest form of Loss Reporting Clause involves advice of loss only, if a percentage figure is added to the clause, e.g. 50%, then the reinsured is obliged to report to the reinsurer all losses attaining or exceeding 50% of the reinsured's deductible. The third form (involving notification of specified serious bodily injuries) is known as an **Extended Loss Reporting Clause**. Some clauses seek to deny liability for a claim that has not been notified within a stated period.

Claims Co-Operation Not all wordings contain such a clause but there is an increasing tendency to include this important facility. These clauses vary from simple expressions of intent that the reinsured *should* co-operate with the reinsurer in the settlement of claims to clauses that actually prohibit the reinsured from litigating without the consent of the reinsurer. Another version is still stronger in its effect, in that the clause allows the reinsurer to take full *control* of settlement of losses that might involve the excess of loss reinsurance. This particular clause is therefore known as the **Claims Control** clause.

Follow the Settlements This usually states that the reinsurer should follow all settlements made by the reinsured and are within the terms of the original policy and further within the terms of the reinsurance. On the one hand, it possibly prevents the reinsurer from "second-guessing" the reinsured and objecting to the terms of the original loss settlement. Conversely, it requires that those settlements are both within the terms of the original policy and within the terms of the reinsurance. Some variants allow for compromise and *ex-gratia* payments to be considered as being within the terms of the original policy and therefore covered by terms of the reinsurance. An *"ex-gratia"* payment is one where liability is either not admitted or where the circumstances of the loss are unclear. As a sign of good faith, the reinsured might settle a claim *"ex-gratia"*. Such a claim is technically not recoverable from any reinsurance. The reinsured is obliged to inform reinsurers that it intends to make an *"ex-gratia"* settlement and it is up to reinsurers to decide whether to pay their share or not.

Readers should be aware that many reinsurers have now changed their opinion of the intent of this clause and attempt to exclude it from excess of loss contract wordings. Excess of loss reinsurance does not necessarily follow the terms and conditions of the original policies it protects. As such, the Follow the Settlements Clause is perhaps more relevant to proportional reinsurance treaties.

Index/Stability Clause This clause has been discussed in detail in Chapter 9 above. It provides for the deductible and limit of liability to be adjusted for the effects of inflation affecting a particular claim and increasing its value over time. This movement in inflation (and apportionment between deductible and limit) is calculated on the basis of an index identified within the clause itself. For legal liability contracts, the index would normally be based upon movements in wages, rather than movements in the cost of living.

Currency Fluctuation This clause applies to any claims that arise in a currency different from the main limits expressed in the reinsurance contract. Devaluations or strong movements in currency exchange rates could increase or decrease the value of a claim when converted into the main currency limits for the contract. The main currency limits are converted into separate currency limits at the rates of exchange ruling at *inception* of the contract period. Those converted currency limits remain in force for the contract period and offer the reinsured (and reinsurer) a degree of certainty. If a currency loss occurs, the loss is set against the converted (and now fixed) currency contract limits and a loss identified in that currency. The currency loss would then be converted into the main currency at the rate of exchange ruling at the date of *settlement*. In this way, the effects of currency revaluation or devaluation would be shared fairly between the reinsured and the reinsurer.

Currency Conversion Readers should be aware that some contracts contain a provision that allows nominated foreign currencies to be converted into the main contract currency at *fixed rates* of exchange. Premiums are converted at these fixed rates, but claims would be settled at the rate of exchange ruling on the date of settlement of any loss. These rates of exchange would also be identified at contract inception and last for the duration of that contract period.

The more normal Currency Conversion Clause simply allows the reinsured to convert foreign currencies into the main contract currency at the various rates of exchange ruling on the dates of its various accounts entries for those transactions. It is often known as the **Rates of Exchange Clause.**

6. Inception and Termination

Inception/Termination Most contracts incept at the beginning of the reinsured's own financial year. As we explained in the proportional section, this date would be 1st January in many countries and for most companies. There are obviously exceptions, many contracts covering Australian business incept at 1st July, whilst most Japanese reinsurances tend to incept at 1st April. Nowadays, almost all excess of loss reinsurance contracts are concluded for a fixed 12 months period. We would suggest that there are now very few excess of loss programmes concluded on a continuous basis. If they were, then such programmes would be subject to the notice of cancellation condition identified in the proportional section.

Special Cancellation (or Sudden Death) We repeat here what we stated in the proportional section. This clause allows for the contract to be terminated immediately on the happening of certain specified events. Such events include war breaking out between the countries of the two parties, the contract being declared illegal, one party becoming insolvent or bankrupt, or not being able to fulfil its contractual obligations. The clause provides for *either* party to give immediate notice of termination to the other and would also identify what happens to unpaid (normally deposit) premiums and known outstanding losses. Special Cancellation Clauses for excess of loss contracts would normally state that obligations or liabilities incurred up to and including the date of cancellation should remain in force until finally discharged or settled.

Readers should be aware that many Special Cancellation clauses now contain a "downgrading of security" provision. This means that if a *reinsurer's* claims-paying ability is reduced by specified rating agencies, then the reinsured has the option to cancel that reinsurer's participation, often from the date of such downgrading. Many clauses stipulate that the cancellation option rests solely with the reinsured, hence our emphasis. This apparently one-sided option is in contrast to the more standard provisions mentioned in the first paragraph of this section. It is also fair to point out that the separate **Insolvency Clause** identifies what would happen if the reinsured became insolvent.

The problem of insolvency is particularly important for

excess of loss reinsurance. Technically, excess of loss reinsurers are only obliged to pay their share of any excess of loss claim *after* the reinsured has settled its own share (and thus created an "ultimate net loss"). Recent legal cases have tested whether *potential* excess of loss recoveries should be considered as an asset by the liquidators of an insolvent reinsured. The liquidator might require reinsurers to settle excess of loss recoveries in the knowledge that the insolvent reinsured would never be able to settle such loss(es). There has been an important change to the UNL Clause for that reason ("… *actually* paid …") and the Insolvency Clause included for just that unfortunate scenario.

Portfolio Many excess of loss reinsurances are on a "losses occurring during the period" basis so that there is no obligation to cover the unexpired period of risks that would be in force at the date of termination of the reinsurance contract. Matters regarding premium portfolio assumption and/or withdrawal should not arise, but please refer to the next important clause.

Run-Off At termination of excess of loss coverage, and especially where such coverage is on a "losses occurring during the period" basis, the reinsured may still have a ongoing liability for unexpired risks for those original policies in force at the date of termination. This is particularly the case for contracts exposed to individual risks. Some clauses allow the reinsured to pay the reinsurer an additional premium so that the reinsurer could offer coverage for a further 12 months period. The "additional" contract would therefore cover losses that might arise on such unexpired risks. The premium could be a fixed amount, identified at the original inception of the contract, or the clause might contain a calculation formula individual to the circumstances of the subject matter of the contract.

In either case, the reinsured should exercise its option to invoke (utilise) the Run Off Clause before termination of the original agreement.

7. Housekeeping

Once again, we repeat both Housekeeping and Disputes from the proportional section. These clauses regulate activities that do not relate purely to what is covered, what premium is paid and how claim recoveries should be made.

Inspection of Records This article allows the reinsurer, or an authorised representative, to inspect the reinsured's records relevant to transactions under the treaty. Premium or loss bordereaux are rarely supplied for excess of loss contracts, so the reinsurer has no idea of the business protected by the excess of loss agreement. This clause allows the reinsurer (or its duly authorised representative) to conduct a reinsurance audit, if it so desires. Many clauses contain a provision to the effect that such audits should be conducted during the reinsured's "normal office hours". Such audits are often helpful to both parties.

Alterations This article allows for amendments to be made during the period of the reinsurance. These are made by mutual agreement, by exchange of correspondence or by issuing a formal addendum. It is important that alterations are agreed in writing between the parties. This should avoid disputes that might arise at some later stage.

Intermediary Where a broker is involved in placing the contract, this article should be included in the wording to allow for correspondence and all transactions between the parties to be routed through the broker.

8. Disputes

Applicable Law This relatively new article identifies the law applicable to the subject matter of the reinsurance contract and the law applicable to the *operation* of the reinsurance agreement itself. It could also identify the legal jurisdiction for any arbitration proceedings. It has tended to replace the older **Jurisdiction** Clause (see below).

Jurisdiction Reinsurances are often transacted between parties in different countries with different systems of law. It is useful for the parties to agree on what system of law should apply to the reinsurance agreement. That could be the legal system of their own country or that of another country.

Arbitration This article provides for a procedure to be adopted for resolving disputes that might arise between the parties. This used to be a relatively informal procedure and was intended to be an alternative to instituting legal action. Sadly, numerous disputes concerning various reinsurance transactions have caused this clause to take greater precedence. Many excess of loss wordings refer to ARIAS, an internationally recognised arbitration panel as being an acceptable provider for the resolution of contractual disputes. Many clauses would also identify where any arbitration should take place and the legal system to be used.

Chapter 17 contains an example of a Motor & General Third Party Excess of Loss reinsurance wording and discusses some of these clauses in further detail.

16

Treaty Wordings – Proportional

The treaty wordings examined below have been chosen because they contain the important items that should be included in such documents. The purpose of our examination is to illustrate the general principles behind the wordings so that these are better understood. In an attempt to reduce costly administration, many treaty wordings now consist of a series of "standard" clauses to which is attached a "schedule" of specific terms and conditions applicable to the individual reinsurance agreement made between the ceding company and the reinsurer. Obviously, certain ceding companies take pride in the preparation of their own treaty wordings and submit these to their reinsurers, whether the placement is made directly with those reinsurers, or through the offices of a reinsurance broker. There is no right or wrong method, only that which is acceptable to all parties involved.

As proportional and excess of loss business differ basically in concept, so do the treaty and contract wordings for those different methods of reinsurance. We have therefore chosen to examine them separately. This chapter deals with proportional wordings and uses a Fire First Surplus treaty as our example. Readers should be aware that there is no set order to the clauses shown and our example is just that, an example.

THE RECITAL (or PREAMBLE) CLAUSE

FIRE AND ALLIED PERILS AGREEMENT SURPLUS TREATY OF REINSURANCE

between the
ABC INSURANCE COMPANY LIMITED of (hereinafter called the Company) of the one part
and
THE XYZ REINSURANCE COMPANY LIMITED of (hereinafter called the Reinsurer) of the other part

WHEREBY IT IS AGREED AS FOLLOWS

This is the preamble and gives the names and addresses of the parties to the agreement so that their identities are established without any doubt.

ARTICLE 1

BUSINESS COVERED

The Company agrees to cede and the Reinsurer agrees to accept by way of reinsurance a fixed share of   % (*number as words* per cent) of all surplus amounts over and about the amount retained by the Company for its own account on all insurances, whether accepted directly or by way of coinsurance or facultative quota share reinsurance by the Company in its Fire Department, against fire or any other peril (as per the list agreed between the Company and the Reinsurer) which may be insured by the Company on risks situated in ...., provided that the share so ceded shall not exceed   % (*number in words* per cent) of the amount retained by the Company for its own account.

The wording of this article addresses both the business covered and the scope of the reinsurance by mentioning the cessions to be made. It also identifies the share of the reinsurer as well as the classes of risk covered and the territorial limits of the agreement. This surplus treaty wording does not state the amount of the ceding company's retention but limits the reinsurance cession to a percentage (effectively a number of lines) of the ceding company's chosen retention on a particular risk. If this were a quota share, the cession would have been identified in terms of a percentage of the whole instead of a number of lines.

EXCLUSION CLAUSE

This Agreement excludes any liability assumed by the Company for the following:

(1) loss or damage directly or indirectly occasioned by, happening through or in consequence of

   (i) War, invasion, acts of foreign enemies, hostilities or warlike operations (whether war be declared or not);

   (ii) civil war, mutiny, civil commotion assuming the proportions of or amounting to a popular uprising, military rising, insurrection, rebellion, revolution, military or usurped power, martial law;

   (iii) confiscation or nationalisation or requisition or destruction of or damage to property by or under the order of any Government or public or local authority; or

   (iv) any act of any person or persons acting on behalf of or in connection with any organisation the objects of which are to include the overthrowing or influencing of any de jure or de facto government by terrorism or by any violent means.

(2) Notwithstanding any provision to the contrary within this Agreement or any endorsement thereto it is agreed that this Agreement excludes loss, damage, cost or expense of whatsoever nature directly or indirectly caused by, resulting from or in connection with any act of terrorism regardless of any other cause or event contributing concurrently or in any other sequence to the loss.

   For the purpose of this endorsement an act of terrorism means an act, including but not limited to the use of force or violence and/or the threat thereof, of any person or group(s) of persons, whether acting alone or on behalf of or in connection with any organisation(s) or government(s), committed for political, religious, ideological or similar purposes including the intention to influence any government and/or to put the public, or any section of the public, in fear.

   This endorsement also excludes loss, damage, cost or expense of whatsoever nature directly or indirectly caused by, resulting from or in connection with any action taken in controlling, preventing, suppressing or in any way relating to any act of terrorism.

   If the Reinsurer alleges that by reason of this exclusion, any loss, damage, cost or expense is not covered by this reinsurance the burden of proving the contrary shall be upon the Company.

   In the event any portion of this endorsement is found to be invalid or unenforceable, the remainder shall remain in full force and effect.

(3) This Agreement shall exclude Nuclear Energy Risks whether such risks are written directly and/or by way of reinsurance and/or via Pools and/or Associations.

For all purposes of this Agreement Nuclear Energy Risks shall mean all first party and/or third party insurances (other than workers' compensation and/or employers' liability) in respect of:

(i) All Property on the site of a nuclear power station. Nuclear Reactors, reactor buildings and plant and equipment therein on any site other than a nuclear power station.

(ii) All Property, on any site (including but not limited to the sites referred to in (i) above) used or having been used for:

(a) The generation of nuclear energy; or

(b) The Production, Use or Storage of Nuclear Material.

(iii) Any other Property eligible for insurance by the relevant local Nuclear Insurance Pool and/or Association but only to the extent of the requirements of that local Pool and/or Association.

(iv) the supply of goods and services to any of the sites, described in (I) to (III) above, unless such insurances or reinsurances shall exclude the perils of irradiation and contamination by Nuclear Material.

Except as undernoted, Nuclear Energy Risks shall not include:

(i) Any insurance or reinsurance in respect of the construction or erection or installation or replacement or repair or maintenance or decommissioning of property as described in (i) to (iii) above (including contractors' plant and equipment);

(ii) Any Machinery Breakdown or other Engineering insurance or reinsurance not coming within the scope of (i) above;

Provided always that such insurance or reinsurance shall exclude the perils of irradiation and contamination by Nuclear Material.

However, the above exemption shall not extend to:

1. The provision of any insurance or reinsurance whatsoever in respect of:

    (a) Nuclear Material:

    (b) Any Property in the High Radioactivity Zone or Area of any Nuclear Installation as from the introduction of Nuclear Material or – for reactor installations – as from fuel loading or first criticality where so agreed with the relevant local Nuclear Insurance Pool and/or Association.

2. The provision of any insurance or reinsurance for the under noted perils:

    - Fire, lightning, explosion;

- Earthquake;
- Aircraft and other aerial devices or articles dropped therefrom;
- Irradiation and radioactive contamination;
- Any other peril insured by the relevant local Nuclear Insurance Pool and/or Association;

in respect of any other Property not specified in 1. above which directly involves the Production, Use or Storage of Nuclear Material as from the introduction of Nuclear Material into such Property.

DEFINITIONS

"Nuclear Material" means:

(i) Nuclear fuel, other than natural uranium and depleted uranium, capable of producing energy by a self-sustaining chain process of nuclear fission outside a Nuclear Reactor, either alone or in combination with some other material; and

(ii) Radioactive Products or Waste.

"Radioactive Products or Waste" means any radioactive material produced in, or any material made radioactive by exposure to the radiation incidental to the production or utilisation of nuclear fuel, but does not include radioisotopes which have reached the final stage of fabrication so as to be usable for any scientific, medical, agricultural, commercial or industrial purpose.

"Nuclear Installation" means:

(i) Any Nuclear Reactor;

(ii) Any factory using nuclear fuel for the production of Nuclear Material, or any factory for the processing of Nuclear Material, including any factory for the reprocessing of irradiated nuclear fuel; and

(iii) Any facility where Nuclear Material is stored, other than storage incidental to the carriage of such material.

"Nuclear Reactor" means any structure containing nuclear fuel in such an arrangement that a self-sustaining chain process of nuclear fission can occur therein without an additional source of neutrons.

"Production, Use or Storage of Nuclear Material" means the production, manufacture, enrichment, conditioning, processing, reprocessing, use, storage, handling and disposal of Nuclear Material.

"Property" shall mean all land, buildings, structures, plant, equipment, vehicles, contents (including but not limited to liquids and gases) and all materials of whatever description whether fixed or not.

"High Radioactivity Zone or Area" means:

(i) For nuclear power stations and Nuclear Reactors, the vessel or structure which immediately contains the core (including its supports and shrouding) and all the contents thereof, the fuel elements, the control rods and the irradiated fuel store; and

(ii) For non-reactor Nuclear Installations, any area where the level of radioactivity requires the provision of a biological shield.

These exclusions are included in almost all treaties. The wordings of these exclusions have changed over the years. The War & Civil War exclusion shown in (1) extends to various types of undeclared war and to terrorism. We have included in (2) an example of a new Terrorism Exclusion. Such exclusion has been included in many reinsurance treaties following the tragic events of 11th September 2001 in New York, Washington and Pennsylvania. The example we have used would be additional to our example of the War and Civil War Exclusion Clause. The Nuclear Energy Risks exclusion in (3) reflects the increased use of nuclear and radiation material in industrial, commercial and medical life. The version shown is now almost universally used for international reinsurance agreements. Other exclusions would depend upon the type of original business covered, the constitution of the ceding company's portfolio, and the state of the reinsurance market at the time of placement.

ARTICLE 2

ATTACHMENT OF LIABILITY

The liability of the Reinsurer upon any one risk shall commence obligatorily and simultaneously with that of the Company as soon as the Company's retention, according to its Tables of Limits, is exceeded.

The Company, in all cases, shall be the sole judge of what constitutes any one one risk and the retention appropriate thereto. The Reinsurer shall accept all alterations, modifications and/or cancellations of contracts ceded hereunder and the consequent adjustment of premium.

The Company shall be at liberty to effect reinsurances elsewhere on any risk normally falling within the scope of this Agreement provided such reinsurance is in the interest of the Reinsurer. The Company may effect excess of loss reinsurance in respect of its net retention on business ceded under this Agreement.

Cessions made hereunder shall not exceed a period of twelve months plus odd time. Such additional odd-time period shall not be greater than 6 (six) months.

This Article expands on the terms set out in Article 1. It states that the ceding company alone should determine what constitutes the extent of any one risk. This should avoid any arguments that might arise with reinsurers. A further point is that other reinsurances arranged by the ceding company on a particular risk would not invalidate the present agreement. Clearly, the ceding company needs to have the capability to effect priority reinsurances, particularly if this would be in the best interests of the reinsurer. Although, technically, the ceding company could reduce its retention to "nil" by the use of further reinsurance, this could be interpreted as an act of bad faith. Many regulators now insist that a ceding company should retain a "meaningful" retention on any risk it accepts. The fourth paragraph limits the period of cessions so that the ceding company could not cede long-term policies to the treaty. It would be acceptable for, say, a three-year policy to be ceded to the three successive treaties, as this would correspond to the initial inception date and the two subsequent (treaty) anniversary dates. Correct cessions could therefore be made and an "annual" premium (one third of the three-year total) ceded to each treaty period.

ARTICLE 3

SELF-INSURANCE CLAUSE

An insurance effected by the Company wherein the Company is named as the Insured either solely or jointly with another party shall not be excluded from the scope of this Agreement merely because no legal liability may arise in respect of such insurance by reason of the fact that the Company is named as the Insured or one of the Insured.

As we have seen, this clause allows the ceding company to obtain treaty protection for its own buildings. A simple example might be the ceding company's head office (irrespective of whether it owns or leases the building).

ARTICLE 4

CHANGE OF UNDERWRITING POLICY CLAUSE

> It is a condition precedent to the Reinsurer's liability hereunder that the Company shall not introduce at any time after the Company enters into this agreement any change in its established acceptance and underwriting policy which may increase or materially extend the liability or exposure of the Reinsurer hereunder in respect of the classes of business to which this Agreement applies without the prior written approval of the Reinsurer and any reinsurance arrangements relating thereto shall be maintained or be deemed to be maintained unaltered for the purpose of this Agreement.

The wording of this clause is intended to apply only to significant changes so that the ceding company does not need to seek the agreement of the Reinsurer to every minor alteration. Please note that this wording also requires priority reinsurances (e.g. facultative quota share protections) to be maintained in force.

ARTICLE 5

REINSURANCE RECORDS

> The Company shall keep at its head office or branch offices:
>
> (a) proper records (herein called "Reinsurance Records") which shall have entries with dates and sufficient particulars made therein of all business effected by the Company in respect of which a reinsurance is effected and alterations affecting the reinsurance premium under this Agreement; and also
>
> (b) proper tables (hereinafter called "Tables of Limits") showing the amounts which the Company ordinarily retains according to the class of risk; and also
>
> (c) no lists of such business shall be provided to the Reinsurer.

CLAIMS BEFORE CESSION ENTRY

> If and whenever the Company receives advice of a claim under any original policy or reinsurance effected by it before entry of the risk in its Reinsurance Records, it shall keep as its retention the proportion of the risk as its records show to have been usually retained on that risk or class of risk and the surplus amount shall be calculated accordingly.

RIGHT OF REINSURED TO ALTER RETENTIONS

The Company may at any time increase or reduce the amount retained upon any risk and also may vary its Tables of Limits and its reinsurances shall be adjusted accordingly, provided it does not do so to the detriment of the Reinsurer as the result of knowledge of the risk having been affected by a loss.

SPECIAL ACCEPTANCES

Special acceptances of risks excluded from the scope of this Agreement are to be agreed by all Reinsurers hereon. Any previously agreed special acceptances are to remain in force as far as applicable and all Reinsurers shall be advised of such previously agreed special acceptances at every renewal of this Agreement.

The first in this series of clauses emphasises the obligations of the ceding company in maintaining proper records and that no lists (bordereaux) would be provided to the reinsurer. The second clause emphasises that "normal" cession practices should be maintained, even if a loss had occurred on an original policy prior to any cession being made. The third clause allows the ceding company to vary its retention or table of underwriting limits, providing that such changes are not to the detriment of the reinsurer. The fourth clause refers to special acceptances. These relate to unusual risks that the ceding company feels it should advise to its reinsurer(s) as they do not fall into the normal pattern of its treaty. The reinsurer might accept or refuse a special acceptance, impose restrictive terms or an additional premium.

ARTICLE 6

ACCOUNTS CLAUSE

Accounts between the Company and the Reinsurer shall be closed quarterly and rendered to the Reinsurer as soon as possible thereafter but in any event not less than within 30 (thirty) days after the end of each quarter, which shall be deemed to close on the 31st March, 30th June, 30th September and 31st December respectively in each year.

Accounts shall be confirmed by the Reinsurer within 15 (fifteen) days of receipt but inadvertent errors or omissions in the account shall not delay the payment of any balance hereunder. Any necessary correction shall be made in a supplementary account to the next periodic account rendered hereunder. In such event, any corrections shall be clearly identified in that supplementary account.

Balances due to either shall be paid within a further 15 (fifteen) days of positive confirmation of the accounts.

CURRENCY CLAUSE

For the purpose of this Agreement currencies other than the currency in which this Agreement is written shall be converted into that currency at the rates of exchange used in the books of the Company or where there is a specific remittance for a loss settlement at the rates of exchange used in making such remittance.

Provision is made in the first part of this article for accounts to be rendered at regular intervals. A time limit is also fixed for confirming the accounts themselves and payments of any amounts due under the accounts.

The second clause indicates the way in which rates of exchange are to be used for the purpose of calculation of any amounts due in foreign currencies. Readers should note that this Currency Clause is probably the most common. It is neither a Currency Fluctuation nor Currency Conversion Clause, since rates of exchange are not identified in advance.

ARTICLE 7

PREMIUMS

The Company shall pay to the Reinsurer the Reinsurer's proportion of the original gross premium of the Company, less only returns, cancellations and premiums for risks excluded from the protection of this Agreement, in respect of all risks ceded hereto.

The Reinsurer shall pay to the Company its proportion of taxes and other charges (other than agents' commissions and associated fees) not recoverable from the original insured or reinsured as the case may be.

COMMISSION

The Reinsurer shall allow to the Company a commission of   % (*number in words* per cent) on the premiums ceded under this Agreement.

PROFIT COMMISSION CLAUSE

The Reinsurer shall also pay to the Company a Profit Commission of _____ % (*number in words* per cent) on the profits arising from all business ceded under this Agreement and included in the accounts of each annual period of this Agreement in accordance with the following formula:

INCOME

(1) Premium included in the accounts for the current year.

(2) Unearned proportion (if any) of the premiums ceded hereunder in the previous year.

(3) Outstanding losses (if any) sustained hereunder as estimated by the Company at the close of the previous year.

Items 1 and 2 shall not apply to the first Profit Commission Statement.

OUTGO

(4) Commission included in the accounts for the current year.

(5) Taxes and other charges included in the accounts for the current year.

(6) Paid losses and loss expenses included in the accounts for the current year including cash loses paid by the Reinsurer during the current year and not brought into account.

(7) Unearned proportion (if any) of the premiums ceded hereunder in the current year.

(8) Outstanding losses (if any) sustained hereunder as estimated by the Company at the close of the current year.

(9) Reinsurer's Management Expenses calculated at _____ % (*number in words* per cent) of the premium included in the accounts for the current year.

(10) Cost of any excess of loss protection effected for the benefit of the Reinsurer (if any).

(11) Deficit hereunder, if any, brought forward and calculated in accordance with the provision shown in the following paragraph.

The difference between the Income and the Outgo represents the annual result on which (if a profit) any profit commission will be calculated.

Any deficit resulting from each year's profit commission calculation shall be carried forward and offset against the profit of the next two years. If at the end of the third year the overall result is still a loss then the loss of the first year and the profits for the second and third years shall be eliminated from any further profit commission calculations. Where the second year is also a loss then the loss carried forward to the fourth year shall be the full loss of the second year less any profit resulting from the combined result of the third year's profit less the first year's loss. Where the third year is a loss then the full loss of that year shall be carried forward and offset against the profit of the next two years in the same manner.

The profit commission shall be calculated annually and the profit commission statement shall be submitted to the Reinsurer within three months of the end of the year to which the profit commission relates and any profit commission due shall be included in that account.

On termination of this Agreement by either party, the profit commission statement for the final period of duration hereof shall be deferred until all cessions hereunder have expired and all losses hereunder have been settled.

The main contents of this article have been discussed at length earlier and need not be examined again. The only new item is contained in the last paragraph of the profit commission clause which provides for any adjustment of profit commission to be deferred in the event of cancellation of the agreement because losses could arise on unexpired cessions (if the portfolio for unearned premium is not withdrawn) and claims might be outstanding which could well be settled after termination, often for either higher or lower amounts. To ensure fairness towards both parties, a calculation should be made only when all liability had been fully settled.

ARTICLE 8

PREMIUM RESERVE DEPOSIT CLAUSE

As security for the Company in respect of the future performance of the Reinsurer for cessions hereunder, the Company shall retain from the Reinsurer a Premium Reserve Deposit in cash calculated at 40% (forty per cent) of the premiums ceded to the Reinsurer in the quarterly accounts rendered hereunder. Such retained Reserve Deposit will be held by the Company and released to the Reinsurer in the corresponding quarterly account of the following year.

The Reinsurer may at any time request the release of the Premium Reserve Deposit retained in cash and its replacement with Bonds and/or Securities acceptable to both parties and the Reinsurer shall receive all dividends, interest and other rights accruing thereon. When a Reserve Deposit is constituted in Bonds and/or Securities the Company shall have the right to debit the Reinsurer and retain in cash any deficiency between the Premium Reserve Deposit required and the market value of the Bonds and/or Securities held. The cash deposit so retained shall be held by the Company until covered by Bonds and/or Securities deposited by the Reinsurer and formal documentation has been provided by the Reinsurer to the Company.

The Company shall credit the Reinsurer in the quarterly accounts rendered hereunder with interest credited at the rate of   % (*number in words* per cent) per annum on the Premium Reserve Deposit retained in cash at any time throughout the relevant period.

It is hereby expressly agreed and declared that cash sums and/or Bonds and/or Securities held by the Company in accordance with the provisions of this Article remain the property of the Reinsurer and are held by the Company as trustee for the Reinsurer. They may only be utilised by the Company in the event of the Reinsurer's failure to discharge its liability under this Agreement, and then only up to the value of cash sums and/or Bonds and/or Securities retained or held by the Company as trustee on behalf of the Reinsurer.

This Article requires no comment as the purpose of the premium reserve deposit has been examined fully earlier. The second paragraph allows for the reserve fund to be retained in Bonds and/or in Securities rather than in cash. Modern practice tends towards banking instruments known as "Letters of Credit", but the effects would be similar. The third paragraph makes it clear that the funds or securities retained remain the property of the reinsurer.

ARTICLE 9

ERRORS AND OMISSIONS CLAUSE

Any delay, error or omission in connection with this Agreement, or in connection with any risk ceded hereunder, shall not be held to relieve either party from any liability that would attach to it if such delay, error or omission had not been made, provided such delay, error or omission is rectified as soon as possible after discovery.

FOLLOW THE FORTUNES CLAUSE

It is the intention of this Agreement that the Reinsurer shall, in all matters falling within the scope of this Agreement, follow to the extent of its interest the fortune of the Company.

ORIGINAL CONDITIONS

All cessions under this Agreement shall be subject to the same terms and conditions as binding upon the Company under the original business, and in all things coming within the scope of this Agreement the Reinsurer shall, to the extent of its interest, follow the underwriting fortunes of the Company.

Errors do happen, even in the best-managed ceding company, and administrative errors or omissions should not invalidate the reinsurance treaty. For example, the ceding company might have a risk that falls into a category where it would normally retain 50%. A typical error might be the situation when the ceding company retains that risk in full. If a claim occurred and a subsequent investigation revealed this error, then the reinsurer would settle half the claim, provided that the error had been corrected immediately upon discovery (and the appropriate half-share of the premium credited to the reinsurer).

The second paragraph confirms the intention of the whole agreement that the reinsurer is bound to follow the ceding company in all matters falling within the agreed terms and conditions of the treaty and should follow the ceding company's fortunes. As we have mentioned, many reinsurers are now reluctant to offer this open facility, but (as with all proportional reinsurances), the reinsurer is effectively an extension of the ceding company's own underwriting capacity. For that reason, we have shown a modern clause known as "Original Conditions". This version is perhaps a compromise between the old clause and modern-day practice.

ARTICLE 10

CLAIMS CLAUSE

A preliminary loss advice shall be sent by the Company to the Reinsurer for all losses where the amount of the amount of the loss is estimated to exceed   together with relevant details and an estimate of the probable cost of the claim. The Company shall keep the Reinsurer informed of all developments likely to affect the cost of any such claims and undertakes insofar as is reasonably possible to consult the Reinsurer with regard to the settlement of such claims.

All loss settlements made by the Company affecting cessions under this Agreement, whether made under strict policy conditions or by compromise or otherwise, including ex-gratia payments, shall be unconditionally binding upon the Reinsurer, and the Reinsurer shall bear its rateable proportion of such settlements and of any expenses relating thereto but excluding office expenses and salaries of employees of the Company. The Reinsurer shall, nevertheless, share to the extent of its interest in any sums which might be recovered by the Company.

The Company may likewise commence, continue, defend, compromise, settle or withdraw from actions, suits or proceedings, and generally do all such matters and things relating to any claim or loss as in its judgement may be beneficial or expedient and all payments made and costs and expenses incurred in connection therewith shall be shared by the Reinsurer in proportion to its liability for the claim or loss and debited or paid in accordance with the provisions of this Agreement.

Where the Reinsurer's share of a loss falling under this Agreement amounts to or exceeds the sum of   the Reinsurer shall, upon receiving a summarised statement from the Company (detailing the payment made or the amount to be paid forthwith as agreed with the original insured or reinsured as the case may be), remit its share of such loss promptly. When such share is less than the amount stated the amount shall be debited in the accounts.

The Company shall as soon as practicable and in any event not later than three months after the 31st December of each year send to the Reinsurer a statement of unsettled claims as at the date of submission of such statement showing the amount for which the Reinsurer might be liable.

This clause makes provision for the reinsurer to be advised of serious claims (i.e. those which are above a certain limit) and requires the ceding company to consult the reinsurer, as far as possible, in the settlement of these losses. Usually, these are the claims that would require special cash settlements from the reinsurer without waiting for the usual quarterly or other periodic accounts. There is also a provision for an advice of outstanding losses at the end of the year.

However, this article states clearly that the ceding company retains all powers of negotiation and settlement of claims, and that costs and expenses involved in the claims settlement would be shared by the reinsurer. Readers should remember that the salaries and expenses of the ceding company's own staff who deal with any claim are not normally recoverable from the reinsurer.

ARTICLE 11

INCEPTION AND TERMINATION CLAUSE

This Agreement shall take effect in respect of all insurances, co-insurances or facultative quota share reinsurances relating to risks covered hereunder issued on or after the 1st day of January 20xx
and shall continue in force until terminated by either party giving three months notice in writing to expire at midnight on the 31st day of December in any year. In the event of either party giving notice of termination then such notice shall be automatically deemed to have been given by both parties.

In the event of either party giving notice of termination of any business ceded in reciprocity (in whole or in part) for this Agreement, then this Agreement shall be automatically deemed to be under notice of termination from the same date notwithstanding that previous notice had not been given in accordance with the above paragraph.

Either party shall have the right to terminate this Agreement immediately by giving the other party written notice:

(a) If the performance of the whole or any part of this Agreement be prohibited or rendered impossible *de jure* or *de facto* in particular and without prejudice to the generality of the preceding words in consequence of any law or regulation which is or shall be in force in any country or territory or if any law or regulation shall prevent directly or indirectly the remittance of any payments due to or from either party,

(b) If the other party has become insolvent or unable to pay its debts or has lost the whole or any part of its paid-up capital, or has had any authority to transact any class of business withdrawn, suspended or made conditional,

(c) If there is any material change in the ownership or control of the other party,

(d) If the country or territory in which the other party resides or has its head office or is incorporated shall be involved in armed hostilities with any other country whether war be declared or not or is partly or wholly occupied by another power,

(e) If the other party shall have failed to comply with any of the terms and conditions of this Agreement.

All notices of termination in accordance with any of the provisions of this paragraph shall be by telex, facsimile or any other means of instantaneous communication that leaves a permanent record and shall be deemed to be served upon despatch or where communications between the parties are interrupted upon attempted despatch.

The Reinsurer shall remain liable for its share of all cessions made and effective up to and including the date of termination of the Agreement, except where this Agreement is terminated in the circumstances provided for in paragraphs (a), (b), (c), (d) and (e) of this Article where the liability of the Reinsurer under current cessions shall cease as from the date of the notice of termination and any relevant adjustment of premium shall be made forthwith.

All notices of termination served in accordance with any of the provisions of this Article shall be addressed to the party concerned at its head office or at any other address previously designated by that party.

The first part of this article is concerned with the time of commencement of the treaty, not of the original risks the treaty protects. The rest of that paragraph provides for a minimum period to indicate any notice of termination so that both parties would have time to discuss any amendment to the treaty or alternatives to the present treaty. Please note that notice of cancellation is given automatically if a reciprocal exchange of business is involved.

The other paragraphs list various important circumstances that could arise. If they do, this clause gives either party the option to withdraw from or cancel their involvement in the treaty. The legal Latin terms mean *de jure* = in law and *de facto* = in fact. This clause differs slightly from the excess of loss version as the problem of unexpired risks and unearned premium needs to be addressed. In both cases, the reinsurer would remain liable for losses that had occurred up to and including the date of termination of the treaty but remained unsettled at that date.

ARTICLE 12

ASSUMPTION AND WITHDRAWAL OF PREMIUM PORTFOLIO CLAUSE

At the option of the Company, the Reinsurer shall assume liability for its share of all cessions current at the commencement date of this Agreement and in consideration thereof the Company shall credit the

Reinsurer in the first account rendered hereunder with a portfolio premium transfer calculated at 40% (forty per cent) of the premiums written in the Company's accounts for the twelve months prior to the inception of this Agreement. Such transfer of portfolio premium shall be made after deduction of commission agreed for the prior period.

At the option of the Company, the liability of the Reinsurer for its share of the risks ceded under this Agreement shall cease at the date of termination of this Agreement and in consideration thereof the Company shall debit the Reinsurer in account with a portfolio premium transfer calculated at 40% (forty per cent) of the premiums written in the Company's accounts for the twelve months prior to the date of termination of this Agreement. Such transfer of portfolio premium shall be made after deduction of commission agreed by the Reinsurer for the period of this Agreement.

ASSUMPTION AND WITHDRAWAL OF LOSS PORTFOLIO CLAUSE

At the option of the Company, the Reinsurer shall assume liability for its share of all losses outstanding at the commencement of this Agreement and in consideration thereof the Company shall credit the Reinsurer in the first account rendered hereunder with a portfolio loss assumption calculated at 90% (ninety per cent) of the Company's estimate of the amount of losses outstanding at the inception of this Agreement.

At the option of the Company, the liability of the Reinsurer for its share of all losses outstanding under this Agreement shall cease at the date of termination of this Agreement and in consideration thereof the Company shall debit the Reinsurer in account with a portfolio loss withdrawal calculated at 90% (ninety per cent) of the Company's estimate of the amount of losses outstanding at the date of termination of this Agreement.

Portfolio entries and withdrawals have been examined earlier. "Clean-cut" treaties provide for automatic assumption and withdrawal of both premium and outstanding loss portfolios. In the above example, the ceding company has the option either to withdraw portfolio or to treat the Agreement as continuing until normal expiry of the cessions. The second option is important because if the treaty is not renewed in whole or in part, then the ceding company (by not withdrawing portfolio) would make existing reinsurers continue their liability until all cessions had expired. Thus, if a large loss were to occur under a particular cession, the ceding company would not be burdened solely with the whole loss. This would be the case if it had withdrawn a portfolio and that withdrawn portfolio transfer had not been taken over by another reinsurer.

In some versions of the outstanding loss portfolio transfer clause, the ceding company has the right to effect a later adjustment if the actually settled loss amounts differ materially from the figure withdrawn as the portfolio. This is important because a claim might be settled for an amount far higher than was originally estimated. A new reinsurer accepting the outstanding loss portfolio transfer from the previous year would therefore be burdened with a greater loss to pay as it had not received a proper consideration within the transfer.

ARTICLE 13

INSPECTION OF RECORDS CLAUSE

> The Reinsurer or a representative duly authorised by the Reinsurer may at any time during normal office hours and at a place to be mutually agreed between the parties, inspect and take copies of such of the Company's records and documents which relate to business covered under this Agreement. It is agreed that the Reinsurer's right of inspection shall continue as long as either party has a claim against the other arising out of this Agreement.

This paragraph safeguards the interest of the reinsurer if it has any concerns over the way it believes that the ceding company might be operating the surplus treaty. It would allow the reinsurer to inspect all relevant records and to take copies. Please note that this clause allows such right of inspection to continue after termination of the treaty and lasts for as long as any liability remains outstanding or unsettled.

ARTICLE 14

ALTERATIONS CLAUSE

> Any alterations of the terms of this Agreement, whether effected by Addendum or correspondence shall be binding on both parties and be deemed to form part of this Agreement.

If the parties make changes to the treaty during its currency, this clause enables any subsequent correspondence or addendum exchanged between them to be given the same legal effect as if those changes had been embodied in the original treaty wording. This relieves the parties from having to prepare a new treaty wording if any changes need to be made.

ARTICLE 15

INTERMEDIARY CLAUSE

> Both the Company and the Reinsurers agree that all notices, correspondence and payments to either party in connection with this Agreement shall be forwarded through (name and address), who are recognised as the brokers for this Agreement.

It might seem strange to include someone mentioned in the wording who is not party to the treaty, namely the broker. In order to avoid any problems on "who might have sent or paid what to whom and when", the intermediary clause identifies the route of all correspondence, accounts, premium and loss settlements. Clauses of this nature used in the US market clearly identify who is liable for what and to whom.

ARTICLE 16

APPLICABLE LAW

> This Agreement is governed by and is construed according to the law of (*name of country*) and subject to the provisions of the Arbitration Article, the Courts of (*name of country*) shall have exclusive jurisdiction over this Agreement.

As we have mentioned, this relatively new clause identifies

that the treaty would be subject to the identified laws of the nominated country (or state, if applicable). Please note that this clause and the Arbitration Clause tend to work together.

ARTICLE 17

ARBITRATION CLAUSE

All matters in difference between the parties arising under, out of or in connection with this Agreement, including formation and validity, and whether arising during or after the period of this Agreement, shall be referred to an arbitration tribunal in the manner hereinafter set out.

Unless the parties agree upon a sole arbitrator within fourteen days of one receiving a written request from the other for arbitration, the claimant (the party requesting arbitration) shall appoint its arbitrator and give written notice thereof to the respondent. Within thirty days of receiving such notice the respondent shall appoint its arbitrator and give written notice thereof to the claimant, failing which the claimant may apply to the appointor hereinafter named to nominate an arbitrator on behalf of the respondent.

Before they enter upon a reference the two arbitrators shall appoint a third arbitrator. Should they fail to appoint such a third arbitrator within thirty days of the appointment of the respondent's arbitrator then either of them or either of the parties may apply to the appointor for the appointment of the third arbitrator. The three arbitrators shall decide by majority. If no majority can be reached the verdict of the third arbitrator shall prevail. He shall also act as chairman of the tribunal.

Unless the parties otherwise agree the arbitration tribunal shall consist of persons (including those who have retired) with not less than ten years' experience of insurance or reinsurance as persons engaged in the industry itself or as lawyers or other professional advisers.

The arbitration tribunal shall, so far as is permissible under the law and practice of the seat of arbitration, have power to fix all procedural rules for the holding of the arbitration including discretionary power to make orders as to any matters which it may consider proper in the circumstances of the case with regard to pleadings, discovery, inspection of the documents, examination of witnesses and any other matter whatsoever relating to the conduct of the arbitration and may receive and act upon such evidence whether oral or written strictly admissible or not as it shall in its discretion think fit.

The appointor shall be the Chairman/Chairwoman for the time being of ARIAS *(name of country)* or if he or she is unavailable or it is inappropriate for him or her to act for any reason, such person as may be nominated by the Committee of ARIAS *(name of country)*. If for any reason such persons decline or are unable to act, then the appointor shall be the Judge of the appropriate Courts having jurisdiction at the seat of arbitration.

All costs of the arbitration shall be determined by the arbitration tribunal who may, taking into account the law and practice of the seat of arbitration, direct to and by whom and in what manner they shall be paid.

The seat of the arbitration shall be in (*name of city and country*) and the arbitration tribunal shall apply the law of (*name of country*) as the proper law of this arbitration agreement and of the above Agreement.

The award of the arbitration tribunal shall be in writing and binding upon the parties who covenant to carry out the same. If either of the parties shall fail to carry out any award the other may apply for its enforcement to a court of competent jurisdiction in the territory in which the party in default is domiciled or has assets or carries on business.

The arbitration clause is important because it provides for the procedure to be adopted if a dispute arises between the parties. Arbitration is now a preferred alternative to litigation. This more modern form of arbitration clause avoids problematic phrases such as "the Arbitrators shall not be bound by any strict rules of law or procedure or evidence" or "they shall interpret this Agreement as an honourable engagement rather than as a purely legal contract". Any reinsurance is a legal contract and, although the procedures might be informal, the law of contract needs to be observed. This form of clause sets out the procedures for resolving the dispute without too many formalities.

SIGNATURE CLAUSE

This Agreement has been drawn up in duplicate and executed by a duly authorised representative of each of the contracting parties.

Signed in　　　　　this　　　　day of　　　　20xx .
For and on behalf of the ABC Insurance Company Ltd

And in　　　　　this　　　　day of　　　　20xx .
For and on behalf of the XYZ Reinsurance Group Inc.

This final paragraph prepares the treaty wording for signature by the two parties.

17

Contract Wordings – Excess of Loss

As we have mentioned, excess of loss contract wordings differ from those for proportional treaties. Some of the clauses/articles are nevertheless similar (e.g. Inspection of Records and Arbitration) and we have only mentioned the names of those clauses here as we have already given full examples in the Chapter 16. We have also tried to use an uncomplicated excess of loss contract covering Motor and General Third Party business in our example. Chapter 11 above discusses various additional clauses used (with examples), especially for catastrophe excess of loss reinsurance protections.

RECITAL (or PREAMBLE) CLAUSE

MOTOR AND GENERAL THIRD PARTY EXCESS OF LOSS AGREEMENT

made between the

ABC INSURANCE COMPANY LIMITED of
(hereinafter called the Reinsured) of the one part

and

Various Insurance and/or Reinsurance Companies and/or certain Underwriting Members of Lloyd's, all as per their individual participations, rights, interests and liabilities as identified in the individual Schedules attached hereto, each for their own part and not one for another (hereinafter called the Reinsurers) of the other part.

WHEREBY IT IS AGREED AS FOLLOWS

This is the preamble and gives the name and address of the Reinsured and states that there are a number of different insurance companies, reinsurance companies and Lloyd's Syndicates involved in this excess of loss placement. Each company or syndicate would sign an individual schedule identifying their individual participation. We have deliberately shown this method to highlight the "each for their own part and not one for another" aspect of reinsurance contracts. Please note that all the following clauses would probably identify the contract terms and conditions in another Schedule (e.g. "limits as shown in the attached Schedule"). For the sake of simplicity we have continued to show the detail in each individual article.

ARTICLE 1

COVERAGE, PERIOD and TERRITORIAL SCOPE

Subject to the exclusions set out in Article 3 hereof, this Agreement applies to Motor and/or General Third Party Liability policies of insurance and/or co-insurance and/or facultative quota share reinsurance written or accepted directly by the Reinsured.

This Agreement shall apply to losses occurring during the period commencing on 1st January 200* and expiring on 31st December 200*, both days inclusive, Local Standard Time at the place where the loss occurs.

This Agreement shall apply to losses occurring during the period hereon anywhere in the world excluding absolutely any losses occurring in the United States of America and Canada.

The rights and obligations of both parties to this Agreement shall remain in full force until the effective date of expiry or termination after which the liability of the Reinsurers shall cease absolutely except in respect of losses occurring during the period of the Agreement the claims for which remain unsettled at that date.

It is understood and agreed that as regards losses arising under the business defined in the Class of Business clause covering on a "claims made" or "losses discovered" basis, that is to say, policies and/or contracts and/or reinsurances where the date when the claim is made or the discovery of loss determines under which policy or contract or reinsurance the loss is collectible, such losses are covered hereunder irrespective of the date on which the loss occurs provided that the date the claim is made or the loss discovered falls within the period of this Agreement.

For the purpose of the foregoing the date a claim is first made or a loss discovered shall be the date applicable to the entire loss provided that such date falls within the period of this Agreement and the Reinsurers shall be liable for their proportion of the entire loss irrespective of the expiry date of this Agreement.

This article identifies the class, period and territorial scope of the business covered by the excess of loss reinsurance contract. Most excess of loss contracts are now concluded for a 12 months period, and we have used that period in our example. The inclusion of the words "both dates inclusive" and "local standard time at the place where the loss occurs" hopefully require no explanation.

Please note that this wording applies to "losses occurring during the period" and within the territorial scope shown. The exclusion of any loss occurring in North America is absolute. Thus, if the reinsured were to insure a manufacturer exporting its products to the United States, there would be no excess of loss coverage if a claim for injury or damage were to occur in that country (or Canada).

The third paragraph identifies the ongoing liabilities of reinsurers for claims that have occurred during the period, but remain unsettled at the termination of the contract. As coverage under original policies changes, many legal liability excess of loss contracts allow for coverage of original policies issued on a basis other than a standard "occurrence" form. To simplify excess of loss coverage, losses occurring on original policies issued on a "claims made" or "losses discovered" basis would be protected by the reinsurance agreement. This provision is contained in the fourth and fifth paragraphs of the example clause. Although we have identified these provisions as paragraphs within the clause, there is an individual clause known as the **"Losses Discovered and Claims Made Clause"** that is often used as an independent article.

ARTICLE 2

INDEMNITY (or LIMITS OF INDEMNITY)

> The Reinsurers hereby agree to indemnify the Reinsured for that part of its Ultimate Net Loss which exceeds ********* (indexed) on account of each and every Loss Occurrence and the sum recoverable under this Agreement shall be up to but not exceeding ******** (indexed) Ultimate Net Loss on account of each and every Loss Occurrence.
>
> The underlying loss stated above shall be retained net by the Reinsured and not reinsured in any way other than under the underlying excess of loss reinsurances, if any, on a Loss Occurrence basis, recoveries under which shall be disregarded in computing the underlying loss and Ultimate Net Loss hereunder.
>
> This Agreement shall be subject to an Annual Aggregate Limit of ********** (unindexed).

This Article defines the monetary extent of the cover given. This cover is to indemnify that part of the reinsured's ultimate net loss (explained later) which exceeds a stated monetary amount up to a further limit of liability. In this example, we have shown that both the reinsured's deductible and the reinsurer's limit of liability are subject to indexation (also explained later in this chapter). Please note the term "Loss Occurrence". The term would be expanded in a later article. Since we have used a simple term here, the appropriate and separate clause might read as follows:

DEFINITION OF LOSS OCCURRENCE

> The words "Loss Occurrence" shall mean all individual losses arising out of one and the same event.

Whatever term is used, readers should be aware of the importance of correctly defining what is meant by "loss occurrence" within the contract wording.

Reverting to our clause, the content shows that the reinsured may not have other excess of loss reinsurances in force on its retention other than layers underlying the individual contract in question. This allows for the reinsured to recover an ultimate net loss from a programme of consecutive vertical layers. Please note that coverage should be on the same basis for all layers within the programme. In this instance we have shown "losses occurring during basis".

The limit of liability restricts the reinsurer's liability for each ultimate net loss, but reinsurers would also limit the number of ultimate net losses that could arise during the reinsurance period. In this example, reinsurers have chosen to offer the reinsured an annual aggregate limit of losses recoverable from the excess of loss contract. Although the limit and deductible are subject to indexation, the annual aggregate limit is unindexed. Readers should consider the implications of this apparent inconsistency in coverage. As the reinsurance is subject to an aggregate limitation then the contract wording would need to include a clause similar to that appearing in Chapter 11.

If an excess of loss programme is placed on a "risks attaching" or "policies attaching or renewing during the period" basis, then a loss could affect two (or more) separate underwriting years of account. There is a clause known as an **"Interlocking Clause"** which fairly apportions a loss (involving policies issued in different periods) between the excess of loss protections and the reinsured's deductibles for those two periods. There are various versions of this clause.

In a similar vein, clauses exist to apportion interest and costs fairly between reinsured and reinsurer. Without such clause, costs or interest would rise vertically through an excess of loss programme, without a layer necessarily being involved in the main ultimate net loss itself. These clauses are known as the **"Interest Apportionment"** and **"Costs Apportionment"** clauses.

ARTICLE 3

EXCLUSION CLAUSES

(1) Notwithstanding any provision to the contrary within this Agreement or any endorsement thereto it is agreed that this Agreement excludes loss, damage, cost or expense of whatsoever nature directly or indirectly caused by, resulting from or in connection with any of the following regardless of any other cause or event contributing concurrently or in any other sequence to the loss;

   (i) war, invasion, acts of foreign enemies, hostilities or warlike operations (whether war be declared or not), civil war, rebellion, revolution, insurrection, civil commotion assuming the proportions of or amounting to an uprising, military or usurped power; or

   (ii) any act of terrorism.

For the purpose of this Agreement an act of terrorism means an act, including but not limited to the use of force or violence and/or the threat thereof, of any person or group(s) of persons, whether acting alone or on behalf of or in connection with any organisation(s) or government(s), committed for political, religious, ideological or similar purposes including the intention to influence any government and/or to put the public, or any section of the public, in fear.

This endorsement also excludes loss, damage, cost or expense of whatsoever nature directly or indirectly caused by, resulting from or in connection with any action taken in controlling, preventing, suppressing or in any way relating to (i) and/or (ii) above.

If the Reinsurers allege that by reason of this exclusion, any loss, damage, cost or expense is not covered by this Agreement the burden of proving the contrary shall be upon the Reinsured.

In the event any portion of this endorsement is found to be invalid or unenforceable, the remainder shall remain in full force and effect.

(2) Nuclear risks in accordance with the following clause:-

NUCLEAR ENERGY RISKS EXCLUSION CLAUSE –
(REINSURANCE) (1994)

(WORLDWIDE EXCLUDING U.S.A. AND CANADA) – NMA 1975 (a)

(Please note that the full text of this clause was used in Chapter 16).

(3) Excess of Loss Insurances and/or Excess of Loss Reinsurance Contracts and original policies with a self-insured deductible exceeding (say)$ 10,000

(4) Obligatory Reinsurance Treaties

As we have explained elsewhere, these exclusions would

be found in most excess of loss contract wordings. We have shown another version of the War and Terrorism Exclusion Clause and shown just the title of the internationally accepted Nuclear Energy Risks Exclusion Clause, rather than repeat the full text again.

Legal liability accounts vary a great deal between different countries and reinsurers have identified their own "wish list" of exclusions, both general (as shown above) and specific. Specific exclusions tend to relate to hazardous risks within the class or classes of business protected. Motor exclusions might refer to vehicles running on rails on not on *terra firma*, vehicles used on or near to airport runways and vehicles used in races, speed tests and rallies. General Third Party exclusions might refer to any form of aviation risk, drilling or operation of oil wells and refineries, mining risks, and any risk involving asbestos (including handling and storage). As a general rule, anything "dangerous" would be excluded. An excluded risk nevertheless has its price. If the reinsured is willing to pay a suitable premium, then reinsurers might be willing to include such a risk on a very controlled basis.

We have explained elsewhere why reinsurers do not normally cover the reinsured's acceptance of inwards reinsurances – whether proportional (obligatory reinsurance treaties) or any form of excess of loss. Please note that original policies involving legal liability often include large excesses. This is a function of price that the original insured is prepared to pay. In other words, by retaining a very large excess, the original insured should expect a substantial reduction in the premium charged. Such a risk might distort the reinsured's normal portfolio, so reinsurers choose to exclude such business. The exclusion is not intended to apply to voluntary or compulsory excesses under "standard" motor liability insurances. Please note that these exclusions still allow the reinsured to accept facultative reinsurance business. In this example, the reinsured would be allowed to obtain coverage for losses occurring on its inwards acceptance of both quota share and excess of loss facultative placements.

ARTICLE 4

ULTIMATE NET LOSS CLAUSE

> The term "ultimate net loss" shall mean the total amount which the Reinsured has actually paid in settlement of all claims or series of claims arising out of one accident or occurrence or event originating from one cause which may occur during the period of this Agreement, including any legal costs and professional fees and expenses (excluding salaries of employees and the office expenses of the Reinsured) reasonably incurred in connection therewith. Recoveries including amounts which inure to the benefit of this Agreement shall first be deducted from such amount to arrive at the amount of the liability, if any, hereunder.
>
> Any salvages, payments or recoveries or payments effected subsequent to a settlement of any such ultimate net loss shall be applied as if effected prior to such settlement and any adjustment as may be necessary shall be made forthwith.
>
> Nothing in this Article shall be construed to mean that claims under this reinsurance are not recoverable until the Reinsured's ultimate net loss has been ascertained.
>
> The liability of the Reinsuers hereunder in respect of each Ultimate Net Loss shall not be increased by reason of the inability of the Reinsured to recover amounts from any other reinsurers for any reason whatsoever.

This Article is important as it defines what comprises the "ultimate net loss". The intention is that the reinsured is allowed to aggregate claims arising from one accident or occurrence and that accident or occurrence in turn arises from the same original cause. The reinsurance of legal liability business often gives rise to a large variety of circumstances under which a reinsurer might become liable to pay a claim. We covered this topic in some detail in Chapter 9 above, and make further references later in this chapter.

The loss payable is calculated after all possible deductions have been made. The wording allows for interim payments and also makes provision for salvages and recoveries obtained after a loss settlement has been made under the Agreement.

ARTICLE 5
NET RETAINED LINES CLAUSE

This Agreement shall apply only to that portion of any insurance or reinsurance otherwise covered hereunder which the Reinsured, acting in accordance with its established practices, retains net for its own account and in computing the amount in excess of which this Agreement applies, only a loss or losses in respect of that portion of any insurance or reinsurance otherwise covered hereunder which the Reinsured, acting in accordance with its established practices, retains net for its own account shall be included.

The Reinsurer's liability hereunder shall not be increased due to an error or omission which results in an increase in the Reinsured's net retention nor by the Reinsured's failure to reinsure in accordance with its normal practice.

The Reinsurer's liability hereunder shall not be increased by the inability of the Reinsured to collect from any other Reinsurer or Reinsurers, whether specific or general, any amounts which may have become due from them for any reason whatsoever.

Where the reinsurance applies only to the net retained portion of the reinsured's business (for example, risk excess of loss reinsurance, or where some form of priority reinsurance is in place), whatever is reinsured under other treaties or contracts is outside the scope of the Agreement. In the same way, the reinsurer is not expected to absorb the credit risk that could result from the reinsured's failure to collect under those other reinsurances or from other reinsurers. Even though there is little prior (proportional) reinsurance protection on many legal liability accounts, the clause is still included in many wordings to guard against some priority reinsurance (whether proportional treaty or facultative) being in force and then failing to respond.

ARTICLE 6

CLAIMS SERIES CLAUSE

Definitions

For the purpose of this clause, a Claims Series Event shall be defined as a series of claims arising from one specific common cause which is attributable to one design and/or specification and/or formula in products and/or services supplied by one and only one original insured.

Basis for Recovery Hereunder

Notwithstanding anything to the contrary contained in this Agreement, and subject always to the specific exclusions contained in this Agreement and subject to the special loss reporting provisions contained in this Agreement, it is understood and agreed with regard to policies of Public and/or Products Liability that where legal liability of one original insured is established in respect of a Claims Series Event as defined above, then for the purposes of recovery hereunder such a Claims Series Event shall be deemed to be one event the date of loss for which shall be determined strictly on the basis as set out below.

Date of Loss

(i) To apply exclusively in respect of policies and/or sections thereof issued on a claims-made basis:

For the purposes of the foregoing, the date of loss of such a Claims Series Event shall be the date that the original insured is first advised in writing of the first claim of the Claims Series Event which contributes to the Ultimate Net Loss applicable hereto. In such circumstances the Reinsured shall include each and every claim which could be taken into consideration for the purposes of establishing the date of loss.

(ii) To apply (a) in respect of policies and/or sections thereof issued on a losses occurring during basis; and (b) in respect of a combination of policies and/or sections thereof issued on a claims-made basis and on a losses occurring during basis:

For the purposes of the foregoing, the date of loss of such a Claims Series Event shall be deemed to be the date that the Reinsured first notifies the Reinsurers hereon in writing of the possibility of a Claims Series Event affecting Reinsurers.

This clause modifies the "event" or "cause-based" nature of the reinsurance to cater for certain forms of liability insurance. For example, many types of Products Liability and Professional Indemnity insurance are issued on an "in all and in the annual aggregate" basis rather than on an accident or occurrence basis. A clear distinction should be recognised between original insurances issued on an aggregate basis and reinsurances issued on an "event" or "occurrence" basis with a limit for any one loss and subject to an aggregate limit per year. Reinsurers do not always favour the Aggregate Extension Clause (AEC) or Claims Series Clause (as we have used here), because of the tendency for "event" coverage to be turned into some form of stop loss or aggregate excess of loss without a suitable premium having been paid. However, as claims under legal liability insurances become more complex, there is a need to adapt the usual form of excess of loss wording to accommodate these more complicated claim situations. There has been a move to replace the AEC with the simpler "Claims Series Clause" and then use various "ACOD" clauses (for occupational disease claims). This is perhaps a topic well beyond the scope of a beginner's guide, but we have nevertheless shown an ACOD clause below.

OCCUPATIONAL DISEASE CLAUSE ACOD/B

The provisions of this Article shall override any provisions of any other Articles contained herein which may conflict.

Insofar as liability is incurred by the Reinsured under an employers' liability policy and/or workmen's compensation policy in respect of legal liability for occupational disease or physical impairment which does not arise from a sudden and identifiable accident or event this Agreement shall provide cover only on the following basis:-

(a) Where the occupational disease or physical impairment results from exposure to a hazard of the employment of the claimant, any one claim in respect of any one employee of an original insured arising out of this exposure shall be considered individually as one event for the purpose of recovery hereunder.

(b) Where the legal liability of the original insured to the original claimant is established on "exposure basis" that is legal liability attaches for the whole or part of the period which the claimant is exposed to the hazard of the employment then recovery hereunder shall be as follows:-

(1) the proportion of the total claim amount in respect of any one employee attributable to any one period of this Agreement shall be that proportion of the total of such amount which the period concerned bears to the total period during which the

employee was exposed to the hazard of the employment and,

(2) the underlying loss of the Reinsured and the limit of liability of the Reinsurers under this Agreement shall be reduced in the proportion which each period of the Agreement bears to the total period during which the employer was insured by the Reinsured and the employee was exposed to the hazard of the employment.

Provided always that the exposure took place during the period of this Agreement which shall be understood to mean exposure between each inception and annual renewal date of this Agreement.

(c) In the event of legal liability being established to an original insured on other than an "exposure basis" as described above then for the purpose of recovery hereunder the date of the loss hereon shall be the date applicable to which such legal liability is established.

ARTICLE 7

CHANGE OF UNDERWRITING POLICY CLAUSE

This clause has been discussed in Chapter 16 above

ARTICLE 8

INDEX/STABILITY CLAUSE

An example of this clause has been given in Chapter 9 above together with a description of how it operates.

ARTICLE 9

CURRENCY FLUCTUATION CLAUSE

An example of this clause has been given in Chapter 9 above together with a description of how it operates.

ARTICLE 10

PREMIUM CLAUSE

The Reinsured shall pay to the Reinsurer premiums at the rate of xx% (*number in words* percent) calculated on the gross premium income of the Reinsured in respect of the business covered hereunder and accounted for by the Reinsured during the period hereon. The term "gross net premium income" shall mean gross original premiums (less only cancellations and returns, premiums for risks excluded from the protection of this Agreement and premiums paid away for other reinsurances, if any, recoveries under which would inure to the benefit of Reinsurers hereon) accruing to the Reinsured from all business falling under this Agreement.

The Reinsured shall pay to the Reinsurer an annual Deposit Premium of $ .... in full at inception of this Agreement. The annual Minimum Premium for this Agreement shall be $ ....

As soon as possible after the end of each annual period of this Agreement, but in any event within three months after the anniversary date, the Reinsured shall supply to the Reinsurers a declaration of its gross net premium income as defined above and if the premium due to the Reinsurer computed on the basis set forth in the first paragraph of this Article exceeds the Deposit Premium, the amount in excess thereof shall be paid by the Reinsured to the Reinsurer. Should the Adjustment Premium be higher than the Deposit Premium, but less than the annual Minimum Premium, then the annual Minimum Premium shall apply, and the Adjustment Premium shall be the difference between the Deposit and Minimum Premium.

This article states how the premium due to the reinsurer should be calculated and that a deposit premium should be paid at inception of the agreement. The minimum premium appears to have been set at a higher figure. This is shown in the last paragraph as it provides for the adjustment of the contract premium and what should happen in the circumstances described.

ARTICLE 11

EXTENDED CLAIMS REPORTING CLAUSE (with CO-OPERATION CLAUSE)

The Reinsured shall give advice within reasonable time, together with all relevant details to the Reinsurers of each accident or event where either the sums claimed or the potential loss amounts to 75% (seventy five percent) or more of the underlying loss stated in the Indemnity Clause, whether or not the Reinsured considers that it has an adequate defence, and the Reinsured shall advise the Reinsurers of its estimate of the probable cost of the loss but failure to give such notice shall not prejudice the rights of the Reinsured in any way.

In addition, the following categories of claims or potential claims shall be reported to the Reinsurers immediately, regardless of any questions of the liability of the insured or the Reinsured:

(i) Fatal injuries unless it is known that there is no dependency.

(ii) Bodily injuries as specified below:-
brain injuries
spinal injuries resulting in partial or total paralysis
total or partial amputations or permanent loss of use of a limb or limbs
severe burn injuries
total or partial blindness
extensive scarring or severe facial disfigurement
all other injuries likely to result in a permanent disability rating of 50% (fifty percent) or more.

(iii) Bodily injuries resulting in payment of any annuity.

(iv) Bodily injuries or property damage for which suit has been filed if the amount claimed by the plaintiff or plaintiffs exceed the underlying loss stated in the in the Indemnity clause.

CLAIMS CO-OPERATION CLAUSE

The Reinsured shall keep the Reinsurers informed of all developments likely to affect the cost of any claim or claims hereunder and undertakes insofar as is reasonably possible to co-operate with the Reinsurers or their duly authorised representative in the conduct and settlement of such claim or claims and in the estimating of claims reserves.

In calculating the liability of the Reinsurers hereunder all loss payments made by the Reinsured within the conditions of the original insurance and/or reinsurance and falling within the scope of this Agreement shall be binding on the Reinsurers. The Reinsurers shall be bound also by ex-gratia payments made with their consent.

The Reinsurers shall remit their share of all loss payments within fourteen days of receiving a request from the Reinsured so to do, upon reasonable evidence of the amount paid having been given by the Reinsured.

The Reinsured shall as soon as practicable and in any event not later than three months after the expiry of this Agreement send to the Reinsurers a statement of unsettled claims as at the date of submission of such statement showing the amount for which the Reinsurers may be liable in respect of each individual claim.

These clauses set out the procedure for advising and settling claims under the reinsurance. This version provides for advice of potential losses exceeding a specified percentage amount of the deductible, 75% in this example. This should provide the reinsurer with an early warning of a possible claim. The second paragraph lists a number of serious injuries that could have a possible major impact on the reinsurance, even if there is a low initial estimate of the cost of the loss (or liability unadmitted or unidentified). This part of the clause is the "extended" section. The third, or "co-operation" section of the clause should be self-explanatory. All claims would be settled as individual cash loss recoveries. The annual statement of outstanding losses would enable the reinsurer to track the development of all incurred losses to the agreement.

ARTICLE 12
ERRORS AND OMISSIONS CLAUSE

This Clause has been discussed in Chapter 16 above

ARTICLE 13
SPECIAL CANCELLATION CLAUSE (amended to include DOWNGRADING of REINSURER SECURITY PROVISION)

It is a condition precedent upon all subscribing Reinsurers who participate in this Agreement that each individual subscribing Reinsurer shall at all times during the period of this Agreement maintain an Insurer Financial Strength (IFS) rating from Standard & Poor's Rating Group of 1221 Avenue of the Americas, New York, New York 10020, USA ("S&P") equal to or greater than the rating that was applied by S&P to that individual subscribing Reinsurer at the commencement of this Agreement.

In the event of an explicit downgrading of any individual subscribing Reinsurer by S&P to an IFS rating inferior to that which was applied by S&P at the commencement of this Agreement, then at the sole option of the Reinsured the Reinsured may elect to cancel the participation of that individual subscribing Reinsurer. The effective date of such cancellation shall be determined at the sole discretion of the Reinsured provided that the date so determined shall not be earlier than the date upon which the relevant downgrading by S&P was announced in New York, USA.

Any individual subscribing Reinsurer who does not have an IFS rating from S&P but who maintains during the period of this Agreement a rating from A.M. Best Company of A.M. Best Road, Oldwick, New Jersey 08858-0700 USA ("Bests") shall also be considered as falling within the terms of this Article. Any explicit downgrading of such an individual subscribing Reinsurer by Bests to a rating less than the rating that was applied by Bests to that individual subscribing Reinsurer at the commencement of this Agreement shall give the Reinsured the same right of cancellation as set out above.

In the event that a rating should be given to an individual subscribing Reinsurer by both S&P and Bests which differ to the extent that one of the ratings is inferior to the other then the rating of S&P shall prevail.

For the avoidance of doubt the status of Credit Watch as defined by S&P or a rating modifier of 'u' (Under Review) applied to a rated Company as defined by Bests shall not, of itself, be construed as a downgrading for the purposes of this Article.

With regard to any Lloyd's Underwriters participating hereunder the rating applicable to each individual Lloyd's Underwriter shall be S&P IFS rating applicable to the Lloyd's Corporation as a whole at the commencement of this Agreement. *(Please note that since this part of the clause was issued, Standard & Poor's has created a special rating method for Lloyd's Syndicates. This method is known as a "Lloyd's Syndicate Assessment" or LSA. We suspect that this part of the clause might change as a result of that new method of assessment).*

If, for a Reinsurer with no rating by S&P or Bests, in the judgement of the Reinsured the security of such Reinsurer has materially deteriorated since inception of this Agreement, the Reinsured shall have the same right of cancellation as set out above.

The Reinsured may also elect to cancel the participation of any individual subscribing Reinsurer that ceases underwriting. The effective date of such cancellation shall be determined at the sole discretion of the Reinsured provided that the date so determined shall not be earlier than the date upon which the relevant Reinsurer ceased underwriting.

Furthermore, either party shall have the right to cancel this Agreement immediately by giving the other party written notice:

(i) If the performance of the whole or any part of this Agreement is prohibited or rendered impossible de jure or de facto in particular and without prejudice to the generality of the preceding words in consequence of any law or regulation which is or shall be in force in any country or territory or if any law or regulation shall prevent directly or indirectly the remittance of any or all or any part of the balance or payments due to or from either party

(ii) If the other party has become insolvent or unable to pay its debts or has lost the whole or any part of its paid up capital or should reduce or call up any of its capital or should go into liquidation or should pass any resolution preliminary to liquidation or if a Receiver should be appointed

(iii) If there is material change in the ownership or control of the other party

(iv) If the country of territory in which the other party resides or has its head office or is incorporated shall be involved in armed hostilities with any other country whether war be declared or not or is partly or wholly occupied by another power

(v) If the other party shall have failed to comply with any of the terms and conditions of this Agreement

After the date of cancellation, under either paragraph A or B above, the liability of the Reinsurers hereunder shall cease outright other than in respect of losses which have occurred prior thereto.

All notices of cancellation served in accordance with any of the provisions of paragraph A and B above shall be by telex or facsimile or any other means of instantaneous communication that provides a permanent record of such communication, and shall be deemed to be served upon despatch or where communications between the parties are interrupted upon attempted despatch.

All notices of cancellation served in accordance with any of the provisions of paragraph A and B above shall be addressed to the party concerned at its Head Office or at any other address previously designated by that party.

In the event of this Agreement being cancelled at any date other than that stated under the Period of the Agreement then the premium due to the Reinsurers shall be calculated upon the Premium income of the Reinsured up to the date of cancellation or pro rata temporis of the flat premium, if applicable. Premium shall include Reinstatement Premium, where applicable.

As we mentioned in an earlier chapter, the first part of this example clause shows the modern "downgrading" of reinsurer security provision. Please note that we have shown two rating agencies, Standard & Poor's Rating Group and A.M. Best Company, within this example *(with grateful acknowledgement to both Companies)*. Other versions of the clause exist. Please note the one-sided option specified in the second paragraph that relates to "the reinsured's sole option" to invoke the cancellation provision in event of the downgrading of any reinsurer. The second part of the clause is similar to the version used in Chapter 16. As mentioned, many excess of loss agreements would include the Insolvency Clause (shown at the end of this chapter) to counter this "sole option" provision.

ARTICLE 14
INSPECTION OF RECORDS CLAUSE
This Clause has been discussed in Chapter 16 above.

ARTICLE 15
INTERMEDIARY CLAUSE
This Clause has been discussed in Chapter 16 above.

ARTICLE 16
ALTERATIONS CLAUSE
This Clause has been discussed in Chapter 16 above.

ARTICLE 17
APPLICABLE LAW CLAUSE
This Clause has been discussed in Chapter 16 above.

ARTICLE 18
ARBITRATION CLAUSE
This Clause has been discussed in Chapter 16 above

SIGNATURE CLAUSE
An example of this Clause has been discussed in Chapter 16 above. The only difference would be the use of the word "Reinsured" in place of "Ceding Company" when excess of loss reinsurances are involved. Many excess of loss reinsurance programmes involve a large number of reinsurers and many contract wordings would use individual signing schedules or individual signing pages. This facilitates administration for all parties concerned.

As we have concentrated in this chapter on an example

contract wording for legal liabilities, we feel that we should mention a few more important clauses that might appear in such excess of loss programmes.

Most reinsurers attempt to restrict two important exposures. The first restriction relates to pollution, whether as a result of an unfortunate incident or what is known as gradual pollution of the environment. The second set of restrictions relate to any form of general third party liability exposure in North America.

Two environmental impairment exclusion clauses are shown in full.

INDUSTRIES, SEEPAGE, POLLUTION AND CONTAMINATION EXCLUSION CLAUSE NO. 3

This Agreement does not cover any liability for:

1. Personal injury or bodily injury or loss of, damage to, or loss of use of property directly or indirectly caused by seepage, pollution or contamination, provided always that this paragraph 1 shall not apply to liability for personal injury or bodily injury or loss of or physical damage to or destruction of tangible property damaged or destroyed, where such seepage, pollution or contamination is caused by a sudden, unintended and unexpected happening during the period of this Agreement.

2. The cost of removing, nullifying or cleaning-up seeping, polluting or contaminating substances unless the seepage, pollution or contamination is caused by a sudden, unintended and unexpected happening during the period of this Agreement.

3. Fines, penalties, punitive or exemplary damages.

This Clause shall not extend this Agreement to cover any liability which would not have been covered under this Agreement had this Clause not been attached.

The clause above relates to sudden and accidental incidents, and the one below to gradual pollution. We have used the non-US version here. The US version is known as the "North American Absolute Environmental Impairment Exclusion" clause, which is hopefully self-explanatory.

GRADUAL ENVIRONMENTAL IMPAIRMENT EXCLUSION (LMC 1B)

With regard to all public liability and general third party liability and products liability (whether written as such or otherwise) under policies covering operations located outside the United States of America and Canada incepting or renewed on or after 1st January 1987, this Agreement does not cover any liability for

1. personal injury or bodily injury or financial loss or loss of, damage to, or use of property directly or indirectly arising out of the discharge dispersal release or escape of pollutants;

2. the cost of removing nullifying or cleaning up pollutants;

3. fines, penalties, punitive or exemplary damages arising directly or indirectly out of the discharge, dispersal, release or escape of pollutants.

Notwithstanding the foregoing, this Agreement shall cover liability otherwise excluded under paragraphs (a) and (b) above which

(i) its entirety at a specific time and place, and

(ii) is indemnified in not more than one annual period of original insurance.

For the purposes of this clause, "pollutants" means any solid, liquid, gaseous or thermal irritant or contaminant, including but not limited to smoke, vapour, soot, fumes, acid, alkalis, chemicals and waste. Waste includes material to be recycled, reconditioned or reclaimed.

We have then listed four clauses that restrict various types of North American exposure and have only given a brief summary of what is contained in the clauses, rather than their full text. All of these clauses could appear in the same agreement, or just selected clauses only.

LGT 397 (1994) North American Operations Exclusion Clause Operations located in US or Canada are specifically defined, as are sales &/or distribution offices.

LGT 398 (1994) North American Export Costs Inclusive Clause Operates in tandem with LGT 397. Defines that costs are included within (not in addition to) the limit of indemnity for public liability and (in the annual aggregate) for products liability.

LGT 399 (1994) Worldwide Punitive Damages Clause

Identifies circumstances where punitive &/or exemplary damages are excluded from excess of loss coverage.

LGT 400 (1994) Worldwide Claims Made Basis Clause
Identifies circumstances where coverage is excluded.

Please note that revised Liability General Text (LGT) Clauses have been proposed, probably with a 2000 date suffix, but we have shown the 1994 date suffix, as these are in common use at the time of writing.

Finally, we have made many references to the Insolvency Clause throughout this book. We have shown an example here and hope that no further comments are required for this intricate clause !

INSOLVENCY CLAUSE

Where an Insolvency Event occurs in relation to the Reinsured, the following terms shall apply (and, in the event of any inconsistency between these terms and any other terms of this Agreement, these terms shall prevail).

1. Notwithstanding any requirement in this Agreement that the Reinsured shall actually make payment in discharge of its liability to its original policyholder before becoming entitled to payment from the Reinsurers

    (a) the Reinsurers shall be liable to pay the Reinsured even though the Reinsured is unable actually to pay, or discharge its liability to, its original policyholder

    (b) nothing in this clause shall operate to accelerate the date for payment by the Reinsurers of any sum which may be payable to the Reinsured, which sum shall only become payable as and when the Reinsured would have discharged, by actual payment, its liability for its current net loss, but for it being the subject of an Insolvency Event.

2. The existence, quantum, valuation and date for payment of any sums which the Reinsurers are liable to pay the Reinsured under this Agreement shall be those and only those for which the Reinsurers would be liable to the Reinsured if the liability of the Reinsured had been determined without reference to any term in any composition or scheme of arrangement or any similar arrangement, entered into between the Reinsured and all or any part of its original policyholders, unless and until the Reinsurers serve written notice to the contrary on the Reinsured in relation to any composition or scheme of arrangement or any similar arrangement.

3. The Reinsurers shall be entitled (but not obliged) to set-off, against any sum which it may be liable to pay to the Reinsured, any sum for which the Reinsured is liable to pay to the Reinsurers.

An Insolvency Event shall occur if:

A. (i) (in relation to 1, 2 and 3 above) a winding-up petition is presented in respect of the Reinsured or a provisional liquidator is appointed over it or if the Reinsured goes into administration, administrative receivership or receivership, or if the Reinsured has a scheme of arrangement or voluntary arrangement proposed in relation to all or any parts of its affairs; or

A. (ii) (in relation to 1 above) if the Reinsured goes into compulsory or voluntary liquidation, or

in each case, if the Reinsured becomes subject to any other similar insolvency process (whether as under the laws of *name of country* or elsewhere) and

B. the Reinsured is unable to pay its debts as and when they fall due within the meaning of the appropriate section of the Insolvency Act or any equivalent legislation (or any statutory amendment or re-enactment of that legislation) in accordance with the laws of *name of country*.

18

Developments Since the Fourth Edition

We identified in the Introduction that as society, technology and consumer awareness (and consumer protection) develop, new insurance and reinsurance products are created to protect and support those changes.

This Fifth Edition would be failing in its duty if we did not comment on the tragic events in New York, Washington and Pennsylvania on 11th September 2001 and the consequent dramatic effects on the worldwide insurance and reinsurance markets. Terrorism is now almost an absolute exclusion for certain classes of business, especially any original insurance product connected to commercial or industrial enterprises. In some markets, terrorism has also been excluded from certain private or personal insurances. Within the term "terrorism", we must include a potential chemical, nuclear or biological attack by fanatical or idealogical organisations.

Many reinsurers have stipulated that they are now only prepared to cover "named perils", whether for property or casualty (legal liability) accounts. In other words, if a reinsured has not identified correct exposures for a particular class and declared an appropriate premium income, then reinsurers would not pay a claim occurring on such an unidentified class of business. Reinsurers' rationale lies in the fact that as they had not been able to quantify an exposure, then no liability would exist as no excess of loss (or other) premium had been charged. No consideration, no identification or transfer of risk, no reinsurance liability.

We have experienced a change in century since the Fourth Edition. This led to many concerns as to "Y2K" or "Year 2000" and whether computer systems would cope with the change of date from 31st December 1999 to 1st January 2000. It appears that there were few problems, but the insurance and reinsurance industry created many "Electronic Data Recognition" clauses. These were created to avoid potential problems if a computer system "crashed" as a result of the date change. The clauses were then adapted to identify that any computer-based problem, such as an infection by a computer virus, worm or similar, would be excluded from any reinsurance protection, unless the problem resulted directly from a peril insured against, e.g. a fire or an explosion. These clauses are often known as "Information Technology Hazards Clarification" clauses, and many versions exist. Another clause name is the "Cyber Liability Exclusion", whilst certain other reinsurers have created their own "Clarification Agreement" or "Letter of Intent".

A new currency, the Euro, was introduced in many European Union countries from 1st January 2002. This led to the creation of two clauses known as the "Currency (or Agreement) Re-Denomination Clause" and the "Currency (or Agreement) Continuation Clause". The former was included in many agreements prior to the conversion date as an advance warning of the change to the Euro, and the latter allowed a reinsured to convert the historic statistics of its various reinsurances from its original national currency to the Euro at the rate of exchange set by the European Union. In other words, both clauses attempted to create a "nothing has really changed" situation.

Many court cases involving insurance and reinsurance have been heard throughout the world. This has raised questions over certain practices that have existed for many years in the worldwide insurance and reinsurance market. An obvious example is the use of the term "as original". This phrase is often used in facultative quota share placements, but has now been tested in a number of legal cases. We offer no solution here, other than an observation that the construction of *any* reinsurance should be properly made. If necessary, the parties should provide examples, in advance, of how the proposed reinsurance is intended to operate, rather than wait for a loss to occur, and discover that one or both parties was unable to agree to a proposed method of settlement.

In a similar vein, there have been a number of legal cases concerning the legal jurisdiction of the reinsurance agreement and where any court case should be heard. The reporting of claims is often the cause of many disputes and whether such a claims-reporting provision is a contractual condition or simply part of the normal administration of the agreement. Care should therefore be taken when including both conditions and their effects should be clearly identified. Similarly, many problems have arisen over the late payment of reinsurance premiums. If a settlement date is not identified, then it would be difficult to argue when that premium should be paid. An obvious suggestion is to incorporate specific dates for the settlement of reinsurance premiums, whether or not they are supported by a premium payment warranty clause. If necessary, the reinsurance should identify the remedies or consequences if that premium were not settled within the specified time provision.

Another example of a clause created following various court cases is the Insolvency Clause. As we have mentioned, there are different versions used for different markets, but they all identify what would happen in the event of the insolvency of the reinsured.

As risks become larger, many reinsurers impose a clause to restrict a reinsured's acceptance of local "Target" or "Market" risks for both property and casualty business. These risks tend to be so large (and important to the national economy of a country) that a single insurance entity could not insure that risk on its own. Effectively, the insurance capacity of that entire country (with probable support from overseas as well) must be utilised to cover that risk. If a reinsurer were to reinsure three or four insurance companies operating in that market, then the reinsurer would incur a potentially massive accumulation on that one "target" risk. This could have disastrous consequences on that reinsurer's retrocession protection(s) if a loss were to occur.

It is clear that reinsurers wish to restrict, or at least control, all their exposures and establish a correct price for the reinsurance product on offer. Throughout this book we have commented on three particular areas of concern:

(i) restricting natural perils exposures under proportional treaties by the imposition of Cession and/or Event Limits;

(ii) assessing flood exposures and whether they are now insurable as a "fortuitous" event (under any form of reinsurance protection);

(iii) unlimited vertical and horizontal excess of loss protection for original policies (such as motor third party bodily injury) which themselves are issued for an unlimited amount in accordance with that country's legal requirements.

We suggest that these three topics will exercise the minds of many insurance companies, reinsurers, retrocessionaires and intermediaries alike, together with any regulatory authorities involved. Readers should be aware of the situation in their own markets and the new solutions available. As we have said before, "everything has its price", but these problems can still be solved through the mechanism of reinsurance.

There are many more instances of reinsurer reaction to worldwide events, whether directly related to the product of insurance, or to the financial world in general. They are too numerous to mention here, and realistically beyond the remit of this publication. Readers should nevertheless follow developments in their own markets, and then on the broader world stage.

In closing this Fifth Edition, I wish all readers a successful and enjoyable career within our industry, whether as insurer, broker or reinsurer. It can be exciting, frustrating, repetitive, innovative, but never boring. There will always be something new to learn. Good luck!